MACHIAVELLI
AND THE RENAISSANCE

MACHIAVELLI
& THE RENAISSANCE

FEDERICO CHABOD
Professor of Modern History in the University of Rome

TRANSLATED FROM THE ITALIAN BY
DAVID MOORE

WITH AN INTRODUCTION BY
A. P. D'ENTRÈVES
Serena Professor of Italian in the University of Oxford

BOWES & BOWES
LONDON

First published 1958 by
Bowes & Bowes Publishers Limited
42 Great Russell Street London W.C.1

Printed in Great Britain by Robert MacLehose & Co. Ltd
Glasgow, Scotland

CONTENTS

FOREWORD

The first of the essays included in this volume was originally published as an introduction to my edition of Niccolò Machiavelli's *Prince* (Turin, U.T.E.T., Classici Italiani, Vol. XXXV, 1924).

The second appeared under the title *Del 'Principe' di Niccolò Machiavelli* in the 'Nuova Rivista Storica' (IX, 1925). It was later reissued as a separate volume under the same title (Milan-Rome-Naples, 1926). Here, however, I have reproduced only so much of this, the longest of my essays on Machiavelli, as concerns our author directly (viz. the first six chapters). Chapter VII, which deals with the anti-Machiavellism of the second half of the sixteenth century, is accordingly omitted.

On the other hand, the third essay, entitled *Machiavelli's Method and Style* and consisting of a lecture which I delivered in Florence in May, 1952, first appeared under the title *Niccolò Machiavelli* in *Il Cinquecento* (Florence, 1955), included in the series published by the Libera Cattedra di Storia della Civiltà Fiorentina.

The essay on the Renaissance first appeared in 1942, under the title *Il Rinascimento*, in the miscellaneous volume entitled *Problemi storici e orientamenti storiografici*, ed. E. Rota, Como, Cavalleri (2nd edition, published under the title *Questioni di storia moderna*, Milan, Marzorati, 1948).

Although the first two essays on Machiavelli belong to a period long past, some of my friends have kindly expressed the opinion that they may still be of some interest. Since I would not wish to modify either their general design or the essential ideas and opinions which they express I have reproduced them here, save for a few minor corrections, in the exact form in which they originally appeared. Here and there

I have thought fit to add a footnote, which I have enclosed in square brackets; but I have purposely refrained from making any additions of a bibliographical nature. The two essays were planned and written at a particular moment; they refer to 'the state of the question' at that moment; and I am anxious that they should retain completely their original character.

I have made a few substantial additions and modifications (also enclosed in square brackets, when it is a question of footnotes) to the more recent essay on the Renaissance. But the most important point here is that I have completely revised and rearranged the bibliography. Planned in 1942 as an aid to the reader, as a preliminary guide to him in his researches, this bibliography could obviously not reappear in its original form in 1957. Accordingly, I have not only brought it up to date, endeavouring in the process to take account of the most important contributions that have been made to the subject since 1942, but have included a number of additional works published prior to that year. In addition, I have somewhat altered its internal design, always with the aim of providing an initial pointer, a bibliographical introduction to the study of the period which will, I hope, prove to be of some service, particularly to students.

My most cordial thanks are due to Mr. David Moore, who has brought so much understanding to the task of translating a text which, in view of its stylistic peculiarities, must have presented considerable difficulty; and to Dr. Conor Fahy, whose collaboration at the final proof stage has been invaluable. And I would like to express my heartfelt gratitude to my old friend and fellow-countryman Professor A. P. d'Entrèves, to whose personal interest the appearance of this English edition of my work is principally due.

FEDERICO CHABOD

January, 1957.

INTRODUCTION

PROFESSOR CHABOD'S essay on Machiavelli's *Prince* has long been a bibliographical rarity. Here in Oxford, the only way to get acquainted with it is to read it in Bodley, in the 1925 volume of the *Nuova Rivista Storica* where it was first published. This however has never prevented tutors from impressing on generation after generation of undergraduates reading the Italian Renaissance that Chabod's essay is indispensable. Such a state of affairs would in itself provide sufficient ground for justifying an English translation.

But this is not the only reason which has made me wish for many years to see Chabod's Machiavelli translated into English. I think that this essay represented at the time of its appearance, and still represents in many ways, a landmark in Machiavelli studies. I also think that it represents, together with Ridolfi's recent biography,[1] the best illustration of what I would call the Italian approach to, and interpretation of, the 'Florentine Secretary': an approach and an interpretation that differ in many ways from those prevailing in Anglo-Saxon countries. The present volume contains, besides the essay on *The Prince*, two other important essays of Chabod on Machiavelli, an earlier, and a much later one. To these has been added the admirable essay on *The Concept of the Renaissance*, and a truly formidable bibliography, specially composed for the occasion – which I can only hope will not act as a deterrent to the uninitiated in the niceties of Continental scholarship! If a link were needed for holding together these various essays, Professor Chabod has provided us with one by remarking that 'Machiavelli is the true test

---

[1] R. Ridolfi, *Vita di Niccolò Machiavelli*, Roma, 1954.

of any view that is held of the Renaissance and of its historical significance'.

I have spoken of an Italian approach to Machiavelli. I
trust that I will not be thought to belittle the importance of
Chabod's work by saying that it is best understood in the
context of Italian historiography, and particularly of Italian
Renaissance studies. Professor Chabod has given us a very
interesting survey of the trend of these studies during the
last half-century in the *Festschrift* for Benedetto Croce's
eightieth birthday.[1] I do not think that we could find a better
introduction to the essays contained in the present volume.

The problem of the Renaissance – Professor Chabod
points out – has always been felt by the Italians as one of the
most crucial problems in their history. They never could
quite accept the fact that the age of Italy's greatest achievements in the field of the arts and the sciences should have
coincided with the loss of Italian 'liberty' and have led to the
establishment of foreign domination over the Peninsula. In
the days of Italy's re-awakening as a nation – the age of
Romanticism and of the *Risorgimento* – Italian historians set
themselves the task of finding an explanation for this tragic
paradox. In their view, cultural history and political history
could not be treated as separate water-tight compartments.
Any judgment on the one necessarily involved a judgment
on the other. Even at the cost of distorting historical evidence, the whole story had to be re-written, and the Renaissance either condemned outright for its corrupting influence, or pushed back in time to the 'real' period of Italian
greatness, the age of the free Communes, of the sea-faring
republics, and of great characters and great personalities
such as Dante. The echo of such emotional re-thinking of
Italian history is clearly perceptible in the interpretation of
Machiavelli. The Florentine Secretary had either to be
transformed, as he had been by Rousseau, Alfieri and Fos-

---

[1] F. Chabod, *Gli studi di Storia del Rinascimento*, in *Cinquant'anni di vita
italiana, 1896–1946*. Scritti in onore di Benedetto Croce per il suo ottantesimo
anniversario. Napoli, 1950. Vol. I, pp. 125–207.

colo, into the advocate of liberty and the denouncer of
tyrants; or his 'immoral' doctrines excused and glossed over,
as De Sanctis attempted to do, in the name of the 'divine
spark of patriotism' that shone forth in them.

In contrast to this romantic idealization and transfigura-
tion of the past, modern Italian scholarship has professed, in
the last fifty years, to be matter-of-fact and scientific. 'In a
calmer historical perspective, national passions became less
compelling, or at any rate they carried less direct implications with them. Once independence and unity had been
secured, the past could be looked at with less bias; the lack
of independence, and of the very desire for it, could cease to
be regarded as a crime. It was no longer demanded from past
ages that they should contain an anticipation of the noble
ideals of the *Risorgimento*; nor were these ideals any longer
used as criteria for historical interpretation. In this new
climate of opinion the connexion between cultural and
political history, if not completely severed, has at any rate
been considerably weakened; and in order to understand
Petrarch's poetry or Masaccio's art or Valla's thought it is
no longer deemed necessary to invoke the ideals of Communal liberty, nor are the sweet harmonies of Ariosto's
stanzas contrasted, as they inevitably used to be, with the
baseness and blindness of the Italians in the early sixteenth
century.'[1] The Renaissance, in other words, ceased to appear as an exclusively Italian affair; the movement of ideas
which, for good or ill, was born on Italian soil, came to be
viewed as something of European, and not only Italian importance. In Italy as elsewhere, Burckhardt's ideas were pre-
dominant; they survived even after the progress of historical
studies had contradicted some of them: thus, to give an
example, the formula of the Renaissance State as 'a work of
art' continued to enjoy credit long after the growth of the
Signorie had been shown to be the result of a slow historical
process rather than the creation of the 'virtuous' Prince.

Nevertheless, the particular Italian concern in the problem

[1] *Op. cit.*, p. 136.

of the Renaissance could never be entirely set aside nor forgotten. It is clearly reflected in the discussions regarding the 'contribution of Italy' to the 'rise of the modern spirit' in Europe, and in the attempts to analyse and define the nature of that contribution in the domain not only of the visual arts, but also of philosophy, religion and politics. Here indeed the most startling claim was that made by Croce, that the 'true and proper foundation of a philosophy of politics' was the work of an Italian. That foundation was due to Machiavelli's 'discovery' of 'the necessity and autonomy of politics, of politics which are beyond good and evil, which have their laws against which it is useless to rebel, which cannot be exorcised and driven from this world with holy water'.[1]

Thus, by a single stroke of the pen, Croce reversed the age-long denunciation of Machiavelli's 'immorality'. What had been too often used as an argument for a negative verdict on the Renaissance no less than on the Italian character, suddenly became one of Italy's greatest achievements. Actually, Croce pointed out that, like all discoverers of unpalatable truths, Machiavelli was deeply aware of the tragic dilemma he was revealing with his shrewd penetration and ruthless quest for sincerity. Croce even went so far as to speak of an 'austere and painful moral awareness' in Machiavelli, the proof of which could be found in the 'galling bitterness with which he underlines his notion of politics and its inherent necessities', in his dream of a 'good society' which may have existed in antiquity or may still be found among the uncouth inhabitants of the Alps, in his very recoiling from the horrors recorded in history, and in his exhortation to follow the good, not the wicked examples of the past. But, clearly enough, the whole emphasis of Croce's argument fell on Machiavelli's supposed 'discovery': well might he have repeated with Bacon, 'we are much beholden to Machiavel'. Croce did not stop to examine what harrowing experience lay behind Machiavelli's clear-sightedness, nor the price which Italy and the Italians were paying, and

---

[1] B. Croce, *Elementi di Politica*, Bari, 1925, p. 60.

would have to pay, for the theory and practice of 'Machia-vellism'.

The influence of these ideas of Croce on subsequent Italian literature about Machiavelli was great and decisive. That influence is clearly traceable in Chabod's essays; writing about them many decades later, he expressly acknowledged his indebtedness to Croce's vindication of the 'autonomy of politics' as Machiavelli's great contribution to political science.[1] Yet Chabod, as a historian, was able to avoid the over-simplifications of many among Croce's followers. Instead of discussing endlessly, as some of them still do, the 'nature of politics' which is 'beyond good and evil', he returned to the earlier tradition of considering Machiavelli and his teaching as a cross-roads in Italian history. In contrast to the separation between political and cultural history which had characterized the latest phase of Italian Machiavelli and Renaissance studies, Chabod shifted the emphasis back to the close connexion between the two. The error of the old romantic theory had been to conceive of that connexion as one of cause and effect; but to deny the causal dependence of one on the other was no excuse for overlooking the contacts and interrelation between theory and practice, 'ideologies' and historical facts. Chabod's purpose, to quote his own words, was 'to present Machiavelli, the author of *The Prince*, as the expression, almost the synthesis of Italian life throughout the fourteenth and fifteenth centuries; to see reflected and clarified in his thought, as it were in its essential outline, the age-long process of development which leads from the downfall of the old, Communal freedom to the triumph of the princely, the absolute State'.[2]

Whether, and to what extent, Professor Chabod succeeded in the task he set himself is not for me to say in a short introduction. As far as his essay on *The Prince* is concerned, I need hardly point out that in over thirty years much work has been done that has either confirmed or called in question some of his conclusions. But this should not

---

[1] F. Chabod, *Gli studi di Storia del Rinascimento*, p. 154.   [2] *Op. loc. cit.*

make us overlook the novelty and freshness of Chabod's viewpoint, a freshness and novelty which the passage of years has not diminished. I do not think it is an exaggeration to say that some chapters in this book – I am thinking especially of the one on *The 'Lesson of Events' offered by Italian History* – have taken their place among the classics of Renaissance history. But there is one point on which I would venture to take Professor Chabod to task in his own appraisal of his contribution to Machiavelli studies. I have said that, by his own account, his was a deliberate return to the older and 'romantic' approach to the problem of Machiavelli and the Renaissance, to the view that 'cultural' and 'political' history should not be divorced from one another. But Professor Chabod is anxious to point out that, unlike the Romantics, he has no use for the 'moral considerations which were so dear to them', and that his was a deliberate attempt to steer clear of any justification or condemnation of Machiavelli 'in the framework of his times'.

I confess that I cannot understand why, unless out of reverence for Croce, Professor Chabod has chosen to present in this light his own masterly reconstruction of Machiavelli's teaching. Surely what gives even to-day an intense pathos to his writing is his personal concern in the story he tells us and the problem he debates. It is good to find him forgetting all about the 'autonomy of politics' when he comes to assessing the tragic significance of Machiavellism in Italian history. Personally, I cannot help feeling that he has given us his *real* conclusion about *The Prince* when he writes, at the end of Chapter IV: 'Other works . . . reveal that in the Europe of those days new seeds of life were germinating. This one, on the other hand, so infinitely superior to all others in its imaginative power and dramatic emphasis, testifies to the passing of a glorious era that has run its course. – Thus *The Prince* is at once a synthesis and a condemnation of two centuries of Italian history; and far more than its supposed immorality, what should have stirred the emotions of the commentators was the thought of the boundless misery which was overtaking our civilization.'[1] Unless I am entirely mistaken, there is contained in these lines a judgment, indeed a 'moral' judgment, which should allay the suspicion that Italians take a cynical pride in the statecraft of the Florentine Secretary.

But this emotional participation in the problem of interpreting Machiavelli and his age can also provide the clue to another characteristic of the Italian approach, which is clearly reflected in Chabod: the tendency to concentrate on *The Prince* in the assessment of Machiavelli's teaching. Here indeed is an objection which I think will not fail to be raised by the English reader of the essays contained in the present volume: why are the *Discorsi* given so little prominence, if not actually belittled or neglected? Why is the emphasis placed entirely on Machiavelli the theorist of absolutism, 'delivering up to Europe the blueprint of two-hundred years of her history',[2] and no account taken of Machiavelli the republican, longing for the free institutions of ancient Rome or of the Swiss cities of his own days? The first and ready answer that suggests itself to questions of this kind is, that the subject of the major essay in this volume is after all *The Prince*; that the first chapter is, too, *An Introduction to 'The Prince'*, and the third a study of *Machiavelli's Method and Style*, and not of the various phases of development of Machiavelli's political thought. But the argument based on the distinction between an 'earlier' and a 'later' phase in Machiavelli's teaching is, I am ready to admit, an invidious argument, for Chabod has made much of his interpretation depend on a particular dating of both *The Prince* and the *Discorsi*;[3] and that interpretation in turn is linked to the assumption of a close interrelation, both in conception and composition, between the two works. Quite recently, the question of

[1] See below, p. 105.   [2] See below, p. 120, note 1.

[3] Chabod's dating of *The Prince* between July and December 10, 1513, is now generally accepted and has never been seriously challenged. It is a pity that his masterly discussion of the problem (*Sulla composizione de 'Il Principe' di Niccolò Machiavelli*, in 'Archivum Romanicum', XI (1927), pp. 330–83) could not be included in the present volume.

the composition of the *Discorsi* has been reopened,[1] and as a consequence the whole problem of ' Machiavelli's last word about politics' has again come to the forefront. Once again, it would seem, is the question of the relationship between the 'absolutist', and the 'republican' Machiavelli open to enquiry.

What matters, however, is that the value of Chabod's reading of *The Prince* remains unimpaired; and perhaps it is also a reminder of the real problem at issue in any assessment of Machiavelli's historical significance. The 'republicanism' of Machiavelli and the 'humanism' of the *Discorsi* may no doubt be of great, even of capital importance for the study of the political thought of the late Renaissance or of the 'Florentine political awareness in the transition from the Republic to the Principate'.[2] But the memory that haunted the men of the following centuries was not that of the scholar who had written a brilliant commentary on Livy, but that of the politician who had ruthlessly laid bare the rules of the unholy game of power-politics. 'Machiavellis Lehre war ein Schwert, das in den staatlichen Leib der abendländischen Menschheit gestossen wurde und sie aufschreien und sich aufbäumen machte.'[3] The teaching that was a dagger thrust in the moral conscience of our forbears was the one contained in *The Prince* and in the chapters of the *Discorsi* which contain the pure doctrine of Machiavellism. It seems only natural that, more than any other nation, the Italians should have been haunted by this particular memory of Machiavelli. Actually, if I may be allowed a personal

---

[1] I am referring to the controversy which was started by F. Gilbert's article, *The Composition and Structure of Machiavelli's 'Discorsi'*, in 'Journal of the History of Ideas', XIV (1953), pp. 136–56; for its latest developments see now H. Baron, *The 'Principe' and the puzzle of the Date of the 'Discorsi'*, in 'Bibliothèque d'Humanisme et Renaissance', XVIII (1956), pp. 405–428.

[2] This phrase is taken from the title of R. von Albertini's admirable recent study, *Das florentinische Staatsbewusstsein im Übergang von der Republik zum Prinzipat*, Bern, 1955 (see pp. 53–74 for the section on Machiavelli).

[3] F. Meinecke, *Die Idee der Staatsräson in der neueren Geschichte*, 2d ed., München und Berlin, 1925, p. 60.

reminiscence, there were good reasons why many of us in Italy some thirty or more years ago should have turned to Machiavelli in despair for an explanation of what was happening around us. It is no mere coincidence that Chabod's study of *The Prince* was composed in the years when Fascist dictatorship was tightening its grip over our country.

I have tried to introduce the English reader to the essays that are herewith made available for his perusal. About their author I have said little or nothing so far. But – apart from the fact that since Chabod delivered the 'Chichele Lectures' here in Oxford in 1951 he needs no introduction to English academic circles — to speak of him as a man would involve me in saying much more than merely listing his achievements as a scholar. For once I had said that Professor Chabod is the Professor of Modern History in the University of Rome, the Director of the [Croce] Institute of Historical Research in Naples, the President of the 'Comité International des Sciences Historiques', the editor of several learned collections and the author of a number of books which have given him fame[1] – I would still feel that I had said little about his personality and character, and I might be tempted to go on speaking of the days of our youth when we used to ramble among the peaks of our native valley, and of the more recent ones when, finding ourselves side by side again, we were given the rare opportunity of testing the accuracy of Machiavelli's statement, that 'if any one in these dayes would frame a Republick, he should find it easier to deal with rude mountainers. . . .'[2] This alone I shall say: that

---

[1] One more writing of Chabod on Machiavelli, not included in this volume, must be mentioned: the article *Machiavelli* in 'Enciclopedia Italiana Treccani', vol. XXI (1934), pp. 778–90. For a further development of some of his ideas on the Renaissance (such as the influence of geographical discoveries on the decline of Renaissance ideals) two other works are of particular interest: *Giovanni Botero*, Roma, 1934, and *Paolo Giovio*, in 'Periodico della Società Storica Comense', XXXVIII (1954), pp. 9–30. I can only make passing mention of Chabod's studies of Politics and Religion in the Milanese State under Charles V, and of Italian Foreign Policy from 1870 to 1896, which lie altogether outside the scope and subject of this Introduction.

[2] *Discorsi*, I, xi (Dacres' translation).

I hope that my admiration for Chabod has not made me unduly biased towards his interpretation of Machiavelli; and that, both as a friend and as a fellow-countryman, I have a very great pleasure in welcoming him in his new and unfamiliar English garb which will I trust endear him to a large number of readers.

A. P. D'ENTRÈVES

Oxford,
November 1956

I

AN INTRODUCTION TO
THE PRINCE

AT the time when Machiavelli first emerged from the
shelter of his familiar circle into a world dominated by
the passions of the mob, the life of Florence was
neither calm nor well-ordered. Between 1494 and 1498 the
various social classes of the Republic had bestirred themselves, seeking, albeit vainly, to rebuild the city-state; and
they had been roused to a high pitch of frenzied excitement
by the resounding, picturesque sermons of Girolamo Savonarola. If at times the biblical figures which the Dominican
friar recalled to life in his addresses seemed remote and intangible, they were pregnant with an obscure meaning; and
the masses believed, even if they did so with a passion that
was purely superficial and without far-reaching significance,
proclaiming with their bold leader their faith in the resurgence of the moral world and of political life.

Niccolò, for his part, would stand aside from the rest. He
would linger, alone and indifferent, in the farthest corner of
the square, and with a faint, ironical smile[1] observe the fluctuations of party passion, discerning beneath the mask of
godliness the human motive that inspired the friar's preaching, coldly and surely analysing his 'lies',[2] immediately perceiving the pitiable helplessness of the people, who vacillated
between one party and the other, now submitting their will

---

[1] Cf. Carducci's rapidly-drawn and beautiful word-picture, *Dello svolgi-
mento della letteratura nazionale*, in *Discorsi letterarii e storici* (Bologna,
1899, p. 153).

[2] *Lettere Familiari* (Alvisi edition, Florence, Sansoni, 1883), III, dated 9
March 1497 (1498).

to the behest of Rome, now succumbing afresh to the swift,
dazzling succession of images evoked by a reformer who
could not easily be quelled. The obscure young Florentine
would not mingle with the mob. The tone of his words was
oddly bitter and disdainful, the cast of his thought was persistently hostile. Yet his hostility is not to be confused with
that of the *palleschi*,[1] which was inspired by practical and
clearly-defined motives. The irony and disdain of Niccolò are
the reactions of a man who is outside the immediate conflict,
and who surveys it with the assurance of a critic, not with the
interested passion of a participant.

And certainly Machiavelli could not foresee amid those
troubles and anxieties that within a short time he too would
be preaching to an uncomprehending and derisive audience,
that he too would evoke biblical images in order to endue his
exhortations with the amplitude and austerity of the divine
warning, and, finally, that his own chiding would end in a
negative verdict, just as the prophecies of Savonarola were
swallowed up in the calm of death. Nor was it granted to
him, in those early days of spiritual awakening, to recognize
that he had a secret, remote affinity with this friar whom he
judged so harshly – to perceive, in fact, the stealthy beginnings of that imaginative development which was afterwards
to find clear expression in the creation of *The Prince*.

For Niccolò's reasoning faculty, revealed in the sureness
and wisdom of his theoretical scheme, and his profound sense
of reality, which finds such a ready outlet in the consummate
dissection of human motives, are fulfilled and transformed
into living, organic, integral thought only through the medium of his all-powerful, inexhaustible imagination – so different, indeed, from Savonarola's, which, having its origin in
a more or less emotional revolt against history, is creative
only in a negative sense. Machiavelli's imagination, however, accepts the legacy of the years, and converts it into an
instrument of positive achievement – a new instrument, but
still an imaginative one. On the other hand, it is nourished

[1] Adherents of the Medici. (Translator's note.)

and illumined by an intense love of political invention – an obscure mental process by which a given situation is endowed with unsuspected possibilities. Accordingly Machiavelli, in his active career, amid the ups and downs of his official life, no longer appears in the likeness of a diplomat (to use the word in its fifteenth-century connotation), but of a statesman whose like Italy had not seen for many years.

Behold him as he stands in the presence of Valentino. He, a poor, unknown ministerial secretary, lacking even the money with which to pay his travelling-expenses,[1] inexperienced in the handling of affairs,[2] and still dazed by the events that have followed one another during recent months in such bewildering profusion, has been sent by the Republic to keep a close watch on the activities of this *condottiere* – mocking, secretive, as close as the fine coat of mail that envelops his body: a domineering figure, thoughtful-looking by virtue of those vivacious eyes set in that pale face, almost austere, were it not for the thin lips which always seem to be repressing a scornful smile. And Niccolò, when he has heard him speak and seen him at work, surrounded by those other lordlings of baser metal, is inclined to forget he is the ambassador of a republic that is anxiously awaiting news. Accordingly his friends have to urge him to pay more heed to his duties; but he, with some relish, ventures to offer an opinion, and even wants to advise his masters. And they, in reply, tell him through the mouth of a friend – the honest, conscientious Buonaccorsi – that he must relate the facts and leave the opinions to others.[3]

[1] *Lettere Familiari*, XXXIII, XXXIV and XXXV. Valori and Buonaccors procure him thirty gold ducats. He describes his financial difficulties himself in the *Legazione al Valentino*, Letters 23, 27 October, 10, 18 December 1502.

[2] So much so that he himself thought it would have been better to send an orator, 'because the situation required a man of greater eloquence and reputation, and with a greater knowledge of the world, than myself...' (*Legazione al Valentino*, Letter 14 December 1502).

[3] *Lettere Familiari*, XXXII: '... it seems to me ... that you are not in a position to form such a positive opinion on the matter ... as you have done; and now that you have discussed, circumspectly and in detail, all that you have reported, leave the expression of an opinion to others...'

Later on he goes to the Tyrol to see the Emperor Maximilian; and first of all he gives the *Signoria* a detailed report on the general course of affairs. But he is not satisfied with reports and despatches. In this new world which he has quickly learned to know there is something that interests him more than the immediate decision of the Emperor. A vast, grave problem unfolds before his mind, of far greater significance to him than minute factual detail. And so we have the *Rapporto della Magna*, the *Discorso* and the *Ritratto*. In the same vein we gather that during his mission to France he was more interested in the nature of the French and of their affairs than in the cautious conversations of the Cardinal of Rouen. He does not forget the precise, concrete event that motivates his thought; and because of this he gradually accustoms himself to the difficult art of diplomacy, which is not quickly learned, and becomes an adept at it, even if, being a diplomat by chance and not by upbringing, he nearly always lacks the most important quality of the skilful poker-player – the ability to free his mind of the immediate impression and to determine the trend of his personal feelings by judicious analysis conducted in an atmosphere of calm reflection. But soon, with ingenuous and miraculous spontaneity, he makes his experience the cue for a long pilgrimage in the company of his creative imagination, which he cannot restrain, even when he has wholly withdrawn from public life and finds himself in the dark and without sure knowledge.[1]

It is hard to compare him with the other diplomats of the time, with the Venetians in particular, or even with such other Florentine merchants as Roberto Acciaiuoli or Francesco Guicciardini.[2] These men are in truth diplomats by nature. It would almost be correct to say that they exhibit the ultimate refinement of a gift for cold deliberation, inherited from a long line of ancestors, who originally were in

[1] *Lettere Familiari*, CXXVIII, to Francesco Vettori [July 1513].
[2] '... two of the sagest minds in Italy ...' (Varchi, *Storia Fiorentina*, Milan 1845, I, p. 313).

the habit of risking money held in trust by the banks, offering as part-security luck and their own nebulous credit, and
who later used to gamble expertly with the fortunes of their
States, serene in the realization of what they were doing.
Even when, in reporting on their stewardship, they show
themselves to be more accurate, more careful and sometimes
even more acute than Niccolò, we discern, deep down within
them, the wholly intellectual curiosity of the artist who
knows that he must etch in a rapid but complete picture, in-
corporating the most varied and most widely-contrasted
motifs. And so we find them trying, with inimitable perspicacity and sublety, to unravel the causes of things, and
dwelling on the mind of the individual man, with the object
of unmasking his most secret motives. But the interest here
lies solely in the effort of critical intuition and in the sagacity
it bespeaks. Their very style – clear and perspicuous, smoothly flowing and without trenchancy of expression – enables
the reader to discern, beneath the faint smile of the ambassador making his report, the narrowness, almost the pettiness,
of the man of affairs, with his reluctance to give himself away
and to enter fully, and therefore also emotionally, into the
game.

And so the greatest of these political adventurers, Messer
Francesco Guicciardini,[1] acts in a perfectly logical way when,
with Consalvo di Cordova in mind, he proceeds to write two
successive memoranda,[2] in the first of which he advises him
to come to Italy, while in the second he tries to dissuade him
from that enterprise; and when he first advises Pope Clement
VII to ally himself with Charles V, and afterwards seeks to
deter him from doing so.[3] He is not primarily concerned

---

[1] [This description of Guicciardini was unjust and erroneous. Latterly I
have modified my opinion, which at the time when I wrote this essay on
Machiavelli was still unduly coloured by the interpretation of De Sanctis.
Vidg my article on *Guicciardini* in the *Enciclopedia Italiana Treccani*, Vol.
XVIII (1933), pp. 224–8.]

[2] *Discorsi Politici*, V and VI, in *Opere inedite*, edited by G. Canestrini
(Florence, Barbera, 1859, I, pp. 244–8.)

[3] *Discorsi Politici*, XIII and XIV, in *op. cit.*, pp. 306–48.

with the realization of his plans or with their practical significance – to which he always seems to allude with a half-
smile, partly sceptical and partly contemptuous. He seeks
rather, with boundless wisdom, to reach the decision itself,
carefully formulating it against the difficult and disconcert-
ing background of his feelings.[1]

But to Niccolò the refined pleasure of periodically discerning the diverse motives of the human mind would be meaningless were it not for the fact that he can afterwards use
the information thus obtained to bring about the new reality,
the further development in which his original analysis loses
its very limited – I was about to say its purely intellective –
character, and acquires an inspirational and hence a moral
significance. The historical fact is not swallowed up in its
immediate context: instead, it is developed as a creative
force. Thus Machiavelli's analytical faculty is less penetrating, less sensitive to the slightest vibration, and less complete
than Guicciardini's. The latter's 'particular' (*particulare*) has a
precision and delicacy of outline, a subtlety of nuance of which
the former's 'general' (*generale*) is certainly not susceptible.
But whereas the lieutenant of the Holy Roman Church is hardly concerned with the reconstruction of the event, which too
often constitutes a mere diversion for his inquiring mind,[2] in

---

[1] Ferrari says of Guicciardini: 'He dwells on the fact, which is brilliantly
described, and is accepted intellectually but never morally . . .' (*Corso sugli
scrittori politici italiani e stranieri*, Milan, Aliprandi, 1862, p. 309); and he
attributes this attitude to a consciously critical outlook – the irony of the
thought that transcends the facts and will not stoop to remould them by its own
vitality, but seeks to avoid trouble of any kind. And indeed Messer Francesco
often seems to resort to contemplation in order to forget the sadness of life and
the misery of the times. His subtle analysis conceals sometimes a repressed
feeling of disdain, sometimes a faint bewilderment, a *discreet* bitterness. But
almost always his intellectual acceptance of facts leads him to forget every other
consideration and even his own humanity. He finds peace and contentment in
his habit of theorization without ever perceiving that thereby he is merely
allaying his inner torment. And so he refuses to create anything new – to be
extravagant; and he consoles himself with his beloved *particulare* and his
discrezione.

[2] Herein too consists the profound difference between the psychological
analysis of Guicciardini and that of Montaigne and of the great French writers

the case of the Secretary of the Council of Ten such research at
once strikes a deep chord of feeling, so that it becomes the
centre of a life that is neither apathetic nor amorphous, and
returns to his thoughts with a new significance, whence his
creativeness springs.

And so, after the official legation, we have the brief note,
the personal memoir, the rapid commentary, in which, beneath the apparent formality, the cold objectivity of the
analysis, behind the syllogistic co-ordination of the narrative,
we discern a lively interest, focused not so much upon the
event described as upon the various human motives which
underlie it, and the writer's need to create for himself ever
new experiences, to broaden the logical framework of his
mind through a constantly renewed study of the concrete
manifestations of human passion. He naturally has occasion
to dwell at length and with insistence on events which another diplomat would have reported, perhaps with even
greater precision, and consigned unremarked to the store-
house of his memories. Thus the mission to Valentino and
the Val di Chiana rebellion suggest to his mind the initial
fragments of his political reflections and provide the first
occasion for the exercise of his rapid and incisive style; and,
while any of those amiable Florentine and Venetian merchants, true *grands seigneurs* in everything – in the inflexions
of their voices, in the serenity and calm of their expressions,
in their wit and their avowed contempt for turbulent passions
– would have preferred to dwell upon that centre of European life, papal Rome, he, amid the tranquillity of his official
mission, puts his legation to Julius II out of his mind, and
instead descants upon the other two matters. It is a more
restricted *milieu*. There are no flaunting favourites here, no
solemn ceremonies, no lively court intrigues or palace gossip.

of the seventeenth century, e.g. La Rochefoucauld (though their method too is
admirable, and at first sight not unlike Guicciardini's in its formal expression).
With them the capacity to probe human motives is itself human in origin –
hence that quality of subdued melancholy which continues to characterize it.
In Guicciardini the same capacity is often purely intellectual in its inspiration.
The *Memoirs* do not become *Maxims*.

Yet what could afford a better opportunity for the acquisition of experience, the re-orientation of ideas and the reconstruction of events than this environment, in which the 'virtue' of the Florentine State finds true standards of comparison and true examples!

As reconstructed by Machiavelli these two events are transfigured for us; but in those days they were not greatly dissimilar from many others, and in particular they did not stand out in the minds of professional diplomats at a time when Ferdinand the Catholic and Louis XII were making their presence felt in Italy. The mere fact that they arrested Niccolò's attention is symptomatic of the profound and substantial gulf that divides him from his fellows, and reveals the complete disparity between their spiritual orientations and his own.

Thus from the start it is not difficult to discern, even in his apparent reserve, the initial development of the Florentine secretary's 'political imagination'. This is clearly apparent in the *Decennali*, a poor thing so far as its artistic merit is concerned, but vivacious and of supreme interest to those who perceive the clear indications which it contains of the author's need to derive from the welter of events a 'lesson' — in other words, a new experience. Here there are no official inhibitions; the reserve that was cultivated so painfully and laboriously has vanished; and we find emerging harsh, unwonted expressions, contemptuous opinions,[1] and later on admonitions and advice – Niccolò concludes the first *Decennale* with an appeal for the adoption of his own military system,[2] that personal creation into which he has poured his experience and his regenerative genius.

Niccolò wants to realize his creation. First he alludes to it in his literary compositions, then he proclaims it in the

---

[1] On Florence: 'You rested here with open beak in expectation of one from France who would bring you manna in the desert . . .' (*Decennale Primo*). And: 'Wherefore, in order to escape such pains, like those who can do no other, you . . .' (*ib.*).

[2] 'But the road would be short and easy if you were to re-open the temple to Mars.'

course of his governmental activities: and so we have the *Ordinance* on the infantry and the cavalry. Here is the true Machiavelli, assembling all the scattered elements of his experience and adapting them to another and more spacious form of existence with which they, viewed in the light of their individual, limited significance, would not appear to be commensurate. Now he recalls to mind the companies of the French archers, the Swiss and German infantry, the Roman militia – classical reminiscence and modern life are alike included in the field of his experience. Then, with an abrupt transition to the circumstances of his own country, he conceives a new possibility for this vision, and transforms what is a purely intellectual motif into a spontaneous emotional impulse. Reason finds its complement in imagination; the abstract vision is integrated by the act of faith.

Consider him, by contrast, in his private life. Here he reveals the same liveliness of sentiment, an identical urge to embrace the most diverse opinions, an equal sensibility. He wants to be agreeable in conversation, courteous towards his friends, ready alike for a joke or for an animated discussion; and he wants to bring his life a little closer to the lives of others, even if his critical mind enables him to perceive the moral wretchedness of his contemporaries. Varchi's story that he died of grief because Donato Giannotti was elected to the secretaryship in preference to himself and because he knew that he was universally hated was destined to become a legend;[1] but this legend gives us a very clear idea of the mentality of a man who, having condemned them in his heart, nevertheless wants to go on associating with those who are in theory the object of his scorn. And we can understand how he was able to dedicate the *Discourses* – 'a work that

---

[1] Varchi, *op. cit.*, I, p. 150. On the death of Machiavelli cf. P. Villari, *Niccolò Machiavelli e i suoi tempi*, Milan, Hoepli, 1897, III, p. 366; O. Tommasini, *La vita e gli scritti di Niccolò Machiavelli*, Rome, Loescher, 1883–1911, II, pp. 900 *sqq*. [The candidate who was preferred to Machiavelli was Francesco Tarugi, who for two years previously had been the first secretary of the Otto di Pratica, now abolished. On the death of Machiavelli, cf. now also R. Ridolfi, *Vita di Niccolò Machiavelli*, Rome, 1954, p. 374 *sqq*.]

certainly deals with a new subject, and of a kind that has
never been attempted ... by any man'[1] – to the friends of the
Orti Oricellari; how they listened to him in awed amaze-
ment; and how, finally, he was not above suspicion of having
incited by his conversation the men who were involved in the
anti-Medicean conspiracy of 1522.

Guicciardini, according to his contemporaries, was 'by
nature extremely arrogant', avaricious, and prompted by
personal ambition.[2] But Machiavelli, for all his scorn and
passing sarcasms, would return to the hurly-burly of life and
seek without hesitation to savour it anew at every moment, so
that he might transform his ideas into actions and his words
into concrete admonitions – so that, in short, he might fill
his mind with other things yet unknown to it, which later, in
the silence of his study, he might use for the construction of
fresh arguments. And so the thinker, whose whole life is a
continual search for experience – political experience – reduces that experience to a logical system, into which he
finally breathes new life by the passion and daring of his
ultimate synthesis.

Further developments take place in Italian life. The domination of Venice is relaxed, and Julius II allies himself with
Ferdinand the Catholic. Ravenna sees the King of France's
vain dreams of hegemony dissolve into thin air, and Prato
paves the way for the collapse of the ephemeral Florentine
Republic. The Medici return; Pier Soderini is banished to
Ragusa; and Machiavelli, not enough of a diplomat to win
the favour of the restored Government, his mind filled with
extravagant notions and bizarre opinions[3] by a restless imagination that renders him suspect, pays for his political pipe-
dreams by leaving the city.

He retires to the Albergaccio. It is a peaceful, lonely villa,
far removed from the world of practical affairs. Here the noise

[1] Nardi, *Istorie della Città di Firenze* (Florence, 1842), Book VII, ii, 86.
[2] Varchi, *op. cit.*, I, p. 245.
[3] *Lettere Familiari*, CLXXXI (from F. Guicciardini, 18 May 1521).

of the crowd is lost in the melancholy calm of the woods, through which he walks, an open book in his hand. And now, in his enforced solitude, there flow from his pen, disjointedly and in no precise order, the first fragments of the *Discourses*,[1] and the letters to Vettori.

Now, in the commentary on Livy the rigour of the analysis and the concentration of the author's thought on a remote world, on the past, may blind the reader to something that fundamentally is neither analytical nor logical – a passionate devotion to the Roman world, which is not merely envisaged, but is glorified and idealized in virtue of its stupendous political genius. Hence, what is assuredly original thought, at once intellectual and emotional in inspiration, seems at times nothing more than a historian's cleverness. On the other hand, Machiavelli's correspondence with his friend in Rome reveals unequivocally not only his overriding need to adhere entirely to political reality and subsequently – guided by his own inspiration – to transform it, but also his determination to make the results of his minute analysis the foundation of a hitherto unrealized Utopia. It is unnecessary to repeat that Machiavelli often deceives himself; that to him the Swiss peril becomes a nightmare, even when the facts belie its existence; and that he dreams of impossible agreements and envisages unrealizable events. The value of what he says does not lie in the exactness of the detail. It lies in his inexhaustible creativeness, which even overlooks known facts, because it strives above all after continual self-development and self-renewal through an ever-widening experience. He must seek this enrichment of his inner life everywhere, even at the expense of minuteness of detail. Hence Machiavelli the historian is sometimes less circumstantial, less precise, and even less shrewd in his reconstruction of single incidents than Guicciardini; yet it is this fact alone that enables him to write his masterpieces – the *Discourses*, *The Prince* and *The Art of War*. For him the important thing is

---

[1] On the composition of the *Discourses* cf. Villari, *op. cit.*, II, pp. 272 *sqq.* Tommasini, *op. cit.*, II, pp. 89, 144 *sqq.*

that any specific pretext should suffice both to make him
question himself and his experience – which embraces classical life and modern life, reminiscences of Livy and fifteenth-
century personalities, Italian and European – and to en-
courage him to make his thought ever more lucid and to
develop it boldly and conclusively.

In this by no means extensive correspondence we have,
then, the essence of Niccolò, who cannot remain silent inde-
finitely and is quite incapable of talking about wool and silk.[1]
First of all he promises himself that he will never again discuss politics and public affairs. Soon, however, he resumes
the argument, waxes enthusiastic, and conjures up mighty
visions, changing after his fashion both Italy and the course
of events.[2] Even his style adapts itself to the vagaries of his
fancy, and becomes as bitter as the indignation that is in his
heart, or as lively and concentrated as his reasoning or the
vehemence of his passion.

These months – July to December – witness the birth of
the treatise *De Principatibus*, known to us as *The Prince*. The
marginal notes on Livy are thrust aside. In the last of them,
incidentally, we can already discern an unwonted attitude of
mind. We find two or three entire chapters[3] in which the
people, who constitute the animating spirit of the *Discourses*,
are replaced by the lonely individual, while the heroic conflict of classes and parties fades into the inner conflict
of a man whose thoughts none may know. The brief treatise
is not meant to be a work of art. Rather is it intended
by its writer to resemble one of those numerous memoranda
or disquisitions on the reform of States which Machiavelli
himself wrote subsequently.[4] It is quickly completed. By

---

[1] *Lettere Familiari*, CXX and CXXVIII.

[2] This by no means implies that all the opinions which Machiavelli expresses in these letters are absurd or without a basis in fact. Very often he had a
truer vision of things than even the most recent of his imitators.

[3] E.g. Chaps. xxvi and xxvii of Book I.

[4] *Discorso sul riformare lo stato di Firenze*. Cf. Villari, *op. cit.*, III, pp. 56
sqq.; Tommasini, *op. cit.*, II, pp. 200 *sqq.* [Cf. now Ridolfi, *op. cit.*, pp. 275–
277, and n. 28, pp. 450–451, where the precise title of the work is also given.]

December the outline of the new man has been sketched in. Already he is stepping on to the political scene – a solitary figure, ruthless, thoughtful, inscrutable, epitomizing in himself the life of the whole State.

For now all other voices are silent. The people have become a scattered mob, awaiting only the 'issue of the event' – an amorphous mass that has brought down upon its head the severe judgment of Philippe de Commynes.[1] The nobility – now a pale shadow of its former self, mournfully reminiscent of Dante's elegy on the passing of the Middle Ages and of Guido del Duca's cry of anguish – is no longer united as a class. It has lost its pride of caste, its clannishness. It is a heterogeneous amalgam of individuals who wish to oppress the people (yet are incapable of doing so) in a way in which the people are unwilling to be oppressed, though they lack the energy to defend themselves unaided. Plebs and *Grandi* alike dissipate their energies in petty, calculating trickery, in desultory strife devoid of any serious plan or purpose, or even of the individual grandeur of personal heroism. The material is there, waiting supinely for the advent of the 'virtuous' prince, who 'by his laws and ordinances' will keep the population active[2] and will instil life where now there are only unwarlike feelings vegetating beneath the surface. The manna is about to fall from heaven; and men await it with open beaks.

This, moreover, will be the natural culmination of Italian history, the logical consequence of the atrophying of the communal spirit, of the weakness of the *Signorie*, which do not rest on a sufficiently broad and strong social foundation, and of the diplomatic skill exhibited by the various principates, which, after their last vain struggles for hegemony, have had to resort to party manoeuvring and to the policy of the 'balance of power' – the *federatio italica*. The people are

---

[1] '. . . et est la nature de ce peuple d'Italie, de ainsi complaire aux plus fors' (*Mémoires*, VII, ix; ed. Dupont, Paris, 1843).

[2] Chap. IX.

cut off from the life of the State, the various social classes have disintegrated, the country is hostile to the town. The prince alone holds the key to the accomplishment of his task. The Renaissance, in its artistic and literary aspect, has come about against a background of social and political decay. The prince is the one figure in this society of *littérateurs* and mediocrities who is alive. Yet he in his turn is alive only in a narrow and limited sense. Diplomacy is the one field open to him. Politics – which connote a capacity for struggle, a consciousness of purpose, a consistency of aim and an inner creativeness – lie far outside his scope.[1]

Hence, not even a prince of exceptional virtue could have accomplished the miracle. The strong State, capable of holding off the 'barbarians' and encouraging the free development of national life, could not be created where no community of interest and sentiment bound the subjects to the master and the mob to the government, making all aware that they were involved in a struggle for the common defence. It was an illusion to suppose that even an exceptional power of human achievement, a special insight and a partial reform of external policy could ensure the existence of an organism that was now dead.

Very pointed, therefore, was the objection raised by Guicciardini, the merchant and diplomat, who avoided the dangers of a too vivid imagination by confining himself to the placid but somewhat melancholy realm of desire. He would have wished Italy to be free; but it was useless to consider the eventuality; indeed, since it was inevitable that the country should be subservient to barbarian overlords it was as well that they should be two in number, so that while they were occupied with their own disputes the subject cities might at least be left to enjoy a more peaceful existence.[2] He

---

[1] I shall deal more fully with this question, as well as with that of the historical and political significance of *The Prince* (here barely touched upon) [see Chap. II]. Meanwhile the student should see the excellent observations on statecraft considered as a work of art in Burckhardt's *The Civilization of the Renaissance*.

[2] *Discorsi Politici*, VIII, in *Opere inedite*, I, p. 264.

develops on an ample scale the concept of the balance of power and party rivalry, applying it to the field of European politics in the hope that it will be the means of preserving the narrower life of the cities, as indeed, in days gone by, it had saved Florence and Ferrara from the insatiable greed of Venice and Naples. But he in his turn fails to perceive how, when the delicate machine changes hands, its rhythm is inclined to change as well.

Niccolò, on the other hand, has just been seeking, for the first time, to identify the glory of Rome with the perennial conflict between her social classes.[1] His soul is still deeply stirred by the thought of those tumultuous struggles between free men, and he has said very clearly that if a State is to achieve greatness those who are brought under its sway by conquest must be turned into citizens, not subjects.[2] In this way he discountenances the entire history of the Italian communes and with a sure touch reveals their inherent weakness. He should accordingly foresee the final ruin of Italy, and seek only to repair her fortunes, so far as that is possible, through diplomatic manoeuvres. Instead, he falls once more under the spell of his imagination, forgets the *Discourses*, and with feverish speed constructs the framework of the new State. Revealing a miraculous power of political invention, he disregards the history of the late fifteenth century and resuscitates the policy of Gian Galeazzo and Ladislao of Naples – the first great 'Seigneurial' policy. With the aid of that power of reconstruction which he alone possesses he integrates it, and advocates its revival, at a time when it is no longer feasible.

He looks about him for some figure who reveals unmistakable signs of excellence. He discovers Valentino, and completes his ideal man after his fashion by adding a dash of Ferdinand the Catholic, Francesco Sforza and Louis XI. He suggests remedies for every untoward happening and corrects the errors of past governments, thinking by such attention to detail to restore an edifice whose foundations have

---

[1] *Discorsi*, I, Chaps. iv, v and vi.   [2] *Ib.*, II, Chaps. iii and iv.

c

collapsed. In fact, he has discovered the real mistake: the cause of all his country's misfortunes is clear. It is the employment of mercenary forces, the great vice of princes, who, content with fine phrases and skilful diplomacy, have renounced their only true *métier* — with the result that Italy has been pillaged, ravished and traduced, and they have become private citizens.

The general character of *The Prince* — not only its formal scheme, but the actual spirit that pervades it — is clearly revealed in these chapters on the creation of a militia. Here is the wound that must be healed. The very style assumes an unusually emotional tone. The writer's grief and indignation, previously expressed in the rapidity of his phrase, in the concealed ending of the period, or even by means of a very subtle irony, so fleeting as to be barely perceptible,[1] now suddenly burst forth in all their vehemence. We witness the first stirrings of his passion, which subsequently, in the highly emotional peroration, upsets the logical pattern of the work, and which later reaches a despairing climax in the concluding passage of *The Art of War*.

In fact Machiavelli, conceiving the possibility of a national militia, in which the arms will be entrusted to the citizens, while the State will be defended by the individuals who compose it, looks beyond the narrow limits of contemporary history and the present state of Italian civilization and treads a new path. In this case he does not merely resume the motifs of Italian political development, but amplifies them. However, he fails to perceive that such a revolution in the military art must have its counterpart in a political and social regeneration. A citizen militia is an impossibility unless the State lives from day to day in the inner consciousness of the people; and so the Principate, as he conceives it, is doomed to disaster. The mere enunciation of the new military theory must inevitably entail the abandonment of the concept of the Prince.

[1] Cf. Chap. xi, *Of Ecclesiastical Principates*: 'These alone possess States, and do not defend them.'

He does not realize the fact, and he leaves his thesis un-completed. He draws his inspiration from the examples of France, Switzerland and Republican Rome, failing to per-ceive that his models possess a hidden quality – the very quality that Italian civilization has now lost. His precepts will be carried out not many years later by a prince who will introduce his race of mountaineers – a rough, impoverished yet hardy breed – to the Italian political scene for the first time in history. But the monarchy of Emmanuel-Philibert is not the Italian principate of Machiavelli's dreams.

And so the prince was not forthcoming; and the little book, written at an anxious time, when miraculous events seemed to be looming up on the distant horizon,[1] met with a contemptuous reception on the part of Lorenzo de' Medici. The feckless nephew of Leo X preferred his hounds to a pamphlet that was not full of 'grandiloquent phrases',[2] and Machiavelli experienced a fresh rebuff.

But he, in his enthusiasm for his work, failed to perceive the fragility of the 'castelluccio' that he was seeking to build; and he continued to write with undiminished fervour.

Thus we have the logical pattern of the book. For quite unlike Savonarola, whose principal theme is one of revolt against the times and the historical situation,[3] Niccolò starts by accepting that situation, at any rate in its essence. His mind, which closely identifies itself with contemporary his-tory, has been sharpened and stimulated by the not un-

---

[1] Apropos of this crisis in Italian history, and of the 'combinazioni' of the Medici and their repercussions on Machiavelli's mind, cf. Tommasini, *op. cit.*, II, pp. 76 *sqq.*

[2] The anecdote is related by Alvisi (*Lettere Familiari*, Introduction, p. xiv).

[3] In the *Discorso sul riformare lo stato di Firenze* Machiavelli does, indeed, revert in some degree to Savonarola's thesis. His insistence on the necessity of re-opening the 'Sala' and governing the city by liberal methods echoes, at least in part, the democratic refrain of 1495. That vague confidence in the Italians of his day – a mysterious sentiment, not a reasoned conviction – which enables him to write *The Art of War* (apropos of which I again refer the reader to the essay already mentioned [Chapter II]) and his love for his native land now open up new prospects before him, and tend to bring him back to that point of view which *The Prince* would seem positively to condemn.

profitable labour of twelve years; and he takes advantage of this unfailing gift of analysis, this serene logicality and realistic observation of life with its variety and intensity, to lay down the broad lines of his picture. The serenity and cautiousness of his reasoning do not conflict with his imagination. The latter alone enables him, once he has picked out the pieces, to re-unite them in a final vision, to refashion them into a perfect organism of which they are the separate ingredients. The others – the diplomats – do not go beyond the first stage; they cannot conceive the possibility of making a fresh start, and their world is bounded by their own subtlety and discretion. Savonarola is incapable of controlling his passions to the point of making them conform to a coherent and cast-iron system and investing them with the imperceptible nuances in which life abounds. Machiavelli, on the other hand, knows how to take advantage of his experience, which by now provides him with a wealth of themes, in such a way as to convert it, with the help of his imagination, into a new political form. This will enable him to leave a wholly personal imprint on the history of political thought, from which succeeding generations – outside Italy – will in their turn draw ampler and more certain conclusions. Of the others, the Dominican friar can only provoke in a few of those who come after him a momentary and rare awakening of conscience, while the diplomats establish the ultimate pattern of Italian civilization, their highest achievement being the inauguration of the life of the Grand Ducal court, with its monotony, circumspection and insularity.

Thus, of the twenty-six chapters of which *The Prince* consists, twenty-five are severely logical. The argument follows a direct course, without digressions or interruptions; the analysis is conducted with incisiveness and subtlety; the thought, which is welded carefully and surely into a unified whole, is discriminating and precise. Step by step the new State emerges. Of its multifarious elements all are subjected to individual scrutiny, and the effective worth of each is duly tested.

For his characters Machiavelli did not have to look very far afield. In that horde of princelings and *condottieri* who harassed the cities of Central Italy he found the scattered fragments of his Prince, the single features that were fit to be reincarnated in that more complete and more coherent figure. His memory was sufficiently agile for him to recall personages from the most recent history – Sigismondo Malatesta, for example, at once fox and lion, *condottiere* and diplomat, adept in frustrating the moves of hostile armies or devising the most subtle schemes to outwit the sagacity of his rivals. It was from these men, and from others too – the excessively calm, untroubled face of Ferdinand the Catholic in the background is disturbing, and there is food for thought in those words of his which speak of nothing but faith and peace, just as we are compelled to wonder at the military capacities of Francesco Sforza – it was from this rich and varied experience, made up of the most diverse elements, that Niccolò derived the details of his picture. Hence, behind the closeness of his thought, through which his principles are systematized and marshalled with calm assurance, we can always detect a living, concrete reality, we can constantly hear the echo of that historical note which is introduced so smoothly into his incisive, almost dictatorial assertions; and we can no longer discern exactly which part represents experience and which the overlay of imagination, nor are we able to separate the voice of the world from the voice of logic and the voice of the author's mind.

We note the freshness and vigour of the slight action, which is true to life and at times concentrated in an image, at times subtly veiled by a clear, concise precept. We note the writer's ability to seize upon the dominant motifs of events and to analyse them, shrewdly and serenely. Finally, we note his imagination, which, just as it has enabled him to conceive the possibility of *The Prince*, now, when he comes to write it, permits him to assemble all his scattered information and reflections, to reintegrate them in a wholly unforeseen unity, and to transform them into a political experience that is new, even if it is only a cherished dream. And there emerges the political struggle, whose existence is affirmed naturally and confidently: the State acts and conquers and destroys, without having to account for its actions to anyone; it is already paramount. For the moment it still lacks a full inner life – a continuous existence in the mind of the nation that is called upon to create it hour by hour. It is therefore formal, just as the political struggle is only external; but meanwhile it no longer looks outside itself for its *raison d'être*. It does not even look for this within itself. It is represented in its moment of equilibrium, which will never return, and which seeks nothing and has no need of justification or explanation.

The creation of the solitary inhabitant of San Casciano is an absurd creation, since it presupposes the possibility of a strong State where no social life is available to sustain it. Here, indeed, by a strange paradox, Machiavelli does not see things clearly – he who has exposed the political degradation of Italy;[1] yet, in another sense, *The Prince* gives a complete and perfect picture to which nothing can be added. It is a brief but impressive synopsis of Italian history with special reference to its ultimate outcome, as conceived by the men of the Renaissance; and if the little book does not deal with particular periods, and if it is not specifically a historical source, at least it catches and explains, and indicates the ultimate consequences of, the spirit that has determined those single moments and integrated them in the course of its development. What this Italian civilization most obviously lacks Niccolò invents – namely, a militia of its own (*milizia propria*), and this is the creative act in which the vital power of his imagination is most apparent. And certainly, if partial reforms of State laws, coupled with manly virtues, had

---

[1] Cf. *Discorsi*, I, vi, xii, xvii, xxxviii, xlv, xlix; II, xix, xxx; III, xxxi; *Arte della Guerra*, Books I and VII; *Decennali*; *Asino d'Oro*, V; *Istorie Fiorentine*, I, xxix ('The Venetians . . . like all the other Italian princes, are the liegemen of others'); *Lettere Familiari*, CXXXI ('As for the union of the other Italians you make me laugh – first, because no union will ever do any good . . .') and CXXXIV ('we Italians, poor, ambitious and despicable . . .') (dated 10 and 26 August 1513).

been all that was necessary to save the Italian domains and
the fortunes of our civilization, the formula for salvation was
to be found, in effect, in *The Prince*.

The argument is closely reasoned until the last chapter but
one. Here, the sentiment and the spirit that inform the book
are already becoming more immediately apparent. At the end
of the work Machiavelli finds himself confronted by Fortune. He has constructed his 'little castle' down to the smallest detail, bit by bit. He has strengthened it with good laws
and good weapons, he has made it more secure by prohibit-
ing useless liberality and empty confidence, which is more
transparent than glass. But now, at the very last, an agonizing question poses itself: Can man accept the warning in a
spirit of faith and hope? Or does Fate decree that it too shall
be in vain? There is a mysterious force, which none of the
historians and politicians of the early sixteenth century can
clearly visualize – at one moment they identify it with the
logic of events,[1] at another they regard it as an intangible
external constraint which comes from above and guides
events blindly, as it wills and where it lists. As a result of its
workings Italy is now seen to be enslaved and reviled and the
fortunes first of the Lombards, then of the Venetians and
Florentines, seem to have deteriorated 'in wondrous wise'.[2]
How is this force to be combated, kept within limits – if
indeed it is possible to set limits to a river in full spate?

This question reflects the spiritual anxiety of the man who,
even when reason and logic have shown the way, remains in
doubt, unable to decide whether to pass on to the final act of
creation or to halt on the threshold, lost in a maze of detail;
the man who, noticing that something is missing, realizes
that he must bridge the gap at a single bound, without
measuring the length of his flight. Here, indeed, is the
dramatic moment of contrast between subtle diplomacy and
the vigorous imagination. The one refuses to make the jump

[1] B. Croce, *Teoria e storia della storiografia*, Bari, 1917, pp. 215–16.
[2] Guicciardini, *Storia d'Italia*, VIII, vii (ed. Gherardi, Florence, 1919).

and, without discussing the ruling principle of the world, Fortune, accepts it implicity, denying the value of the general rule and adapting itself to the particular situation. The other presses on, for a moment abandoning logic and prudence in the hope of reaching the final stage of creation. At this point Guicciardini pauses, deep in thought, then, breaking into a half melancholy, half cunning smile, warns us that it is useless to persist. On the other hand, Machiavelli advances, and pens his exhortation to the Italians to free their country from the barbarians.

The chapter on 'Fortune', and indeed the mere suggestion of a discussion of its power, signifies that the agonizing doubt is already virtually resolved. Niccolò discusses the matter at length and, with some reluctance, half-acknowledges the authority of the goddess who has come to life during this ultimate phase of Italian civilization. But notice how the only purpose of his ratiocination is to ensure that his thought has that consistency of form and practical validity the existence of which in his heart he has long recognized. Notice, too, how the significance of human activity is already affirmed.[1] The thinker's insistence on a logical approach, his need to convince the Seigneur to whom the work is to be addressed on this point also, and the necessity of opposing something clear, precise and positive to the vague pessimism and flabby indifference of the mob, which is not least to blame for the present misfortunes, induce him, here as before, to define the limitations and to analyse the influence of party activity. But already his emotions are stirred, and they find expression in a clarion call that is intended to rouse the sleepers and to pave the way for the new greatness of Italy. Observe how the digression on Fortune is almost immediately robbed of its doctrinal severity by the interpolation of a vivid simile, how it terminates in a vigorously expressive

---

[1] The problem of Fortune has in effect been resolved already in the course of a simple allusion to the subject: '. . . these princes of ours who held sway for many years should not blame fortune for the subsequent loss of their principates, but their own slothfulness . . .' (Chap. xxiv).

image. The abstract scheme is first thrown into confusion by the onrush of the swollen, turbid river, then disappears completely in face of the almost sculptural representation of the woman who allows herself to be beaten and submits to young men. This imperceptible transition from reasoning to imagery, from the concept to the effigy, from the systematic argument to the rapidly-drawn picture, is typical of Machiavelli, who is now dominated by his imagination and his emotions. And suddenly there comes the final exhortation, already implicit in that half logical, half imaginative analysis of Fortune, implicit for that matter in the entire treatise, from the first deduction to the last, from the most trivial comment to the boldest theorization.

For the mere fact that Machiavelli conceived the possibility of political reconstruction amid that welter of events which revealed ever more clearly the irremediable weaknesses of Italian society and politics and the vacuum in which the constitutions of the principates had taken shape; the fact that he followed up this possibility, made it the subject of rational argument, gave it concrete life within a framework of analytical subtleties – all this was already a call, a heartfelt, tragic appeal which broke the closed circle of logical observation and let in a passionate emotion, a palpitating, restless hope. And if in the end his faith and importunity can no longer be suppressed, if they vent themselves in a sudden outpouring of feeling and find their complement in that enslaved, beaten and disrupted Italy which compels pity, this is nothing but the final expression of that non-logical, non-intellective world which has been growing within the rational world all through the work. Having put reality and the conventional interpretation of history behind him, Niccolò must needs return to them with that new germ of life which he has engendered by transforming his experience into creativeness and his memories – both classical and modern – into a renewed political consciousness. Thus the worlds of logic, imagination and emotion, sureness of coordination and observation, vigour of synthesis, and the will to action, are blended into a single organism, so compact that if you detach the smallest element the whole will crumble in your hand.

Such is the spiritual unity of which *The Prince* is born. And the rapid, excited, almost feverish way in which the author's mind opens on to those vast and ever broadening horizons, the close reasoning, the intensely dramatic character of the thought, due to the continual and progressive blending of the two worlds, the logical and the imaginative – these have their counterpart in the graphic, incisive, and intensely vivacious quality of the formal expression.

However, the headings of the various chapters are in Latin. In this, in the persistence of the legal custom, we detect almost an unconscious need on the author's part to regulate the force of his imagination, to contain it within the tranquil limits of a formula which through long literary usage had acquired an austere, almost solemn quality. As he explicitly says, Niccolò does not seek to create a work of art, nor to adorn his dissertation with 'turgid parentheses or grandiloquent phrases'. Such is not his aim. He seeks to revive political wisdom, not literary finesse, to convince, not to win applause, to stir men's feelings, not to soothe them by the elegance of his style. And so it is right to frame the treatise in a solemn and orderly setting of ceremonious forms, which must lend an air of gravity and calm reasonableness to the style and restrain the liveliness of the sentiment. In this way the work may in fact become acceptable reading to those who govern.

Again, in the course of his analysis he employs Latin words, legal forms, expressions that are an echo of Roman law[1] – minor interpolations, light touches in which at first sight one can perceive nothing but pedantry, the last vestiges of an outmoded fashion; yet they introduce into the ceaseless argument the homely familiarity of the letters,[2] and

[1] Thus 'iure hereditario' (Chap. xix).

[2] In which they appear continually and constantly. Cf. especially the letters to Guicciardini, who also uses them himself.

they give us a vivid picture of Niccolò, who in his writing immediately seizes upon the expression that is running through his mind after long conversations, spread over many years, with colleagues in the Chancellery and officials of the Republic, and imbues it with the spontaneous vivacity of his own temperament. On the other hand, however, this style bears the indelible stamp of tradition: it is the echo of a wide experience in the past. Hence, at times the Latin word seems, as it were, to slow down the tempo of the period, to moderate its ardour in such a way as to facilitate the solemn introduction of the historical reminiscence.[1] We have, at one and the same time, a nonchalant familiarity and a traditional dignity, and we notice that the thought, naturally direct in its expression, is nevertheless kept within the limits of a decorous and simple form. Just as the classical image merges completely into the experience of the writer, colouring the abstract vision which in its turn imparts to the image its own essential dynamism, so in the Latin words, sandwiched between two phrases, we discern the absolute blending of reminiscence and sentiment, of tradition and everyday life. Hence the style – a mixture of the familiar and the lofty, the immediate and the considered, clearly illustrating the ceaseless alternation of the various phases of thought, which nevertheless are always closely integrated. There is no effort, no striving after effect. The ancient and modern motifs which inform Niccolò's experience and logic are so inseparable that the seemingly archaic phrase is sometimes the only one in which the idea can be directly and unequivocally expressed.

In their turn, dialectal forms intrude themselves. The loftiest phraseology is succeeded by the forthright language of the people – vivacious, fresh and concise, just as the thought is vivacious and concise. At the end of a dignified passage the author for a moment allows himself to give vent to his inmost feelings. Then the period collapses. At times we are left in suspense by a prodigious anacoluthon. There

[1] Thus 'In Italy we have, *in exemplis* . . .' (Chap. ii).

are abrupt transitions from one subject to another, from singular to plural. Yet the argument always appears lucid and closely-reasoned, since what is clearly before the writer's mind is the fundamental theme, not the detail or the parenthetical observation, which he introduces in telescopic form, at times leaving it incomplete so that he may return without ado to his principal line of thought. This follows an undeviating course; and we are conscious of the initial clarity of the author's vision, into which these side-issues insinuate themselves one by one, being admitted only in so far as they suffice to add colour to the central idea, then left in mid-air if their full treatment would in the slightest degree detract from the powerful unity of his conception.

At certain points, when logic becomes too rigid a vehicle for the sentiment, the style suddenly becomes lighter. We may encounter a piece of intense irony, so subtle and perfect that it begins and ends between the subject and the verb and needs no adjective to lend it colour.[1] Or the writer will pronounce a sorrowful malediction, which derives its fervour and its force from four stressed participles.[2] Here too Machiavelli the artist scorns the adjective, the ornament, and forces the bald, simple noun to create the image unaided.

So we come to the last chapter. This epitomizes and sets the seal upon the logical world and makes it the theme of a vehement and sublime peroration. In the same way, its initial note of dismay and anguish, the subsequent quieter arrangement of the period, the religious simplicity of the Biblical image, and finally the broken, almost timorous prayer, interrupted by a rapid series of questions—for the author's passion is mounting—symbolize the successive transitions from hope

[1] Chap. xi, *Of Ecclesiastical Principates*: 'These alone have States, and do not defend them; subjects, and do not govern them; and their States being, undefended, are not taken away from them; and their subjects, not being governed, care naught for them, and neither think, nor are able, to secede from them.'

[2] Chap. xii: 'And the result of their *virtù* is that Italy has been laid waste by Charles, plundered by Louis, violated by Ferrando and abused by the Swiss.'

to sadness, from faith to despondency, from calm to excitement, which form the pattern of *The Prince*. The first chapter has the economy and the flexibility of a syllogism; but this, the last one, with the introduction of Biblical reminiscences opens out on to limitless horizons; when the writer allows his hopes to revive and lifts his eyes from his beaten and enslaved Italy it aspires to the austere emotion of a religious warning. At the end the periods follow thick and fast like hammer-blows. The image, subdued for a moment by the serenity of the Biblical reminiscence, re-asserts itself forcefully, with a vehemence that is wholly human, breaking up the period – until the writer, unable to find a concluding sentence that is sufficiently incisive, has recourse to Petrarch's heart-cry.

So ends *The Prince*. Machiavelli's imagination has created his masterpiece. Later on, it will create *The Art of War*; and it will be veiled then in an introspective melancholy, for the princes do not listen; they 'persist in the same error, and live amid the same disorder, heedless of warnings and the lesson of events.'[1] When he wrote *The Prince* Niccolò had faith: now he has none left. The events that have unfolded between 1513 and 1519 have shown him the emptiness of his dream. France has returned to the plains of Lombardy; Lorenzo de' Medici, with the utmost difficulty and by shabby expedients, has succeeded in saving his Duchy of Urbino; and Machiavelli, though he cannot see what constitutes the real weakness of his creation, of his *principate*, nevertheless perceives that it is unrealizable. He ascribes the blame to the futility of the princes,[2] without appreciating that 'futility', in other words incompetence, is a characteristic of the whole of Italian society – in the form in which it has emerged from the life of the Communes – and not merely of individual men. *The Art of War* has its origin, then, in the disappointment of a hope.

---

[1] *The Art of War*, VII.

[2] 'I am now starting to write again, and I vent my feelings by indicting the princes, who have all done everything possible to bring us to our present pass' (*Lettere Familiari*, CXCIX, letter written to Francesco Guicciardini in 1525).

The author's imagination confines itself to its intellectual function; it loses the passionate faith which contemplates reality and seeks to alter it. Machiavelli writes 'for the satisfaction of those who are lovers of ancient exploits'.[1] There is still the capacity for reconstruction, but the will to act is lacking.

Hence the very style has an air of peacefulness and melancholy. In the construction of the sentences, which are linked more closely to those that precede, in the sometimes slow and pensive rhythm of the period,[2] in the quiet opening stresses of an imaginative passage,[3] we detect this new sense of disillusionment and self-withdrawal. Even the denunciation of the princes, which takes the form of a symmetrical, ample period, fully developed and complete in every particular, lacks the excited, abrupt tone of the curt reproof in *The Prince*.[4] This relaxation and self-withdrawal is even more pronounced in *The Life of Castruccio*. Observe the slow, almost solemn beginning of the dying Castruccio's speech.[5]

[1] Preface to *The Art of War*.

[2] 'When they had arrived and sat down, some on the grass, which in that place is very fresh, some on the seats, which thereabouts stand in the shade of some very tall trees, Fabrizio praised the place as being delightful; and having looked at the trees, and failing to recognize some of them, he remained in suspense . . .' 'I thought it was as you say, and this place and these meditations reminded me of certain princes of the Kingdom, who delight in these ancient plants and shadowy groves. And having paused for a while, as if absorbed in his thoughts . . .' (Book I).

[3] 'And I grieve when I think of nature . . .' (Book VII).

[4] Chap. XII: 'And the result of their *virtù* is . . .'

[5] 'If I had believed, my son, that Fortune wished to cut short at the half-way stage my journey to that glory which my numberless successes had led me to count on, I should have exerted myself less; and I should have bequeathed to you a smaller State perhaps, but even fewer enemies and fewer jealous rivals; for, content with the dominion of Lucca and Pisa, I should not have subjugated the folk of Pistoia, nor irritated the Florentines by inflicting upon them so many injuries. But having won the friendship of both these peoples, I should certainly have had a quieter, if not a longer life, and the State which I bequeath to you, if smaller, would undoubtedly have been more secure, more firmly based.'

[I feel bound to point out that in the *Italia* edition of Machiavelli's works (1813), as well as in *Le opere di Niccolò Machiavelli*, II, ed. Passerini and Milanesi, Florence-Rome, 1874, the paragraph quoted above is printed as a

Notice, too, how in the prolongation of the admirably constructed period all vehemence of passion disappears, leaving only the melancholy of the backward glance into the past.

Little by little, slowly but without pause, Machiavelli's imagination slides back into the past, loses its creative vigour and assumes the form of an interpretative faculty. And so we have the *Florentine Histories.*

The mere contemplation of this turbulent past nearly always has the effect of weakening what is Niccolò's true strength, namely his imagination; his analytical shrewdness and his logicality, forced to be self-sufficing, do not always attain the subtlety, or enable him to achieve the stupendous clarity of outline, which characterize Guicciardini's reconstruction of history. In the same way, however, instead of the taut and incisive diction of *The Prince* we often find the perfectly articulated period, the flowing sentence, the discriminating word, with its polish and precision. Usually we miss that ability which is apparent in *The Prince* – the ability to force the individual word and the construction to contribute to the rapid expression of the idea.

When he confines himself to the evocation of Italian history Machiavelli becomes less than himself.

single sentence, whereas in *Tutte le opere storiche e letterarie di Niccolò Machiavelli,* ed. G. Mazzoni and M. Casella, Florence, 1929, and in the more recent editions of Machiavelli's works prepared by A. Panella, Vol. I, Milan, 1938 (*I classici Rizzoli*) and by F. Flora and C. Cordié, Vol. I, Milan, 1949 (*I classici Mondadori*), a full stop has been inserted after *meno invidia* ('fewer jealous rivals'). However, I consider that neither the sense, nor the continuity, nor the symmetry of the period is in any way affected by this division. It seems to me that even in the new reading the passage fully retains its air of solemnity and restraint.]

II

THE PRINCE: *Myth and Reality*

I. THE GENESIS OF *THE PRINCE*

IN the early months of 1513 Machiavelli, still smarting
from the effects of his brief imprisonment,[1] had retired to
his villa near San Casciano, a small village situated on top
of a hill between the Val di Greve and the Val di Pesa. In this
peaceful, lonely spot the passionate sense of life which had
troubled the last days of his public career gradually lost its
intensity, and his thoughts, ridding themselves completely of
their emotional content, stood out in bolder relief, the personal element being kept within clearly-defined limits. Florence was now far away, dimly outlined with its towers
against the misty background of the sky, and to Niccolò it
was at last given to contemplate his own work and that of
others with the serenity of the critic. Hitherto he had
thought about it only at the instant of its performance, with
that sense of urgency which is characteristic of the government official.

The truth is that he had at first sought to avoid any preoccupation which might renew, even indirectly, his contact
with a world of which he retained far from happy memories;[2]

[1] P.Villari, *Niccolò Machiavelli e i suoi tempi*, 3rd edition, Milan, 1912–14,
II, p. 211; O. Tommasini, *La vita e gli scritti di Niccolò Machiavelli*, Rome,
1883–1911, II, pp. 80 *sqq.*

[2] *Lettere Familiari* (Alvisi edition), CXXVIII. Quotations from Machiavelli's works refer to the *Italia* edition of 1813. Only in the case of *The Prince*
have I adhered to my own edition (Turin, U.T.E.T., 1924).

[For the reader's convenience, when quoting from the *Florentine Histories*, I
have indicated the numbers of the chapters as given in P. Carli's critical edition
(two volumes, Florence, 1927). Moreover, to conform to modern usage I have
altered the old title *Ritratti delle cose di Francia* to *Ritratto di cose di Francia.*]

but since fate had not granted him the temperament of a wool-merchant nor sufficient experience to talk about the profits and losses of a banking-house, it remained for him either to languish in silence or to talk about the State, building his 'little castles'[1] in the manner to which long years of arduous activity had accustomed him. Languish in silence Machiavelli could not; and so he began to reflect upon political matters.

Such is the origin of the first fragments of the *Discorsi*.[2]

[1] *Ib.*, CXX.

[2] On the composition of the *Discorsi* cf. Villari, *op. cit.*, II, pp. 271 *sqq.*; Tommasini, *op. cit.*, II, pp. 89, 144 *sqq.* It may be regarded as certain that at the time when Machiavelli started work on *The Prince* the first book of the *Discorsi* was already largely complete. Perhaps, too, he had already written certain other passages which were included in the later books, although by virtue of their content they belong rather to the first. In Chap. II of *The Prince* there is an explicit admission of the work already done: 'I will refrain from discussing Republics, because I discussed them at length on an earlier occasion.' Moreover, that the arrangement of the *Discorsi* does not always conform to a precise, orderly and logical system (Tommasini, *op. cit.*, pp. 146–7) is clearly revealed by various passages that are unrelated to the adjoining chapters. Again, the example given of Francis I (Book I, Chap. xxiii) proves that the passage in question was written after 1515, and hence that the first fragments of the *Discorsi* were also completed after an interval.

[In recent years the problem of the composition of the *Discorsi* has been re-examined and presented in a new light by several scholars.

It had always been accepted that the opening of Chap. II of *The Prince* ('I will refrain from discussing Republics, because I discussed them at length on an earlier occasion') was a reference to the *Discorsi*. However, F. Gilbert (*The Composition and Structure of Machiavelli's Discorsi*, 'Journal of the History of Ideas', XIV, 1953) has advanced the hypothesis that this remark refers not to the *Discorsi*, but to a lost manuscript dealing with republics, which Machiavelli subsequently used for the first eighteen chapters of the first book of the *Discorsi*. These latter, Gilbert continues, consist in essence of a commentary on Livy: this commentary, begun in 1515, when Machiavelli began to frequent the Orti Oricellari, was arranged in its present form and completed in 1517.

Subsequently, J. H. Hexter (*Seyssel, Machiavelli and Polybius VI: the Mystery of the Missing Translation*, 'Studies in the Renaissance', III, 1956), taking as his starting point Chap. II of the first book of the *Discorsi*, which is derived from Polybius, has pointed out that Machiavelli did not know Greek, and could not have been acquainted with the sixth book of Polybius, in the translation of Janus Lascaris, earlier than 1515. Finally, H. Baron (*The Principe and the Puzzle of the Discorsi*, 'Bibliothèque d'Humanisme et Renaissance', XVIII, 1956) has maintained that the opening sentence of Chap. II of *The Prince* was added after the composition of the rest of the work, probably

Niccolò transforms the dismay and desperation which make his daily existence a misery into a spiritual refreshment, an exaltation of the past, a vivid recollection of a political virtue such as no one had ever been able to recall to life. And the tedious days, spent in the company of love-poets and amid the shouts of carters, the yells of trick-track players and the wrangling of woodmen, end in sudden crowded visions of the figures of other days. The room in which the exile dons his curial robes opens on to horizons undreamed of.[1]

Nor was it simply because of his delight in humanism that the evocation of things Roman became a mental habit.[2] Machiavelli's sole consolation in those days was his passionate belief in a strong, healthy State, permeated by lively energies and sustained by the excellence of its people. His faith had been intensified by his recent disillusionment, so that he was obliged to meet the brutal lesson of events with the theoretical strength of his sincere belief, which could only find concrete expression in the recollection of former times. A single glance at distant Florence, wrapped in the mists of sunset, sufficed to supply a bitter answer: the salvation, even the salvation – more a hope than a certainty – of which his embittered soul stood in need was not to be found there.

Nor was it to be found in the history of Italy. For if the thinker did not always have a comprehensive vision of the life of the Communes and its inner development, he did at any rate succeed in discerning its ultimate weakness and the

in 1516, when Machiavelli dedicated *The Prince* to Lorenzo de' Medici. According to Baron, the *Discorsi* were written in 1515–1516.

The problem of the relationship between the composition of *The Prince* and the *Discorsi* would thus be completely reversed. But, despite the ingenious, and often over-subtle arguments put forward, I do not think it is possible to accept the foregoing hypotheses. I remain of the opinion that the opening sentence of Chap. II of *The Prince* is a precise reference to the *Discorsi*, that it is not a subsequent addition, and that, as a consequence, when Machiavelli began work on *The Prince*, he had already written at least a part of the first book of the *Discorsi*.]

[1] Letter to Francesco Vettori, dated 10 December 1513.
[2] Cf. R. Fester, *Machiavelli*, Stuttgart, 1900, p. 139.

negativity of its political achievements, just as he was conscious of the ethical and social disintegration of his time;[1] and the only period of human history characterized by that continuing inner life, unrestricted in theme and rhythm, from which the State derives its greatness, was the age of Republican Rome. Here the contrast between the classes, between patricians and people, both equally active and capable, had shaped the ever glorious and vivacious existence of the State organism – an existence, in fact, such as the former Secretary of the Council of Ten had fondly envisaged for his own city. Here alone could that spirit of regeneration, whose revival the conditions of the time had placed beyond the bounds of hope, he made to live again in the form of a memory.

Livy offered the margins of his *Decades* as a repository for the first embryonic notes. The *Decades* were a lofty eulogy of political life in the form in which it develops in a society that is free of corruption. Such a society is, by definition, rich in collective energy, the uninhibited release of which results in the progressive evolution of State laws and institutions.

But now, when this reconstruction is at its height, Machiavelli comes to a stop, and another vision rises before him, to assume a definite outline in the course of his lonely meditations. Between July, 1513,[2] and the early months of

[1] See, for instance, how he judges Florence: 'Florence . . . has led an organized existence for two hundred years . . . without ever having had a constitution in virtue of which it can truly be called a republic' (*Discorsi*, I, xlix and also xxxviii), and the other Italian States: 'Therefore I say that no happening . . . could ever make Milan or Naples free, because those States are wholly corrupt' (I, xvii). Naples, the district of Rome, Romagna and Lombardy have never had 'any political existence' (I, lv). On Italy in general: 'Nor should you put any trust in those arms which you say might one day achieve results in Italy, for this is impossible' – *Lettere Familiari*, CXXXIV (dated 26 August 1513); and in the same Letter: 'We Italians, poor, ambitious and despicable . . .' Similarly: 'As for the union of the other Italians, you make me laugh – first, because no union will ever do any good . . .' (Letter dated 10 August 1513, No. CXXXI).

[2] On the probability that this was the period during which the work was begun cf. Lisio's Introduction to the school edition of *The Prince* (reprint), Florence, 1921, pp. xvi, xvii.

1514[1] he produces the treatise *De Principatibus* – our *Prince* in its almost complete form.[2]

The fragmentary reconstruction of the Roman world is abandoned, and instead we have a systematic, rapid, vivacious return to present-day life, in the background of which

[1] That the process of expansion and polishing to which Machiavelli refers in the famous letter of 10 December 1513 was not yet complete in January 1514, is proved by the words of Vettori: 'I have seen the completed chapters of your work, and they please me beyond measure; but *unless I have the whole book* I am unwilling to pronounce judgment' (dated 18 January 1514, *Lettere Familiari*, CXLI). [But cf. the end of n. 2.]

[2] I do not, in fact, agree with Tommasini's opinion that the treatise *De Principatibus*, mentioned in the letter to Vettori, is only a rough draft which was followed in 1515 by the definitive edition (*op. cit.*, II, pp. 87, 89, 105). The reasons which he adduces in contradiction of Lisio (*Intorno alla nuova edizione del Principe di Niccolò Machiavelli*, Rend. Acc. Lincei, 1900, pp. 322–3) are not very convincing, and they conflict with historical arguments too weighty to be lightly disregarded (and such arguments did in fact form the basis of Lisio's preface to the critical edition of *The Prince*, Florence, 1899, pp. lxii–lxiv). Not only, indeed, are there no allusions to the events of the summer of 1515, the period during which such a revision must have been carried out, but there are specific references which would be inconceivable if Machiavelli had recommenced work on his book after the early months of 1515. The allusion in Chapter XI ('...and now a king of France trembles before her, and she has succeeded in throwing him out of Italy') cannot be explained except as referring to the conditions prevalent in the summer and autumn of 1513 – conditions which in fact impelled Louis XII to come to an agreement with the Pope in December of that year. It could not possibly refer to the situation in 1515, when Francis I entered the struggle. Similarly, the allusions in Chapter XIII ('which error. . . is, as we now see in practice, the cause of the perils which surround that realm', and 'as a result of this the French cannot hold their own against the Swiss') can only be reconciled with the situation that arose after the Battle of Novara, and would be out of place in 1515. However, the allusion in Chapter XXI to Ferdinand the Catholic ('he has *lately* attacked France') puts us back to 1513, and could not be justified in 1515. Finally, how could Machiavelli have referred to Louis XII in 1515 as a *present* king of France (Chapter XVI), when he had been dead since January? Note that we are not dealing with men and events of secondary importance, such as Machiavelli might have forgotten about, but, in fact, with happenings on which his attention was unceasingly concentrated. Undoubtedly, then, he would have modified, if not the thought, at least the expression, if he had in reality prepared a second edition of his work. And since he was addressing *The Prince* to a Medici, how could he have used the words 'one *hopes*' with reference to Leo X after the latter had been Pope for two years, during which he had become noted not only for his 'goodness' but also for his incessant political intrigues? In 1515 the expression would clearly have been different; and it seems to me

that the correction would have been of some significance, coming from a Machiavelli who had been spitefully treated by fortune and who was anxious to re-enter public service.

For these precise historical reasons I do not think it is possible to speak of a rough draft and a second edition. That there may have been slight amendments here and there, though without conforming to any definite system of general re-arrangement, is another question. And in this connection I feel I must recall a passage which may provide a cue for discussion: 'Francesco Sforza, in virtue of the fact that he was equipped with arms, rose from the status of a private individual to that of Duke of Milan; his *sons*, in order to avoid the discomforts of soldiering, were relegated from the status of Dukes to that of private individuals' (Chapter XIV). These 'sons' (for which read 'successors') can only be Ludovico the Moor and Massimiliano Sforza, who lost his territories following the Battle of Marignano (13 and 14 September 1515). This allusion would take us, then, to the end of 1515, unless we choose to regard the plural 'sons' as a purely stylistic amplification, and hence to limit the allusion, as a statement of historical fact, to the Moor. But the allusion in question seems to me so specific, so insistent in its fundamental note – 'in order to avoid the discomforts of soldiering' – which would be meaningless unless the sons had *all* given practical proof of indolence during a clearly-defined period of rule, so precise in its final assertion, in which reference is made to dukes, i.e. to princes already acknowledged as rulers, that I am inclined to accept for preference the first interpretation. Nor is there anything surprising about such an addition, even though it is an isolated case, if we remember that it occurs right in the middle of *The Prince*, and that it supports the idea that is uppermost in Machiavelli's mind, viz. the necessity of citizen armies, and also lends the weight of facts taken from the history of a neighbouring State to the advice which the writer offers the prince regarding the chief exercise of his calling. It occurs, in fact, in the chapter which more than any other must have been in Machiavelli's mind when, in 1515, he saw Lorenzo de' Medici, captain-general of the Church, perhaps giving a first example of that princely repentance which he had preached for so long, with the result that he was impelled to persist in his advice. On the other hand, the allusion to Massimiliano Sforza is not illogical if we bear in mind that Machiavelli keeps his eyes fixed upon the plains of Lombardy and recall the harsh opinions that he expresses about him (*Lettere Familiari*, CXXIV, CXXXI, CXXXIV; cf. Vettori's opinion, *ib.*, CXXXII).

This would imply an addition to the first draft, and in conclusion it seems to me possible to assert that while the treatise, written between July, 1513, and January-February, 1514, remained unchanged so far as its fundamental structure was concerned, it must have been the subject of a number of amendments, of which it is difficult to-day to form the most elementary idea. This would explain a number of more concise, less detailed readings to be found in the Corsinian and Gothan MSS., which did not take into account the subsequent amendments. But it is a far cry from this to the theory of a rough draft and a definitive edition; and I should be inclined rather to think that the corrections made after 1513 were not numerous, and above all not important – this for the historical reasons just mentioned.

we see clearly outlined the harsh, astute figure of the new Prince. The quiet labour, still confined for the most part to generalities, becomes a feverish improvisation of thoughts and notes which give clear shape to a conception seemingly opposed to that which informed the fragments now laid aside.

Now this transition from one line of argument to another was not contradictory, but rather the result of a prolonged and unceasing spiritual struggle, the first evidence of which is in fact already discernible in the rough notes of the *Discorsi*.

Again, the thesis upheld by Meinecke, *Anhang zur Einführung* (in the edition of *The Prince* and minor writings, Berlin, 1923, pp. 38–47) that the 1513 version of *The Prince* went as far as Chapter XI, and that only afterwards did Machiavelli add the other parts, is ingeniously defended, but does not seem to me admissible. Apart from any other reason, the doubt is resolved in Chapter III: 'And if others point to the promise which the king had made to the Pope . . ., I reply with the observations which I make later regarding the promises of Princes and the attitude to be adopted towards such promises.' In other words, the reader is referred to Chapter XVIII; and it is impossible to see in this remark a connecting-link such as Meinecke sees in the similar remark in Chapter X ('and I shall say what is necessary on the subject in due course'). To the question raised by the statement: 'To avoid war King Louis ceded Romagna to Alessandro and the Kingdom to Spain', Machiavelli replies that one should not connive at an act of violence in order to avoid a war. To the second objection, which concerns the prince's moral conduct, he replies by anticipating the argument which will determine not merely the method by which principates should be acquired and maintained but also the prince's personal mode of action. This means, then, that from the very beginning he saw clearly the form which his *Prince* would eventually assume. As he wrote the chapter on 'principates' he was already considering what he was going to say about the prince's own personal *condottieri*.

Finally, we cannot regard Chapters XII–XIV as a repetition of Chapter X. The latter deals first and foremost with the organization of what may be called 'quantitative' defence, the other two with 'qualitative' defence. Even when a prince has his own forces it is not asserted that he can always fight a 'pitched battle', if he lacks an 'abundance of men'; and so we have the rules to be observed by those who are compelled to shut themselves up in a fortified city. In Chapters XII–XIV the dominant motif is different.

[I have since reverted to the problem of the composition of *The Prince* in my essay *Sulla composizione de 'Il Principe' di Niccolò Machiavelli* (*Archivum Romanicum*, XI, 1927, pp. 330–83). Here, after a lengthy analysis, I came to the conclusion (which somewhat modifies the theory expounded above) that *The Prince* was written between July and December, 1513, and that it subsequently underwent no revision, either complete or partial.]

For it is not hard to detect, in Book I, an uncertainty that is not present in the early chapters, the all-pervading theme of which is the glory of a strong people. This uncertainty becomes steadily more apparent, reaching its climax when the author turns to considerations of a different character. Thus there are whole passages in which the analysis of human motive follows a new method and for the first time emphasis is laid on individual virtue, portrayed through the medium of maxims. Unlike the early ones, which have the scope and form of generalities, these maxims are specific to a degree.

The solitary thinker could not, indeed, stray too far from the reality of the times, which constantly obtruded itself upon him, without concealment, or rhetorical equivocation in all its irremediable precariousness. His very yearning to take refuge in the past, that he might draw from it a new vital strength, compelled him to enter into the sorrowful experience of the present, which was beginning to confine his creative faculty within narrower limits; and the ancient world was gradually obliged to retreat before the modern world, which imposed itself through his ceaseless conversation with his friend Vettori – a conversation that echoed ever more loudly the present feeling of Italy. Thus even these comments on Livy are unobtrusively interspersed with precepts whose theme is no longer the healthy State but the corrupt organism, and the classical examples are replaced by men and events taken from contemporary history.[1] Political life is circumscribed by individual virtue, and at times Machiavelli's exaltation of Rome is sobered by the bitterness of the thought that glimpses beneath the ancient grandeur the misery that surrounds its own development.[2]

---

[1] E.g. I, xxvii, which centres round the figures of Julius II and Gian Paolo Baglioni.

[2] What a sorrowful note of misgiving there is in a brief allusion which transports us back from ancient Rome to the Italy of the day: 'But when, either from negligence or from lack of prudence, they (Princes) remain at home in idleness and send captains (to the wars), I can offer them no other precept than that which their own conduct teaches them' (*Discorsi*, I, xxx).

Thus new conceptions were ripening. A new world was being created – a world not yet subjected to analysis – though its setting and its outline were vague;[1] and it only remained in shadow because of what, after all, was to Niccolò a human necessity – the necessity of seeking escape from his dismay in the recollection of a glory that was past. If anything had happened to cause a psychological *revirement*, then the new line of thought, as yet disjointed, would have assumed a precise and definite form, no doubt interrupting the work originally begun.

And the *revirement* did take place. Looming up on the horizon was the shadow of stupendous, if uncertain, political

---

[1] Chapter XIX of Book I of the *Discorsi* contains the following passage: 'Let this be a warning to every Prince who rules a State – that he who resembles Numa will or will not keep it according to whether the times or Fortune are favourable; but he who resembles Romulus, and like him is armed with prudence and the weapons of war, will keep it whatever happens, unless it is taken from him by relentless and overwhelming force.' Here is a first direct allusion to the type of Prince who will be described in detail in Chapters XIV, XXI and XXIV of our treatise. Similarly: 'And when a people falls into this error of doing honour to a man because he chastises those whom he hates, if that man is astute he will invariably become tyrant of that city. For he will await the moment when, with the approval of the people, he can destroy the nobility . . .' (*ib.*, I, xl). Here we seem almost to discern a prelude to Chapter IX of *The Prince* – a prelude which, however, is foreshadowed in Chapter XVI of Book I of the *Discorsi*: '. . . for he who has incurred the enmity of the few makes his position secure easily and without stirring up great dissensions; but he who has incurred the enmity of the mass never secures his position. . . . So that the best remedy that exists is to seek to gain the friendship of the people. . . . If, therefore, a prince desires to win over a people. . . .' The example of the King of France, here cited, will recur in *The Prince* (Chapter XIX) with the same implication. And Machiavelli himself perceives this change in his reasoning: 'And although this argument is different in form from what precedes, since I am speaking here of a prince and there of a republic . . .' (*Discorsi*, I, xvi). These are, in short, all scattered elements, still drowned by the living voice of the people and by the din of party strife, which will soon become in their turn the dominant theme of a new embryonic theory: 'For all the reasons cited above it is difficult or impossible to maintain or restore a Republic in a corrupt city' (*Discorsi*, I, xviii). Machiavelli, then, was again turning his attention from Rome to the *corrupt* society of his own day; his receptivity and his imagination, having been moulded and developed by the civilization of the Ancients, were being applied once more to present-day life, for reasons both practical and emotional. And so we have *The Prince*.

happenings, of which the Medici were to be the inspiration.[1]
For our exile there was the possibility of a return to active

[1] I do not, however, agree with Villari (*op. cit.*, II, pp. 366 *sqq.*), who has
been followed by others, when he seeks to attribute the writing of *The Prince*
to a widespread desire to see the Medici established as personal rulers of Parma,
Piacenza, Modena and Reggio. In the first place the ambition of Giuliano
and Lorenzo was less specific, and at the time when *The Prince* was being
written it was once more dissolving in a cloud of vagueness and indecision. At
one moment there was a desire to make Giuliano King of Naples, while for
Lorenzo nothing less was hoped for than the entire Duchy of Milan; at another, more modestly, men's minds turned to matrimonial alliances, to Piombino and Siena (Tommasini, *op. cit.*, II, pp. 76 *sqq.* Cf. Pastor, *Geschichte der
Päpste*, IV, 1, pp. 54 *sqq.*). Giuliano himself, a man of unbridled and extremely uncertain whims, was so fickle of purpose that the object of his desires
could not with certainty be determined. But if from July, 1513 onwards Leo
X could envisage the creation of a State for his brother and his nephew in
Northern Italy, based on Parma and Piacenza or on Modena and Reggio
(Luzio, *Isabella d'Este nei primordi del Papato di Leone X*, Arch. Storico Lom-
bardo, 1906, pp. 121 *sqq.*), this does not mean that Machiavelli was so well-
informed on the subject as to decide to write with precisely that end in view.
The first time he reveals an awareness of such designs is on 31 January, 1515
(*Lettere Familiari*, CLIX), and the terms in which he expresses himself prove
that the information, gleaned from 'hearsay', was not in his possession before.
In the whole of his correspondence with Vettori during these years there is no
other trace of a similar line of argument; and this would certainly not have been
so if the two friends had had a sure basis for discussion. Note that Vettori says
nothing definite when he refers on 12 July, 1513 (*Lettere Familiari*, CXXVII),
to the rabid nepotism of the Pope, who proposes 'by all means' to create States
for his kinsmen, since they are dissatisfied with Florence. 'I do not want to
start speculating as to what sort of State he has in mind, because in this matter
he will change his plans as the occasion arises.' Indeed, in Vettori's view Leo
X's action in regard to Parma and Piacenza is inspired by a wish to 'conserve
the territories and the pre-eminence of the Church'. The writers only allude
in the most general terms to the possibility that the Church's power may
in due course be diminished in favour of the Medici, without, however, giving
concrete expression to this surmise by the slightest reference to Parma and
Piacenza. Their tone is always vague. To sum up, I should rather be inclined
not to look overmuch for specific reasons for the writing of *The Prince*. There
is enough to constitute a casual motive in the considerable disquiet with which
men's minds were filled by the continual disturbances, in the ambitions – still
not clearly defined – of the two Medicean princes, and in the fact that the
present Pope was 'young, rich and reasonably desirous of glory . . . with
brothers and nephews who are without dominion' (*Lettere Familiari*, CXXIV:
Machiavelli to Vettori, 20 June, 1513).
  On the practical purpose of *The Prince* cf. Meinecke, *Angang zur Einführung* (already cited), pp. 31 *sqq.*

life, to the cares of government[1] – a possibility which intensified his insistent and natural urge to raise his voice in an effort to point the way of political success to possible rulers. And all these influences, blending into a single incentive in which we can no longer distinguish the purely utilitarian element from the emotional, nor the casual motive from that which had become part of the writer's mind, caused the isolated thoughts to take definite shape, to subordinate themselves to a guiding principle, to become part of a rational pattern. Within a few months the treatise, inconsiderable in length, was complete. Under the stimulus of a practical and immediate interest those 'little castles' had at last been integrated into an organic whole. But for that, they would still – and perhaps for a long time – have remained mere scattered fragments in a larger work.[2]

[1] But Dubreton exaggerates when, ascribing a purely utilitarian motive of this kind to *The Prince*, he says: '. . . il (Machiavelli) se fait alors professeur *d'inganno* (deception). Enseigne au maître le moyen d'être plus sûrement le maître, trahit ses compagnons, sa classe, exactement sa classe d'humble fonctionnaire mal payé – bref, redemande à crever de faim avec honorabilité et décence' (*La Disgrâce de Niccolò Machiavelli*, 2nd edition, Paris, 1913, p. 190). Obviously *The Prince* is something more than just the petition of a functionary who is ready 'à crever de faim'!

[2] Villari (*op. cit.*, II, pp. 366 *sqq.*) has well illustrated the spiritual genesis of *The Prince*, noticing also its points of coincidence with the *Discorsi* (*ib.*, pp. 271 and 363); but he exaggerates when he goes on to assert that if *The Prince* had been lost we could reconstruct it *in toto* (cf. also Fester, *op. cit.*, p. 134). If Machiavelli was not contradicting himself when he passed from the *Discorsi* to *The Prince*, this is not to say that his thought did not develop along different lines in the two works. The points which they have in common should not blind us to the fact that their general background is not the same – far from it. There is, on the other hand, a tendency among the most able of recent critics (Mayer, Ercole, Meinecke) to recognize the common basis of the two works, viz. the 'virtue' which adapts itself to the 'material' of the subject under review, while always preserving its essential character. This conception replaces – justly from one point of view – the well-worn notion of a contradiction between *The Prince* and the *Discorsi* – a notion which has been badly interpreted in the past. Nevertheless, it is a conception that sometimes assumes an excessively abstract and rigid character. Suppose that individual 'virtue' is also the basis of a republic; suppose too that it is the essential stimulus of all energy, being divided into a first and a second category: the fact remains that in the one case it forms part of the collective life-force, the 'virtue' of the citizens, while in the other it maintains with absolute rigidity its

The Republic yielded place to the Principate; the people, capable of dictating its wishes and of leaving its own impress on the State, gave way to the single man with his individual energy and the resources of his own ability; the vision of past glory – a vision clouded by nostalgic regret – was replaced by the theoretical prospect of Italy's political recovery.

II. THE 'LESSON OF EVENTS' OFFERED BY ITALIAN HISTORY

The 'Seigneurs' and the Regional States

In truth, the Prince was the supreme creation of Italian history up to this time.[1]

It was not that the ruler had all at once obtained the *plenitudo potestatis*. This had been the epilogue. But previously, and for a great part also of the fourteenth century, the life of the seigniorial governments had been characterized by a

individual character. Machiavelli was not an abstract theoretician who developed, first in one sense, then in another, a concept that had been completely articulated from the start, but a politician and a man of passion who gradually unfolded and defined his ideas in the light of his activities, his hopes and his practical aims at different moments. In the same way, it remains for us to see what variation of meaning is necessarily to be found in an apparently rigid criterion, and hence how 'virtue', in the inner life of the writer, either loses its individual character and re-appears in the mass of the people, or else through its personal manifestation constitutes a lone standard. Now it cannot be denied that the orientation of Machiavelli's inner life, and hence of his thought, is different in the two works. This does not mean that the author of the *Discorsi* is a democrat in the modern sense, for he watches the tide of collective life not so much from the point of view, and in the particular interests, of the various groups as from the general viewpoint of the State, i.e. of the Government (this extremely acute observation comes from Meinecke, *Die Idee der Staatsräson*, Munich and Berlin, 1924, p. 40); and indeed the true and profound continuity of Machiavelli's thought consists in this fact. It means, on the contrary, simply that in the notes on Livy political life assumes a breadth and a strength of motive unknown to *The Prince*, breaking the bounds, as it were, of the schematic concept of 'virtue', which, by contrast, is fully brought out in the shorter treatise.

[1] Here I am thinking essentially of the historical evolution of Northern Italy, in other words of the region in which *The Prince* had come clearly into the limelight.

long, lingering travail. Often they were torn by bitter dissensions, even if these were not made public by the clash of arms. They were founded on the resistance of the ancient ruling cliques, who were bent on defending the last remnants of their seigniory. Originally mere party-leaders, whom the members of their faction entrusted with dictatorial powers in order to save their own skins, the 'Seigneurs' had soon appeared in the rôle of saviours of the urban *bourgeoisie*. This class had been compelled to renounce its full control of affairs by the relentless pressure of the inferior classes, by the necessity of finding a remedy for civil war and financial embarrassment, and by the need to safeguard its life and property – the latter being threatened particularly in the outlying districts, which were daily ravaged by different gangs of outlaws. It was forced, then, to request the decisive intervention in public life of men whose hands were strengthened sometimes by economic power, sometimes by the favour of the populace, rural or urban, sometimes by fiefs and arms, and, finally, sometimes by all these factors at once. But in spite of its difficulties it had tried to preserve as much as it could of its erstwhile authority.[1]

Hence that characteristic attachment to the old municipal institutions, which still survived, even if they had now become mere empty shells,[2] almost a symbol of the conflict that beset minds torn between vain dreams of government, a desire for peace and order, and an annoyance – which at

---

[1] See, for example, the treaty under which Asti was surrendered to Luchino Visconti in 1342, with its clauses in favour of the Commune and the citizens, i.e. the former rulers (F. Cognasso, *Note e documenti sulla formazione dello Stato visconteo*, Boll. Soc. pavese stor. patria, XXIII, Parts I–IV, pp. 118 *sqq*. of the extract). The seigniorial governments are the subject of a notable essay, concise and comprehensive, by A. Anzilotti (*Per la storia delle signorie e del diritto pubblico italiano nel Rinascimento*, Studi Storici, XXII, 1914, pp. 76–106.

[2] Cf. F. Ercole, *Comuni e Signori del Veneto*, Nuovo Arch. Veneto, New Series, XIX, 1910, pp. 255–338; also P. Torelli, *Capitanato del popolo e Vicariato Imperiale come elementi constitutivi della signoria Bonacolsiana* (Mantua, 1923), where the constitutional development of the seigniory is very clearly outlined.

times led them to the point of courting opposition – with the dictator who allowed himself to restrict civil liberties,[1] to recall exiles, to attempt the pacification of the rival factions, to admit men from the outlying districts to membership of the civic councils,[2] and to reform the system of rates and taxes,[3] thereby obeying the logical dictates of his own personal *raison d'état*.

As soon as those who had previously controlled the Commune perceived the significance of their renunciation, as soon as they saw the last bulwarks of their former dominance gradually crumbling away, they tried to resume the offensive in whatever way they could, endeavouring, tenaciously if unsuccessfully, to ensnare that same government which they had themselves constituted. This led to a historical development full of seeming contradictions, as when the original supporters of the Seigneur became after a short time his enemies, while his former adversaries, the exiles of yesterday, set themselves up as the bodyguard of the man who might at some remote period have sent them scuttling to the countryside. This paradoxical state of affairs was variously coloured by emotional and religious factors, so that sometimes a man of the Church would rise up to defend the languishing Communal society.[4] At certain moments it was

---

[1] On the annoyance of the people of Bologna with the Visconti, and, conversely, their satisfaction with Giovanni da Oleggio, who showed more respect for the rights of the Commune, cf. L. Sighinolfi, *La Signoria di Giovanni da Oleggio in Bologna*, Bologna, 1905, pp. 44 *sqq*.

[2] On the resistance offered for this reason to the Caminesi cf. G. B. Picotti, *I Caminesi e la loro Signoria in Treviso dal 1283 al 1312*, Leghorn, 1905, pp. 213–14 and 312–13. The recall of exiles is characteristic of the measures taken by seigniorial governments. It was, for example, one of the administrative acts of Azzone Visconti: '. . . *ob cuius meritum possidet Paradisum*' (Galv. Flamma, *Opusculum de rebus gestis ab Azone, Luchino et Johanne Vicecomitibus, R.I.S.*, XII, 1040).

[3] On the opposition of the '*maiores*' of Pavia to financial provisions made by Filippo Maria Visconti cf. P. Ciapessoni, *Per la storia della economia e della finanza pubblica pavesi sotto Filippo Maria Visconti*, Boll. soc. pavese stor. patria, VI, 1906, pp. 192 and 221–2.

[4] Thus Friar Giacomo Bussolari at Pavia in the middle of the fourteenth century. Cf. G. Romano, *Delle relazioni fra Pavia e Milano nella formazione della Signoria Viscontea*, Arch. stor. lombardo, 1892, pp. 579 *sqq*.

rendered acute by particular external conditions, which resulted in an intensification of fiscal pressure and the adoption
of harsher police measures by the Seigneur, to the discomfi-
ture of his ill-disciplined subjects. Finally, it was protracted
in some places by the weakness of the dictator, who was incapable either of strong action or of a shrewd diplomatic
manoeuvre.

Gradually, however, the opposition grew feebler, petered
out in insignificant skirmishes, narrowed itself down to com-
plaints and murmurings. There was an urgent need of a
strong power to keep the streets safe, to protect property
and, through the medium of its conquests, to create wider
outlets for trade and new centres for the supply of victuals;
and the Seigneur, fortified by the support of the urban populace, as also of the rural masses to whom he was at last offering some help, fortified too by the vacillation and inconsis-
tencies of his adversaries, vindicated his authority once and
for all, incidentally furnishing it, through the imperial vicar-
iate, with a basis in law, so that it was no longer subject
merely to the will of the citizens.

And so towards the end of the century there emerged the
principate, which henceforth also enjoyed formal recognition, and was sanctioned by the imperial seal.[1] This meant
that the Emperor confirmed not merely another principle of
common law, but also in a certain sense the regional, as distinct from the municipal, character of the prince's authority,
and that he recognized simultaneously the victory of the
internal dictator and the conquests of the *condottiere*. The
municipal seigneur was replaced by the territorial seigneur.[2]

This was a legitimate acknowledgment of the work accomplished over several generations by the strongest and most

[1] On the historical and juridical significance of the principate system cf. the
acute observations of Ercole, *Impero e Papato nella tradizione giuridica bolog-
nese e nel diritto pubblico italiano del Rinascimento* (fourteenth and fifteenth
centuries), in Atti e Mem. Dep. stor. patria Romagne, 1911, pp. 164 *sqq.*

[2] Torelli does well to note the tendency of the seigneurs to obtain the
Emperor's recognition of the 'territorial nature' of their authority (*op. cit.*,
p. 95).

able rulers, who had soon begun to indulge in expansionist dreams. These were suggested on the one hand by the economic interests of the subject cities themselves, but they were also rendered inevitable by considerations of personal advantage. A large domain signified for the Seigneur the possibility of virtually eliminating the various resistance movements in the cities. These movements sprang up independently. They lacked co-ordination and were animated by meanly parochial sentiments. All, then, were destined to be mutually antagonistic; and in the meantime he – the Seigneur – would practically have made himself supreme in every one of the cities – which elected him individually – by virtue of the fact that he was master of the rest. Bergamo and Pavia, besides increasing the general power of the Visconti and satisfying their ambition, which was as great as that of all young popular leaders, also served to strengthen their rule in Milan; and the seigniorial policy of conquest or peaceful penetration was not determined only by the resolve to establish a strong base for the purpose of warding off external dangers. The exuberant vitality of national life, allied to the personal interest of the rulers, became an incitement to expansion.

Accordingly there sprang up more or less rapidly, especially in the valley of the Po, a number of large domains in which it was possible to discern the beginnings of the regional State. The establishment of a bureaucracy, sometimes truly remarkable for its powerful structure; the reforms – economic, juridical and fiscal – to which all the Seigneurs devoted their attention with differing degrees of skill and to a varying extent, observing principles of a somewhat general nature whose application was calculated to bring about truly fundamental changes throughout their domains; the ever-growing tendency of powers and prerogatives to revert to the central administration – all these things constituted in very truth the first beginnings of a unitarian political set-up, which was strengthened particularly by the spread of laws from one city to another and by the promulgation in ever greater numbers of decrees whose terms were universally enforced, so that there slowly grew up a body of common law over and above the various municipal laws which were still valid in individual localities. Moreover, during this process of unification the supremacy of the city in which the Seigneur had his headquarters would already be growing apparent. This city, which saw some of its statutes being applied to the less important parts of the domain,[1] would gradually become the capital, the political and economic centre around which it was desired to group the whole in accordance with a policy of absorption and centralization; for such a policy was essential if the Seigneur was to make his domain into a compact unit, controlled by a single will and capable of resisting any blow from outside.

The Internal Rift

Had such a movement succeeded, it would have led in fact to the unitarian State as we know it to-day; but it was destined in great part to fail. It is true that an apparent unification was achieved through an administrative system which became ever more uniform and well-ordered; but fundamentally the situation developed along different lines.

Economic disputes and rivalries might cease abroad, where an affinity of financial and commercial interests and the special conditions existing among the 'Lombards' beyond the Alps, who were often at grips with the native populations, had long since resulted in a union of the merchants — the only real and lasting union of Italians during these years.[2] But they remained very bitter within the individual domains,

---

[1] On the seigniory of the Visconti and the application of Milanese mercantile statutes to the other cities of the domain cf. Gaddi, *Per la storia della legislazione e delle istituzioni mercantili lombarde*, Arch. stor. Lombardo, 1893, pp. 290–1; A. Lattes, *Degli antichi statuti di Milano che si credono perduti*, Rendiconti Ist. Lombardo, XXIX, 1896, pp. 1064 *sqq.*; and, for general reference, Lattes, *Il diritto consuetudinario nelle città lombarde*, Milan, 1899, p. 75.

[2] F. Schupfer, *La società milanese all'epoca del risorgimento del Comune*, Arch. Giuridico, VI, 1870, p. 146.

especially among small traders and the artisan class; for these were fighting in every single place against the competition of neighbouring cities, which were nearly always engaged in similar kinds of work. They had another profound reason for their existence in the inveterate quarrels about the ownership of the land, to which the life of every community seemed inseparably linked, with the result that the outsider who became a landed proprietor within the limits of his jurisdiction incurred the hostility of the local populace. They continued to interfere seriously with the policy of the Seigneurs, who aimed at unification and social levelling, but found themselves still confronted by another factor making for inequality – the 'gentry', in other words feudalism, which was still strongly entrenched in many places, especially in the mountainous regions of the peninsula.[1] Moreover, that policy was rendered almost desperate by the persistence of the civic spirit, which was so deeply ingrained that it showed itself on the slightest provocation.[2] It was a cliquish spirit, compounded of economic and emotional elements and based on the conflict of interest between artisans, merchants and farmers, on a continuing hatred of the enemies of yesterday,

[1] On the struggle between the Seigneurs and the feudatories cf., for example, N. Grimaldi, *La signoria di Bernabò Visconti e di Regina della Scala in Reggio*, Reggio Emilia, 1921, pp. 132 *sqq.*, 166 *sqq.* Other feudatories were springing up alongside the old ones – friends of the Seigneur, to whom he granted not only villas and lands but authority too: cf. L. Simeoni, *L'amministrazione del distretto veronese sotto gli Scaligeri*, Atti e Memorie Acc. Verona, 1904–5, p. 287. Grants were also made in 1377 and 1378. In addition there was the personal rule of the Seigneur (*ib.*, pp. 280 *sqq.*). Again, at moments of crisis feuds and honours had to be granted as a reward for services rendered. A typical case occurred in the Milanese in 1412–13, when grants of feuds, or confirmations of earlier grants, by the Duke Filippo Maria alternated with the oaths of loyalty taken by communities and individuals under his sway (G. Romano, *Contributi alla storia della ricostituzione del ducato milanese otto Filippo Maria Visconti (1412–1421)*, Arch. storico Lombardo, 1896, Vol. VI, pp. 240 *sqq.*). It is understandable, then, how the annual revenue from the lay feuds in the Milanese could rise in 1499 to 600,000 ducats (G. Pélissier, *Louis XII et Ludovic Sforza*, I, p. 462).

[2] On the annoyance of the people of Reggio with Bernabò Visconti, who had offended their susceptibilities as well as damaging their interests, v. Grimaldi, *op. cit.*

E

and on enduring memories of an erstwhile autonomy which had only disappeared in very recent times.

This policy of transplanting laws and regulations from one city to another was limited chiefly to penal and procedural law.[1] It was impossible, however, to eradicate that part of the law which was firmly grounded in local customs and statutes and which afforded concrete evidence of the mutual divisions and enmities of the Communes. Thus the law continued to testify to the initial disruption that had accompanied the birth of the new régime,[2] which sought to overcome the most bitter opposition, using the jurists as a weapon against what was a fundamental cause of disunion – consuetudinary law.[3]

But the persistently fragmentary character of the régime found expression most of all in the attitude of the inhabitants of the lesser cities towards the capital. Beneath the cloak of the Seigneur's personal supremacy the latter tended to impose its hegemony, under which all local traditions would have been reduced to a single level. The former, however, haughtily reaffirmed their independence, which they yielded

[1] Lattes, *Degli antichi statuti*, etc. (cited above), p. 1075. It is well to recall that the legal codes of the various Communes already revealed common characteristics and general similarities, which, however, engendered a mutual antagonism and were responsible for the exclusiveness of city life. Essentially, then, the Seigneurs' decrees, which in fact became more numerous as the central power was strengthened, were able to exert a unifying influence.

[2] For example, the statutes published at Bergamo in 1391 reaffirm the well-known clauses dealing with the 'incapacity' of a woman married outside the Commune and with that of a foreigner to take the place of a subject of the Commune (Lattes, *Il diritto consuetudinario*, etc. (cited above), pp. 261 and 456); while in San Salvatore di Monferrato the principle still held good that a person not a subject of the Commune might not possess a house, nor build one, nor even let one unless he had first taken a pledge *de 'bene vivendo'* (*Statuta Oppidi S. Salvatoris Ducatus Montisferrati*, (fourteenth and fifteenth centuries), in the *Rivista di storia, arte, archeologia per la provincia di Alessandria*, April–June, 1924, p. 30). Note also the persistence of the Duchy of Monferrato's municipalism, which is analysed by Bozzola, *Appunti sulla vita economica sulle classi sociali e sull'ordinamento amministrativo del Monferrato nei secoli XIV e XV*, in Boll. stor. bibl. subalpino, 1923, pp. 4 *sqq.* of the offprint.

[3] Lattes, *Il diritto consuetudinario*, etc. (cited above), p. 23.

only to the ruler in person, recognizing his superior, individual authority alone.[1]

The regional State, then, became personified in the Prince, the sole ruler of a vast territory whose constituent elements, however closely they might be integrated, still preserved their own individual character. *The government was essentially personal.*

The Lack of Moral Unity

Such a phenomenon, however, was perfectly logical in this age of transition and the laborious expansion of the city State. But in order to obviate the manifest dangers to which such a disruption of the State exposed the entire domain the times would have demanded a living spiritual force capable of reconciling minds that were divided in the practical field — a profound faith in which men could discover a sure basis of harmony and concord. To rid the Prince of his unduly restricted and immediate character it would have required the power of a tradition whose continuity embraced the figure of the ruler, making him seem almost a fragment of an uninterrupted historical existence, almost part of a complete process of evolution that had originated in an age now leg-

[1] Examples are not lacking. In 1447, when the Ambrosian Republic was constituted, nearly all the other cities in the domain of the Visconti took independent action, refusing to obey a city *which was not nobler than they* (G. Pélissier, *op. cit.*, I, p. 90). In September, 1499, the provisional Government of Milan agreed to submit to French domination; but, fearing that the Duchy would be dismembered, it requested Trivulzio, should the occasion arise, to oppose the separation of Pavia from Milan, since that would be too great a humiliation for the citizens to endure (*ib.*, II, p. 268)! The old divisions remained (on the municipal sentiments of the citizens of Pavia and their consquences in the fourteenth century cf. also Romano's work, already cited). Again, there is extreme significance in the conflict between Perugia and Orvieto after the latter ceased to be under the jurisdiction of Braccio. In the course of one particular controversy the representative of Perugia speaks contemptuously of Orvieto as a city only just liberated from the domination of the Umbrian capital, which had been the seat of Braccio's Government; but the people of Orvieto reply: 'Verum fuimus sub magnifico et excelso domino Braccio qui, esto quod nobis dominaretur ad plenum, tamen nos non ita depressit, ut iurisdictioni civitatis Perusii subiugaret' (R. Valentini, *Braccio da Montone e il Comune di Orvieto*, Perugia, 1923, p. 202).

endary, so remote that it coincided with the first flowering of the life of his people, and indissolubly linked to the dynasty of his leaders.

Such precisely was the fundamental spirit of the French monarchy, which was created 'in the very bowels' of the people[1] – that monarchy which bore the stigmata of a national sentiment first expressed in the world of chivalry and in the *Chanson de Roland*. The king was the sacred, anointed descendant of those who had guided France in her primaeval struggles; he was a link in a long chain; he was first and foremost the custodian of the memories and the glory of France; and his person presented itself against a background still enlivened by the figures of the past. His identity was submerged beneath his *Royauté*.[2]

The Italian seigniories lacked a spiritual force of this kind.

When, in 1272, the citizens of Milan buried the remains of the ancient belfry destroyed by Frederick Barbarossa and the great blocks of stone on which they had once sat during meetings of the *Arengo*, which were held outside the city church,[3] they rejected the living and heroic world of their municipal tradition, putting behind them the remembrance of past struggles and of a freedom won at the cost of blood, the memory of their sufferings and triumphs, and the primitive tradition which from those ruins addressed itself to the hearts of men. These were the days when the foundations were being laid of the Visconti's seigniory!

Now what sentimental leavening did the new masters bring, capable of transforming itself in the hearts of their subjects into passion and hope and faith? What accents could they find to stir the souls of men who were so weary, so hungry for peace, what accents to fill the multitude not only with a love of bread and circuses but also with emotion and

---

[1] This vivid phrase was coined by Reginon *Chronicon*, A.D. 888, *Script, Rerum German. in usum schol.*, Hanover, 1890, p. 129.

[2] The prevalence of this belief is clearly demonstrated by French political writings, especially those of the sixteenth century.

[3] Giulini, *Memorie della città e campagna di Milano*, 1855 edition, IV, p. 605.

with the faith which in heavy hours uplifts the human consciousness and warns the masses that they must face a
struggle without quarter?

What memories could they conjure up before the people's
minds, these men who came from the ranks of the citizens, or
from a feudal caste that had long been resisted?[1] What
tradition, what glory could they recall that would make their
subjects conscious of a spiritual affinity with their forbears?
What faith could they offer, they who were not of the Lord's
anointed, not priests of God, not sanctified in accordance
with the Divine Will?[2] The faith, perchance, that was inspired by the Imperial credentials which they were constantly soliciting?

Too trivial was the fervour which they aroused, that the
people might bestir themselves; and it is not to be wondered
at that in Milan itself, capital of the most powerful of the
seigniorial States, there was a lack of those popular songs,
vibrant with party passion, in which the soul that is deeply
stirred gives vent to its feelings. Emotion had vanished now,
nor was there anyone who could revive it. The ill-tempered
outbursts of the Communal *bourgeoisie* were the last furious
mouthings of an age that was swiftly declining, an age whose
calm had been shattered by the sudden advent of a new order
of things. Zeal for the fight was replaced by a love of peace
and quiet toil.

The masses were very tired. What they asked for now was
security for their possessions and persons, both in the
countryside and in the streets. And the Seigneur could provide it; but what he could not provide was a stronger emotion, one that would sustain even those weary souls and make
them capable of revival, or a word that would lessen their
bewilderment and raise them up again.

[1] The absence of tradition among the seigniories is, incidentally, one of the
characteristics most frequently observed by critics of the Renaissance.

[2] In my opinion this sacred quality, which was possessed not only by the
Empire but also by the national monarchies, is of the most vital significance.
Among our Seigneurs it was entirely lacking.

The Italian Middle Ages had been unable to offer a great tradition, a great national spirit, save only those inspired by the lesser glories of the municipalities. As a result, when men had to delve into the past in order to find some memory to cling to, in order to seek out a remote bond of union, no figure presented itself except perhaps that of an Emperor who had become a symbol of greatness.[1] No ancestral legend offered itself as a rallying-point for the emotions of the people, who were compelled to look beyond the confines of their inner life. When the faith of the Communes languished, and the Empire and the Papacy were no longer able to sustain the spiritual life of the people, that life collapsed and was destroyed.

The humanists endeavoured to revive it, seeking out a tradition for the Seigneur to whom they owed their academic leisure. And as in all ages in which there is a decline in the strength and spontaneity of feeling, so that men are unable to find in their own lives and consciousness the spiritual leavening that is the spur to action; as in all eras in which a multitude that has grown bored with itself finds its political passions and emotions stagnating, so in the fifteenth century men searched among the ruins of another world for the foundations of the glory of their time, creating a spurious religiosity which would never have been capable of stimulating the inner fibres of the nation, had a struggle become inevitable.

So it was that the intense individualism of the seigniorial domains was not subordinated to any spiritual influence through which the subject cities, while preserving their separatist traits, might nevertheless have become aware of a powerful unifying force not subject to the fluctuations of a human life. Their eyes remained fixed on the figure of the ruler who was the one symbol of unity. But if by any chance

[1] And it was Charlemagne, the mythical hero of another nation, who attracted the attention of those who looked back. Ezzelino da Romano boasts of wanting to accomplish in Lombardy deeds greater than any that have been done there since the far-off days of that Emperor (*Cortusiorum Historiae*, *R.I.S.*, XII, p. 772. Cf. Verci, *Storia degli Ecelini*, Bassano, 1779, I, p. 133).

he disappeared, or seemed to have succumbed to external pressure, then the regional State disintegrated, and the administrative co-ordinating machine did not avail to keep its members together. They fell apart, and there ensued a period of anarchy, which lasted until a new sovereign came on the scene whose 'virtue' was sufficient to restore order and to re-unite the broken threads. The disorder that prevailed in the Duchy of Milan on the death of Gian Galeazzo and Filippo Maria shows how the most *modern* and organic of the Italian States was in reality built on sand.[1]

The Weakening of Political Consciousness and the Figure of the Ruler

The Prince, then, remained the one firm support on which regional life rested; and to magnify the shadow of his individuality there followed another development of vast importance – the gradual decline of the political faculty of the Communal classes. For if the fact that free institutions had been renounced so that a party leader might be invested with dictatorial powers was an early sign of a weakening of will-power and political consciousness in men who had long and jealously defended their prerogatives and the autonomy of their government;[2] if such an enfeeblement of the ruling classes had first led to desperate appeals for peace, which could only be secured through the intervention of a king – 'unum proprium et naturalem dominum qui non sit barbarae nationis et regnum eius continuet naturalis posteritas successiva';[3] and if the seigniories had owed their triumph specifically to the decline of political 'virtue' in Communal

---

[1] It is obvious that this phenomenon occurs chiefly, not to say solely, in the great territorial seigniories. That of the Visconti furnishes a typical example. On the other hand, in the case of those that brought together only a few places, and above all did not incorporate cities which had had a Communal life of their own and were centres in themselves, it is impossible to speak of dismemberment. The very material to be dismembered was lacking.

[2] On the conflict between the 'dictatorial' trend and Communalism, which lasted for much of the thirteenth century, cf. Salzer, *Über die Anfänge der Signorie in Oberitalien*, Berlin, 1900, pp. 61 *sqq.*

[3] Cognasso, *op. cit.*, p. 6.

society, then their work marked a further and final stage – completed with a smoothness that was impressive – in the annihilation of the political consciousness of the people.

The Seigneurs had first emerged as party leaders of a class that was certainly willing to acknowledge a single master, but had not yet entirely abandoned its vain dreams of pre-eminence. Accordingly, their position was as precarious and insecure as could be imagined. Impelled by a desire to make their régime stable and enduring, they had at once been obliged to try to put a check on the very people who had chosen them and who were liable to constitute a ceaseless threat to their supremacy; and here they found themselves in sympathy not only with the aims of the party that had been proscribed but also with a vaster, more vigorous movement, originating among the common people in both town and country, all of whom were oppressed by the classes formerly in power. The exiles returned to their cities, providing the Seigneurs with a powerful offensive weapon against their principal electoral supporters of yesterday. Such a source of power always remained partisan in character; thus, sooner or later, it might in turn become a menace to the dictatorial régime – once the faction had recovered its full strength or some fresh cause of friction appeared. The masses, on the other hand, constituted quite a different foundation of authority. Incapable by themselves of facing a decisive struggle, and therefore always obliged to seek a leader, they were nevertheless ready and able, given inspiring generalship, to keep the common enemy, the old ruling class, under control.[1]

The policy of the Seigneurs was therefore twofold. On the one hand they curried favour with the scattered multitude who dwelt in the back-streets of the cities or in the fields – not a very difficult task, for the latter's principal requirements were bread and peace, and fiscal reforms, effective police measures or judicious management of the corn-supply

---

[1] Cf. the pertinent remarks in Ercole's recapitulatory essay, *La lotta delle classi alla fine del Medio Evo*, in *Politica*, October, 1920, p. 228.

in times of famine were all that was necessary. On the other hand they aimed to destroy, or at least to transform completely, the juridical and political institutions behind which the ruling classes of the old Communes were taking refuge. The re-assessment of rates and taxes,[1] the struggle to do away with the fiscal privileges of the upper classes, from whom the new governments tried to exact larger contributions,[2] and a more rigorous tutelage of justice were making the Seigneurs the friends of the common people.[3]

On the other hand, the skilful and relentless methods of the rulers gradually deprived the Guilds of their political character, transforming and abolishing their dangerous power,[4] fatally curbed the political organizations of the urban *bourgeoisie*, and reduced the function of the municipal constitutions, which still formally survived, to that of internal administration pure and simple, even as the last republicans were clinging to these relics of the past as a last line of defence.

Such pressure from above, coupled with a natural weariness after the long civil wars and their need of leisure to devote all their energies to trade or alternatively to save themselves from economic ruin, produced a gradual deadening of political consciousness in the *bourgeoisie*. Opposed,

---

[1] The reform of the rating system seems to have been almost a miracle-cure for all ills. Note a curious case at Pisa during the seigniory of Gambacorta, when the rates were fixed and re-fixed, to the dissatisfaction first of the rich, then of the less well-to-do (P. Silva, *Il governo di Pietro Gambacorta in Pisa*, Pisa, 1912, pp. 116–17 and 124–6).

[2] The fiscal policy of the Visconti provides a typical example. *V*. Ciapessoni, *op. cit.*, Boll. pavese, Part III, pp. 383 *sqq.*

[3] Rizzardo da Camino 'plebi sue gratus habebatur' (Ferreto, *Historia rerum in Italia gestarum*, ed. Cipolla, Rome, 1914, II, p. 127). Matteo Visconti 'maioribus obviat, illis opponens plebem'; he is 'audax ex vulgi robore' 'et plebis captivat colla latenter' (from the short poem by Pace del Friuli, of Torri), Cognasso, *op. cit.*, pp. 9 and 10. And think of the 'gentem rusticam et enormem' who supported the Carrara family in 1325 and burned the 'iura Communis' (*Cortusiorum Historiae, R.I.S.*, XII, p. 835).

[4] See, for example, the shrewd analysis of the work of Taddeo Pepoli in Rodolico, *Dal Comune alla Signoria. Saggio sul governo di Taddeo Pepoli in Bologna*, Bologna, 1898, pp. 84 *sqq.*

albeit covertly, by the Seigneurs and beset by the swarming
hostile mass of the inferior orders, they renounced their past
and sought an outlet for their restless energies in work, content now merely to maintain their social position. The
political disintegration of the old ruling class was hastened
by the departure of many of the most estimable citizens, who
entered the seigniorial administration[1] or were summoned
to join the diplomatic service or the Princes' Councils;[2] and
if in spite of this the State still lacked internal unity, considerable numbers were diverted from the ranks of the former governing classes. It was aggravated by the prevalence
of the mercenary system. True, this had itself been largely a
consequence – and not the least serious consequence – of the
moral exhaustion of the Communal classes, of an aversion
which the *bourgeoisie* seldom overcame to an occupation that
constituted a waste of precious time better devoted to business, and finally of the advent of dictatorial governments; yet
it helped in its turn to accelerate the political dissolution of
urban society, providing the Seigneurs with a weapon independent of the mob over which they ruled, and depriving the
latter of their chances of making a fighting comeback.

Thus the old political world was falling apart. At the same
time, however, economic activity remained intense; indeed,
it increased, thanks to the development of industry, which
was skilfully protected by the Princes, to the new productiv-
ity of those families to whom public life was now closed,[3] and
above all to the creation of vast domains. And the establishment of the principates came as final proof of the disappear-
ance of that mighty Communal consciousness which had
contrived to triumph in face of the Empire.

[1] Cognasso, *op. cit.*, pp. 44 *sqq.*

[2] Thus, among the personages who made up the Council of Gian Galeazzo
Visconti we find Poterio Rusconi, Andreasio Cavalcabo, Bertrando Rossi da
Parma and Andreolo Arese of Milan – names well known in the history of the
Communes. *V.* G. Romano, *Niccolò Spinelli da Giovinazzo diplomatico del
secolo XIV*, Naples, 1902, p. 375. On the diplomacy of Mantua cf. A. Luzio,
L'Archivio Gonzaga di Mantova, Verona, 1922, pp. 80–1.

[3] Cf. Segre, *Storia del commercio*, Turin, 1923, I, p. 136.

There now remained only the most abject parochialism, well calculated to perpetuate the divisions that existed between one place and another, and sometimes a nostalgic regret, which might take the form of rhetorical appeals, but could not inspire a fresh enthusiasm. Occasionally there were sudden outbursts which seemed to indicate a return of youthful vigour; and sometimes, when particular circumstances afforded the opportunity, an insurrection occurred, and there was a momentary return to the forms of liberal government. But the latter's altered character was already apparent in the very name of its custodians, who were known as the 'principes libertatis',[1] as if to remind people that dictators were now necessary; and it soon collapsed, making way for new *condottieri*, who used to enter the cities surrounded by soldiers carrying bread.[2] There was no longer a strong ruling class, but only 'a brute beast, which, not being accustomed to feeding itself, nor knowing the hiding-places in which it might take refuge, becomes the prey of the first man who tries to recapture it'.[3] Nor, certainly, could the conspiracies of the time be regarded as evidence of the existence of a vigorous corporate spirit!

This eclipse of a political class was not counterbalanced by the appearance of another party with a capacity for action. The emergence of a rural *petite bourgeoisie*, for instance, was impossible because the land remained to a great extent in the power of feudatories, great and small, or of urban proprietors, besides bearing the full weight of the endless guerrilla warfare and devastation which were a feature of the age. The external policy of the Seigneurs often bore terribly hardly on the country folk, who, cajoled by the administrative measures adopted, subsequently paid for their master's favour by enduring a long martyrdom at the hands of hordes of plundering mercenaries. Nor was there any sign of the emergence of a strong, united artisan class. The very economic system pre-

---

[1] In the Ambrosian Republic of 1447; Pélissier, *op. cit.*, I, p. 90.
[2] Entry of Francesco Sforza into Milan, *ib.*, I, p. 93.
[3] Machiavelli, *Discorsi*, I, xvi.

vented this: it was based not on a genuine industrial capitalism, which would have led to a concentration of work and so
have permitted the formation of a solid organization of wage-
earners, but generally on a commercial capitalism which controlled a dispersed industry;[1] and it was dictated by the
necessity of importing raw materials, by the need of vast
supplies of capital, which had become a monopoly of the
mercatores, and by current methods of manufacture; but it
had the effect of dividing the working class into so many tiny
groups that its integration was impossible. This scattered
multitude could indeed offer the Seigneur support of a kind;
it could also, at times, break out into rioting of a violence
such as only suffering can provoke; but it certainly did not
constitute a class capable of lending the State solid support
and of imposing its will upon it, depressed as it was by its
hard and lonely life. And even if from time to time the seeds
of a movement appeared there were the rules of the Guilds
to put a check on its aspirations, which were likewise curbed
in his own interests by the Seigneur; for the latter was content enough to govern a formless multitude, and certainly
did not want to contend with an enlightened class organization.

Thus a mighty political consciousness had withered away.
There remained the social groups, mutually antagonistic and
deeply divided by reason of the contempt with which the
bourgeoisie traditionally regarded the common people,[2] by the
latter's hatred of the rich, and finally by the harsh and derisive attitude of city-dwellers of all conditions towards uncouth rustics.[3] There remained the people, gazing in awe at

---

[1] Cf. H. Sée, *Remarques sur l'évolution du capitalisme et les origines de la
grande industrie*, in *Revue de Synthèse historique*, XXXVII (1924), pp. 48
and 66.

[2] Schupfer, *op. cit.*, in *Archiv. Giurid.*, VI, pp. 164–5. All writers, from
Ferreto and Matteo Palmieri to Guicciardini, adopt the same tone.

[3] Few indeed were the voices raised in sympathy, and these were nearly
always inspired by literary motives (I cannot attach much importance to the
majority of the examples of goodwill cited by Zabughin, *Vergilio nel Rinascimento italiano*, I, Bologna, 1921, pp. 233–4 and 244 *sqq*. Perhaps only the

the favourites of the Princes,[1] who in their turn intensified
the general enfeeblement by their paternal policy – all solicitude for the prosperity of their subjects[2] – while Court life
and humanistic culture inculcated into men's minds a serene
indifference to every form of violent emotion. There remained the masses, who very rarely felt themselves freshly
inspired by the spirit of their *condottieri*. Finally, there remained a social and political structure whose unity was expressed almost exclusively in the person of the Seigneur and
in the administrative system. This structure no longer possessed integrated forces capable of fighting, but only individual figures, who might carry on vain struggles among
themselves.

During the second half of the fifteenth century even
external policy seemed to reflect this exhaustion of creative
energy within the States. In the Trecento certain Seigneurs,
and in particular the Visconti, had known how to embody
their aims in a programme which steadily became more organic and complete, thus creating an illusion of ever-increasing
power. In the early part of the new century other adventurers
had inherited the standards and the ambition of Gian Galeazzo, making a bid for final hegemony in Italy or seeking a
kingdom along the valley of the Tiber. But latterly these
attempts had grown more modest, disintegrating into isolated *coups de main* or getting lost in a web of petty intrigues,
while the influence of foreign States on political activity in
the peninsula became ever stronger. The Venetians, formid-

Mantuan was sincerely sympathetic in his attitude to the peasantry). Nor could
this division of the masses be completely healed by the more liberal and
indulgent outlook that prevailed in Court circles, i.e. in the restricted *milieu*
in which the Prince moved. (On the love of the country exhibited by Milanese
courtiers and by the Sforza cf. Malaguzzi Valeri, *La corte di Lodovico il Moro*,
I, Milan, 1913, pp. 596 *sqq.*).

[1] Cf. P. Monnier, *Le Quattrocento*, Paris, 1901, pp. 39, 40. On the
favourites of the Gonzaga *v.* Luzio, *op. cit.*, p. 67.

[2] Luzio, *ib.*, p. 51. On the democratic forms which were sometimes ostentatiously observed at the Court of the Sforza cf. Malaguzzi Valeri, *op. cit.*, I,
p. 456.

able – 'formidolosi' – throughout Italy by reason of their hegemonic aspirations,[1] were preparing for an assault on Ferrara. Alfonso of Aragon found himself beset by the Italic League of 1454.[2] Finally, the 'balance of power' policy supervened to demonstrate the impotence to which the Italian States were reduced.[3]

It was the diplomats who now held the stage – in particular those merchants with hard, secretive profiles who live again in Masaccio's frescoes. These men had long been used to discussing the allocation of financial loans, and they had subsequently been impelled to remedy the shortcomings in communal life. Their calculations no longer had to do with money but with men: they assumed the form of a psychological inquiry, and found concrete expression in subtle, specific precepts, which were all the more shrewd in that those who formulated them were so skilled at reading the faces of their adversaries, at deducing their inmost feelings from a mere contraction of their facial muscles. This emphasis on all that is superficial in human relations led men to cultivate a discretion, a composure so exquisite, serene, almost marmoreal,[4] a style so perfect that 'it produces an illusion of decorum and greatness, while the general impression is that of a bottomless abyss'.[5]

In a contest of this sort the technique of government, the art of the few, acquired a prodigious refinement. Nothing

---

[1] Guicciardini, *Storia d'Italia*, I, 1.

[2] Cf. G. Soranzo, *La lega italica* (1454–1455), Milan, 1924.

[3] 'Accordingly life in Italy was very peaceful, and the chief care of those princes was to watch one another, and to make themselves mutually secure by means of matrimonial alliances, new friendships and leagues' (Machiavelli, *Florentine Histories*, VII, xxiii).

[4] This naturally struck foreigners, who were less refined and to whom 'style' came less naturally: '... et de leur costé (i.e. that of the Italians) ne parloit nul que ledict duc (Ludovico the Moor) et du nostre, ung; mais nostre condition n'est point de parler si posément comme ilz font, car nous parlions quelquesfois deux ou trois ensemble, et ledict duc disoit "Ho, ung à ung" ' (Commynes, *Mémoires*, VIII, 16).

[5] Burckhardt, *La civiltà del Rinascimento*, 3rd ed., Florence, 1921, p. 102. On the foreign policy of the Florentines in particular cf. Luchaire, *Les démocraties italiennes*, Paris, 1916, pp. 241–6 and 290 *sqq*.

remained hidden from the gaze of the Venetian and Florentine ambassadors, who were the most to be feared because,
as merchants, they were diplomats by nature, sent on their
missions for the purpose of obtaining information for the
'Serenissima' (Venice) or the Seigniory (Florence). Accordingly the theoretical maxims of Guicciardini are merely a
rationalization of a century of adventures, in which the sole
criterion was the life of the emotions and of the human
intellect.

The isolated figure of the Prince came more and more to
the forefront. He was the only living thing left in Italy. He
was in truth the artificer, whose daily task it was to weigh up
the most varied sets of circumstances, to detect the machinations of his adversaries, and to plan every step with care.
Beneath him there was no popular opinion which could
triumph over his individual judgment.

III. *THE PRINCE*

The Essence of The Prince

The primordial, ultimate character of this world – devoid of
great moral and political motifs, uninfluenced by the masses,
having its being solely in the isolated virtue of scattered individuals, who left their own imprint on material that was
flabby and incoherent – finds its true expression in *The
Prince*. The latter is not exactly a history of the Seigniories
and Principates, if by history we mean the detailed examination and the minute and constant assessment of specific
events. Rather does it summarize and illustrate the consequences of history, revealing them in broad outline, stripped
of all irrelevancy. Naturally, it does not go into details –
Machiavelli is not at all concerned now with writing history
– and these must be sought elsewhere, just as we have to look
elsewhere for a precise, factual account of the course which
Italian life pursued in the fourteenth and fifteenth centuries.
Here we have merely the fundamental principle which determines and informs the various immediate manifestations

of that life – a principle that is at the same time a consequence.

But Machiavelli, with that powerful creative imagination of his,[1] manages to escape from the realm of mere diplomacy, to which Guicciardini, on the other hand, will confine himself exclusively. He sees beyond the Court events of the last fifty years and, by a wonderful intellectual effort which remained incomprehensible to his contemporaries and caused him to be described as 'extravagant to a degree in his opinions and a discoverer of new and unusual things',[2] succeeds in re-creating the possibility of a great political struggle.

Just as the expansion of the seigniorial State had not been accompanied by a corresponding increase of political virtue, so he too deals only in superficialities; but at least that is something. The grandiose ideal which the Visconti had sought to realize – the establishment of a unitarian State in the Po valley – recurs in Machiavelli as an intellectual concept. Indeed, its realization becomes a certainty; it is seen as the object of a faith that reveals all the passion in the writer's soul – for his discretion and composure are not always sufficient for him to conceal the true nature of his feelings. Not for him the cut-and-thrust of diplomacy, the ebb and flow of negotiations in which the point of equilibrium is sought through the shrewd assessment of possibilities, but rather the clear, positive affirmation of a system which, while availing itself to the maximum degree of the arts of government, human speculation, and back-room intrigue, aims not at a balance of forces but at its own undisputed supremacy. Such are Machiavelli's guiding principles; and in this way he abandons the limited aims of the Italic confederation and of Lorenzo de' Medici and goes back to Gian Galeazzo Visconti and Ladislao of Naples.

Accordingly, he will reject neutrality as being the most

[1] On Machiavelli's 'political imagination' see Chapter I.

[2] He was thus described by Messer Francesco Guicciardini (Letter to Machiavelli dated 18 May 1521, Machiavelli, *Lettere Familiari*, CLXXXI).

pernicious of doctrines,[1] and will refer to the Italian political
equilibrium of former years as a mistake that should be
rectified and consigned to oblivion.[2]

Such is the origin of the treatise *De Principatibus*, in which
political strife, in its most blatant connotation of a struggle
for victory and power, is reduced to a schematic form; but
experience brings with it a new vigour, which, accepting the
basic principle, seeks to carry it out in the surest way possible, and so exposes the uncertainties and mistakes of the
past.

There could be no doubt as to the correct ways of putting
the idea into practice. In the complete absence of any collective force by which the new edifice could be supported,
and assuming, as Machiavelli did, that the virtue of the
Prince was to be the supreme controlling factor of life, it was
essential to follow the paths already trodden by man,
through whom the revival must be brought about. Hence the
minute, cold, incisive analysis, centring round the figure of
the presumed ruler; hence, too, the careful examination of
the position in which the latter would find himself in relation
to his subjects and to foreigners. The details necessarily preserve that personal quality which characterizes the points of
departure and arrival.

And just as for two hundred years of her history Italy had
been dominated by the figures of the great Seigneurs, who
were unsustained by the power of tradition or of any myth,
so in the treatise the thing that serves to illuminate the
general background of events, even if the latter are not deter-

---

[1] *The Prince*, Chapter XXI (where the writer develops an idea already put
forward in the *Discorsi*, I, xxxviii). Indeed, to justify his political principle
Machiavelli comes out with a moral and human assertion ('Men are never so
dishonest that they will embarrass you with such an example of ingratitude')
which is far from consistent with others made elsewhere, e.g. in Chapter
XVIII ('But because they are wicked, and would never keep (faith) with
you . . .').

[2] Chapter XX: 'In the days when Italy was in a certain state of equilibrium
this was surely a good policy; but I do not think that it can be held up as an
example to-day . . .'

F

mined solely by an individual, is the character of the Prince, all sinew and thought, cold and impenetrable, like one of those fine suits of armour made of delicately-wrought steel in which warriors used to encase themselves before a battle: the *new* Prince, sustained not by the memory of his ancestors, not by the recollection of long years of suffering shared with his people, but solely by his own wit and strength of will, his warlike prowess and diplomatic wisdom. Men are more 'beholden' to virtuous actions than to 'ancient blood'.[1]

The people, who bring the first book of the *Discorsi* to life and condition its thought, so much so that Machiavelli justly regards the struggle between patricians and plebs as the source of Rome's greatness, are absent from *The Prince*. They do not even appear in the distance as a social and political entity. We have the Prince's subjects, isolated beings, fragments, as it were, of a vast whole which no longer exists, opposed to the sovereign, but as man to man. Hence the necessity for the Prince to humour them, not to dishonour them or violate their property, to keep their friendship.[2] But where is there any reference to the strength that derives from collective action? When the author seems at first sight to be returning to the theme of the organizing capacity of the masses[3] we find ourselves confronted not with the people but with a confused rabble, not with a party, rich in native energy, abounding in enterprises of its own, seeking to fulfil clearly-defined political aspirations and therefore capable of facing the disputes and the free clashes of opinion on which the fortunes of the Republic depend, but with a mob that 'does not wish to be oppressed' and judges 'a thing by its result'.[4] Compare Chapter IX of *The Prince* with the passage in Chapter IV of the first book of the *Discorsi* in which Machiavelli speaks of the struggle between patricians and

---

[1] Chapter XXIV.

[2] To keep the friendship of the people, who are fundamentally amiable – that is the secret of the Prince's success. Cf. also Chapters X, XX and XXIV.

[3] As he does in Chapter IX and also, briefly, in Chapters XIX and XX.

[4] Chapter XVIII.

plebs in Rome, or with Chapter VI.[1] These last-named chapters breathe a living force, ever-present and self-conscious,
a force that creates its forms of life and overcomes individual
passions by welding them into the compact unity of a
common passion, a force that can also err 'through excessive
love' of its liberty – but in a Republic that is not corrupt
its very error is a source of great good 'and enables it (the
Republic) to lead a free life'.[2] In Chapter IX of *The Prince*,
on the other hand, we have an amorphous, scattered and
truly anonymous mob, in which nothing has any significance
except the feelings of individual persons, who are incapable
of perceiving the collective mind that transcends their own,
or of aspiring to the grandeur of political resolution, even if
the latter be expressed in the communal strife of parties. We
have once more 'a brute beast, which . . . not being accustomed to feeding itself, nor knowing the hiding-places in
which it might take refuge, becomes the prey of the first man
who tries to recapture it'.[3]

Nor is the nobility any less irresolute and aimless. It is
reduced, in short, to engaging in a battle of wits with princes
and people, to hatching plots designed to further only
immediate interests of limited scope, beyond which there is
now nothing. These Italian *Grandi* lack even the pride – a
pride not devoid of a certain heroic quality – which united
the French feudatories against the Monarchy; the latter at
any rate had a pride of caste – as Machiavelli noted.[4] Hat-
reds and passions are aroused by personal, trivial and there-

---

[1] 'Whether it would have been possible in Rome to set up a constitution
which would have destroyed the enmity between the people and the Senate',
to which Machiavelli replies 'No', because 'if the Roman State became more
peaceful, there followed this disadvantage, that it was also weaker'.

[2] *Discorsi*, I, xxix.   [3] *Discorsi*, I, xvi.

[4] *Ritratto di cose di Francia.* Chapter LV of Book IV of the *Discorsi* introduces
the gentry, whom Machiavelli accuses of being the ruin of many Italian
provinces and blames for the fact that those provinces lack any political organization. But even in this passage reference is made to isolated disorders, not to
the organized and conscious opposition of a class of persons bent on supporting
general and collective interests and resolved that clearly-defined aspirations of
their own shall take precedence over all others.

fore fleeting dissensions. The *Grandi* cannot mould their
desire to dominate the people into a clear line of conduct, and
in the end they bow the knee to the Prince, after which fresh
disorders quickly supervene.

Finally, the Prince must gain the friendship of the people,
so that he may keep them 'alive';[1] but the mob must derive
this 'life' from a virtue that is outside itself, from a power that
stands above it. For what life remains in those 'guilds' or
'tribes', the ancient and glorious corporations of arts and
arms, potent symbol of the creative capacity of the Communal *bourgeoisie*? The Prince must take these people into
account,[2] so that he may sometimes talk to them and give
examples of humanity and magnificence, as if he were a
juggler who has to win the favour of an indifferent public.[3]

The emotional invocation at the end itself brings out, once
and for all, this lack of spiritual energy: 'Here is great virtue
among individual members of the community'; but meanwhile these are not capable of any action unless the genius of
a single *condottiere* is forthcoming to arouse them; and they
wait 'open-mouthed' for the 'manna in the desert'.[4]

Machiavelli, then, is impelled to keep his eyes fixed on the
Man alone; and while he propounds some of the general
principles that have occurred to him as a result of his long
meditation – above all that of the necessity of a State militia,
which he regards as fundamental – he is faced with the task
of discovering the specific human laws on which the difficult
art of government will henceforth be based. In this way the

---

[1] *The Prince*, Chapter IX. Fester notes that here even the affection of the
people is no more than an instrument of government (*op. cit.*, p. 165).

[2] *Ibid.*, Chapter XXI.

[3] We get the impression here of a certain demagogic shrewdness – an impression reinforced later when the author cites the example of Valentino, who
has left his subjects 'stunned but satisfied' by his theatrical punishment of
Ramiro de Lorqua (Chapter VII). Such criteria of government vary between
the absolutist and the demagogic, as Zabughin has acutely observed in connection with Valentino himself (*Storia del Rinascimento cristiano in Italia*,
Milan, 1924, p. 267).

[4] *Decennale*, I: 'You took up your station here open-mouthed, waiting for
one who would come from France bringing you manna in the desert. . . .'

treatise on Principates takes the form of a relentless analysis, a kaleidoscope of humanity.

Not that we do not discern even in this the continual expression of a creative imagination that is induced to reconstruct analytical detail through its own power of synthesis. Moreover, the inexorable necessity of reducing an impression that is beautifully complete in itself to the form of a rigid principle is clearly revealed. Just as Machiavelli transforms the historical fact into a theoretical precept, so he remoulds the closely-observed detail into the maxim of unvarying significance,[1] with the result that the contrast with the 'discretion' of Francesco Guicciardini becomes newly apparent; but in the event the axiom, possessing a clearly-defined factual foundation, has a vitality that often disguises its general character, making it as immediate as a psychological observation.

Thus the argument is coloured by human impressions, rapid, clear and complete. Machiavelli, who has spent many years in the service of the Florentine Republic, has met a great number of men, especially the kind of men who hold the tangled threads of the political skein in their hands. Perhaps he is not by nature very diplomatic, not inured to subtle disputations in which care is always taken to keep the language within the limits of a formality that never yields place to the Horatian *fides perlucidior vitro*. Perhaps he lacks the temper of a merchant, having acquired through long practice the habit of remaining impassive and indifferent, with an indifference that terrifies those who have to face it. Perhaps he does not always succeed in restraining the vehemence of his feelings with that calm, lordly mastery which is characteristic

---

[1] It is true that Machiavelli's psychology often assumes a rational character, seeking the man-type rather than the living man (E. W. Mayer, *Machiavelli Geschichtsauffassung und sein Begriff 'virtù'*, Munich, 1912, pp. 39 *sqq.*); yet such is the writer's lively humanity, such is his adherence to the realities of life, that his rationalistic inquiry is itself largely informed by a sense of the concrete which accordingly prevents the figure of the individual from becoming too rigid and restores its mobility. This is also noted by Meinecke, *Die Idee der Staatsräson* (already cited), p. 187.

of Guicciardini. Yet the sometimes painful experience of many years has removed his rough edges, made him civilized, enabling him to perform the most difficult manoeuvres with ease and accustoming him to assume that cold inscrutability which is essential to those who wish to gamble at Court with the lives and destinies of nations. Sometimes, it is true, he forgets what he has learned, and has sudden outbursts of enthusiasm and bitterness which a true diplomat would never permit himself; and indeed his natural confidence re-appears in *The Prince* alongside the acquired manner, moulding the calm and severe analysis into periods that are often animated, vivacious and unexpected. But at any rate the prolonged constraint of public life, combined with the natural perspicacity of his judgment, have taught him to measure carefully the acts and words of those who sit in government over cities and to calculate exactly the effect of the subtle interweaving of the sometimes discordant thoughts and feelings from which the event proceeds – though the process is invisible to the mob.

And so, even when the axioms seem general to a degree, we discern the concrete, precise foundation, unwavering in its detail. The very turn of the clear, laconic phrase, whose every accent is endowed with colour and form, reveals the perfection of the psychological inquiry, which permeates the canvas on which the new State is gradually taking shape.

Moreover, Niccolò does not have much trouble in describing the characters and sketching in the lines of the different figures. It is enough for him to fix his gaze on the various Italian princes, on that crowd of men who had in many cases risen from the humblest circumstances to prosperity, as was possible in those days, by rapid jumps – men who had made themselves the wonder of their contemporaries and had appeared before Machiavelli himself in the privacy of a closed room, like Valentino,[1] or in the crowded halls of another Seigneur, like the princes and ambassadors at the Court of Maximilian.[2] Such fragments of human life present

---

[1] Legation to Valentino, Letters 9, 12, 15, 17 October 1502, etc.
[2] Legation to the Emperor.

themselves almost automatically, ready to be re-assembled
into an organic whole, to one who recalls, for example, men
like Sigismondo Malatesta or Federigo da Montefeltro, both
'fox' and 'lion' at once. Failing all else there is the portrait of
Piero della Francesca; the living image of the Prince with his
broad face, prominent canine jaw, and glassy, impassive
stare.[1] As for his mind, Machiavelli can reconstruct it with
certainty merely by contemplating the image as it appears
roughly outlined against the luminous background.

He finds Valentino truly perfect[2] – partly because in the
character of this son of a Pope, 'le plus desloyal filz de
Prestre qui fut onques',[3] perfect poise was combined with a
prodigious blending of cold calculation and passion, so that
he was able to indulge his passion for sensual pleasures without prejudice to his wise imperialistic plan; but most of all
because Caesar Borgia tried to create a strong unitarian
State, pursuing that goal to which, in the solitude of his villa,
the writer's thoughts were likewise directed. Final ruin can
barely dim the brightness of the vast stage upon which
moved the figure of the *condottière sans peur et sans remords.*
Machiavelli explains his ruin as a caprice of fortune –
'fortune' being an obscure, indeterminate idea to which he
never succeeded in giving clear expression in a bold spiritual
affirmation, sometimes regarding it as the force and logic
of history, but more often as a mysterious, transcendent

[1] R. De la Sizeranne, *Le vertueux condottière*, in *Revue des Deux Mondes*
1 and 15 December 1923, 15 January 1924.

[2] Meinecke (*Anhang zur Einführung*, already cited, pp. 27 *sqq.*) maintains
that the true heroes of *The Prince* are the heroes of Chapter VI, Moses and
Romulus, and not Caesar Borgia. They reappear in fact in Chapter XXVI,
where they are held up to the national Prince as models. But they remain
remote, just as the 'kingdom' will remain remote. They are the 'most excellent
ones', to whose virtue the Prince must aspire, but only so that he may reproduce 'some suggestion' of it; and since excellence is for the present too
much to expect, the human figure on whom *The Prince* hinges is Caesar
Borgia. And we must remember that even at a later date Machiavelli looked
upon the Borgia as the model of the new Prince (*Lettere Familiari*, CLIX),
i.e. of such a Prince as might emerge from the Italy of the day. On Machiavelli's idealization of Valentino cf. Fester, *op. cit.*, p. 63.

[3] J. Bodin, *Les Six Livres de la République*, ed. Paris, 1578 (Preface).

grouping of events, whose incoherence is unintelligible to the human mind.[1] Fortune has 'reproved Valentino'; and the writer is not concerned to examine the fundamental justice of her condemnation.

Thus the picture remains serenely sculptural. It is dominated from afar by the mocking figure of the Borgia, inscrutable in his smile as in his meaning look, with his great black beard that climbs up his pale cheeks and gives his face a sombre setting, even as his mind is circumscribed by his fixed imperial resolve, which is dimly reflected in his every gesture.

He dominates the picture, yet only from a distance; for *The Prince* is no more a glorification of Caesar Borgia than of all those other Seigneurs who come upon the scene – some returning again and again, so that we glimpse the hard, angular features of Francesco Sforza and Ferdinand of Aragon. But since the State can only be founded upon a specific personage – for it has to be conditioned first and foremost by the virtue of an individual, and the inert material awaits the imprint of an 'excessive' excellence – it is natural that the analysis should centre round a figure who will confer on the scattered fragments, which are endowed both with reason and with emotion, a sense of community; and naturally the dominating figure is the son of Alexander VI, who has so often been reviled by the Republicans of Florence.

[1] Croce, *Teoria e storia della storiografia*, Bari, 1917, pp. 215–6. Fortune intervenes when things cannot be explained rationally (Mayer, *op. cit.*, pp. 38–9). Cf. also Ercole, *Lo 'Stato' nel pensiero di Niccolò Machiavelli*, I, Studi Economico-Giuridici della R. Università di Cagliari, VIII (1917), pp. 17 *sqq.* of the excerpt; Meinecke's analysis, *Die Idee der Staatsräson* (already cited), pp. 45 *sqq.*; and Ferrabino's note, *L'universalità della Storia* (*Giornale critico della Filosofia Ital.*, IV, Part II, p. 137). The latter would see in Machiavelli's penetrating discussion of virtue and fortune a search for a *principium universalitatis* in history, whereas it is more likely that Machiavelli never clearly envisaged any such speculative undertaking. The discussion simply reveals the uncertainty of one who cannot satisfactorily account for the changes that occur in a world in which precision and individual will are everything, and the Florentine Secretary's uncertainty is perfectly in keeping with the historical thought of the period. (On this point see Fueter's acute and just observations in *Histoire de l'historiographie moderne*, translated by Jeanmaire, Paris, 1914, pp. 70 *sqq.*)

The Hope of Machiavelli

Such was the foundation on which the solitary inhabitant of the villa at San Casciano was building his 'little castle', giving it concrete form as he awaited the hoped-for final outcome. This was grandiose in conception: for the Italian princes of the late Quattrocento had largely forgotten their idle dreams of hegemony, and had confined themselves to diplomatic warfare and to the achievement of a balance of power; Venice, still ambitious, had found herself compelled to conceal her hand and to resort to deception; and meanwhile Machiavelli had reverted to the idea of the great warriors of the Trecento, bringing to bear upon it his experience and imagination and once more pointing out the necessity of open strife and hence of the kind of powerful State which Valentino had lately sought to realize in practice.

Not that he proposes the complete unification of Italy.[1] The memory of the Kingdom is vividly present to his agitated mind; and he curses those who have destroyed it and thus robbed Italy of her life. But here we have after all only a nostalgic recollection of a time that has passed, only a distant vision, clouded with regrets and bitterness — a vision that does not present itself as a plan for the present and offers no possibility of realization.

The Kingdom comes into the picture as a natural result of the author's reflections on ancient Rome, that Rome which was able to unite beneath its sway the whole of the peninsula, leaving upon it its own creative imprint;[2] and Machiavelli lives again with such passionate intensity in the spaciousness and glory of the Republic of long ago, he applies himself so wholeheartedly to his reconstruction of history, that he conjures up a picture of Italy's lost happiness, and at the same time heaps curses on the heads of those who are to

---

[1] As is maintained, not for the first time, by Ercole, *Dante e Machiavelli*, in *Politica*, July, 1921, p. 136.

[2] *Discorsi*, I, xii. Here Machiavelli, prompted by the example of Rome, uses his experience and his creative gift to envisage a unity which he then finds has been destroyed by the Church.

blame for her ruin. At the outset of his last historical narrative the Monarchy will be alluded to again and again in connection with the achievements of Theodoric, who is surrounded by that glorious halo.[1] It will appear – already torn
by dissension – in the course of references to the Longobards;[2] it will be introduced reluctantly for the last time
when the author comes to discuss Charles of Anjou.[3] And
always there is bitterness in the memory – the bitterness of
one who is conscious of Italy's present plight. Then it ceases
to be mentioned.[4]

Unity is now a memory, an echo of the past – at best a

---

[1] 'He kept all the barbarian Kings who had occupied the Empire within
their own frontiers – not by resorting to the chaos of war, but solely by means
of his own authority. He built towns and fortresses *between the shore of the
Adriatic Sea and the Alps*, so that he might the more easily impede the passage
of the new barbarians who wished to attack Italy' (*Florentine Histories*, I, iv).

[2] 'It was because they had received this advice (viz., to have no more kings
after Clefi) that the Longobards never occupied the whole of Italy and that
their kingdom did not extend beyond Benevento' (*ibid.*, I, viii). And a little
later the writer returns to the theme that runs through Chapter XII of the
Discorsi: 'All the wars that were waged by the barbarians in Italy at this time
were mainly caused by the Popes, and all the barbarians who poured into the
country were usually summoned by them. This mode of action has lasted into
our own day, and as a result Italy has been kept, and remains, weak and
disunited.' (*ibid.*, I, ix).

[3] Who once again finds himself opposed by the Papacy: 'And so the Popes,
now for Religion's sake, now in order to satisfy their own ambition, never
ceased to summon new trouble-makers to Italy and to stir up new wars. And
after they had built up the authority of a prince they would regret it and seek
to encompass his ruin, and would not allow that province, which because of
their weakness they could not dominate themselves, to be dominated by others'
(*Florentine Histories*, I, xxiii).

[4] 'For which we Italians are indebted to the Church, and to the Church
alone' (*Discorsi*, I, xii). Machiavelli refers almost incidentally to Gian
Galeazzo's attempt to establish a *kingdom*, apparently without perceiving its
presumed importance (*Florentine Histories*, III, xxv). 'This man thought he
could make himself King of Italy by force. . .', with the result that the author
can say, alluding to his relations with Florence: '. . . the final outcome was far
less disastrous than the frightful war had been. For when the Duke . . . had
made ready the crown with which he was to be crowned King of Italy in
Florence, he died' (*ib.*). Here there is not even an expression of regret. In the
same way we are afforded a glimpse of Ladislao of Naples, but only in his
dealings with the Florentines: '. . . his death had more power to save them than
did any virtue of their own' (*ib.*, III, xxix).

melancholy aspiration whose vanity is recognized.[1] It is a
conception that makes no impact on a pattern of thought
concerned with positive action in the present. *The Prince* was
written in a moment when the possibility of a monarchy was
farther remote than ever; it was composed, moreover, in
anticipation of specific events – events which would certainly
not prelude such a consummation. Finally, it is permeated
with an actuality that could not easliy be disregarded. Hence,
we cannot divorce it from the context of the times, nor
ascribe to it an unduly wide field of application, in order to
fit it into a picture that is by now out-of-date. The very style
of the work, the fact that it is dedicated to and partly written
for the Medici, who assuredly did not aim at the peninsula's
unification, the specific references in which it abounds[2] –
none of these things can give rise to dreams of unity in the
modern sense. And Machiavelli, who in his reconstruction

[1] E.g. in *L'Arte della Guerra* : 'And I assure you that whichever of the
present rulers of Italy first enters by that road will be master of this province
before any other....' (VII). Here the general tone of Machiavelli's language,
first scornful, then resigned and lugubrious ('. . . and I grieve when I think of
nature. . . .'), and his denunciation of princes who 'live in the same atmosphere of disorder', reveal the true nature of his hopes. In the same way,
Varchi makes a brief reference in passing to the 'overlordship' of Italy as if it
were a sublime subject on which it were pointless to dwell (*Storia Fiorentina*,
Milan, 1845, I, p. 65, l. ii). Cf. a number of just observations by Ferrari,
Histoire de la raison d'État, Paris, 1860, pp. 256–7. On Machiavelli's attitude
to the Kingdom cf. also Fester, *op. cit.*, pp. 145 and 151.

[2] The State which Machiavelli envisages is that which Caesar Borgia
attempted to realize. 'And as regards the acquisition of new territories, he had
planned to become master of Tuscany, and he already controlled Perugia and
Piombino, and had assumed the protection of Pisa. And as if he did not need
to pay any regard to France . . . he seized Pisa. After this, Lucca and Siena
capitulated at once . . . The Florentines had no defence against him: and if
things had gone his way . . . he would have acquired such strength and such a
reputation that he would have stood on his own feet and would no longer have
depended on the fortune and strength of others, but only on his own power
and virtue' (*The Prince*, Chapter VII). Similarly: 'And having heard . . . that
he (Giuliano) is making himself master of Parma, Piacenza, Modena and
Reggio, I feel that this Seigniory would be excellent and powerful and capable
of being maintained in the face of any eventuality if it had been well governed
in the beginning' (*Lettere Familiari*, CLIX). The Seigniory is excellent and
powerful: *The Prince's* aim is to administer such a State well in the first place.

of the past dwells with such feeling and animation on the Italian monarchy, on the ancient unity that has been destroyed by the Papacy, cannot imagine a complete re-union of Italians under a single leader when he writes his treatise, in which he is concerned with the present and regards the most recent historical developments as something to be exploited, not denied.

The 'national' significance of the Prince lies elsewhere. We find it above all in the re-affirmation of the necessity of open and uninhibited political strife, which alone can avail to revive the greatness and glory of a land that has been 'ravaged, plundered, violated and reviled'. We find it in the insistent call for a new disposition of political and military forces, which, leaving out of account all forms of rhetoric and humanism, can alone restore happiness to a 'scattered' nation of 'slaves and bondsmen'.

At this point we leave the realm of literature and witness the creation of a political consciousness. And herein lies the essential morality of Machiavelli: he may well condemn Princes who retire to the solitude of their offices to think out fine phrases, seeing that he himself abandons the 'style' of the Renaissance, creates the new style, and gives the Italians an initial lesson in social ethics.

But he is eager to see established a State which, though territorially spacious, will above all be re-organized and made secure by the virtue of its overlord, a State strong in the possession of its own militia, fortified by its ruler's clarity of purpose, practical determination and administrative sagacity – in short, the kind of State that will be able both to impose its supremacy on the other Italian princes, thus restoring peace and social order where there is anarchy, and to ward off every threat from abroad, expelling the barbarians from the Motherland.[1] For Machiavelli is not turning into 'a Transalpine in Italy – a Francophile, an admirer of foreign might.[2] Above all, he wants a State that can defend Italy

---

[1] Cf. Nourrisson, *Machiavel*, Paris, 1875, pp. 257 *sqq.* and especially 266.
[2] *Discorsi*, Preface to Book II.

from the barbarians: that is his cardinal postulate, and it is transformed into a hope and a faith by the intense fervour of a mind uninhibited by discretion.

Not complete unification,[1] then, nor even a confederation – the Italic *foederatio* of the Quattrocento, by virtue of the very fact that it revealed the impossibility of conquering the various States, is not greatly beloved of the writer – but a dominion that centres around an 'ancient State', possibly the Florence of the Medici, i.e. around a ready-made nucleus, dominating Central Italy and secure in the possession of outlets to the sea, passes across the Apennines and clearly-defined frontiers, and solidly constructed within thanks to the energy of its creator. In short, a régime capable of keeping the 'minor potentates' of Italy in their places, of humbling the 'dignitaries' who disturb the life of the community, and of driving out 'foreign potentates', who are ever ready to take a surreptitious hand in domestic struggles with the aim of imposing their yoke.[2]

The creation of such a powerful régime had been the aim

[1] Which incidentally was prohibited by the profound discrepancies between the various regions of Italy – on the one hand Naples and Milan, breeding-grounds of noblemen and rotten to the core (*Discorsi*, I, xvii and lv), on the other Florence, 'where there is the greatest equality' (*Discorsi*, I, lv, and again in the *Discorso sul riformare lo Stato di Firenze* and the *Florentine Histories*, III, i, in which we read: 'There inequality has been replaced by a marvellous equality'). Milan is specifically contrasted with the Florentine Republic in the *Discorsi*, I, lv, and in the *Discorso sul riformare lo Stato di Firenze*.

[2] Machiavelli's lengthy consideration (*The Prince*, Chapter III) of the need for the Seigneur of a 'heterogeneous province' (as Italy then was in the matter of customs and institutions) to set himself up as the leader and defender of neighbouring 'minor potentates,' to weaken those who were powerful in his own domain, and to take care lest 'by any mischance a foreigner as powerful as himself should be admitted' embraces the entire programme of the new Prince. The latter will bring peace to Italy and will heal her wounds, he will cleanse her of those sores which have been festering for so long; but he will do so in the exact way that is prescribed for a conqueror in a foreign land who at the same time reconciles himself completely to the existence of a national Prince, keeping the other potentates quiet and subdued by his own superior strength, and thus preventing the barbarians from making any further forays across the Alps. And we can understand how in the final exhortation of *The Prince* this supreme aim of liberation from the barbarians is transformed into a bitter hatred of those hard, disdainful and odious races, and

of Valentino,[1] whose stature on that account seemed to Machiavelli all the greater. This was the kind of State whose establishment the writer, reduced to the status of a would-be counsellor, meant to suggest to the Medici. For in the intention of Machiavelli, who conceived it in feverish haste, *The Prince* is not a work of art, nor is it merely an essay in the theory of political organization. It is, in addition, a compen-

how Machiavelli refers to all Italy as awaiting her Redemption and her liberator. Incidentally, the other historians of the time held a similar view. Nardi, indeed, refers to Valentino as a claimant to the seigniory of Italy. In Book IV of the *Istorie della città di Firenze* (Florence, 1842, I) it is stated in connection with the death of Caesar Borgia: 'And such was the end of this wicked man, who had so arrogantly aspired to be *monarch* of Italy, as has been made evident by his deeds and designs' (p. 395). Let us, then, examine the nature of those deeds and designs: '. . . for Valentino was seen to assemble his troops, and from the fact that he enlisted fresh recruits it was known beyond a doubt that the Pope and he planned to stay behind with the said troops and not to enter the Kingdom (of Naples, in 1503) to help France. . . . And all this was done so that he might chastise those he had planned to chastise, who in truth were, primarily, the Florentines . . . and also so that he might later attack the said French, as the opportunity arose, when they had met with some disaster, and so drive every man of them from Italy, leaving himself *almost sole arbiter and master* of her destinies. . . . Valentino had invested the whole of our domain (i.e. of Florence) to the north, and in the direction of the Church lands, surely intending, when the French Army had passed by on its way to the Kingdom, to proceed to Perugia, and to attack the city forthwith from that side . . . so carrying out the plan which the Duke and the Pope had always had in mind . . .' (*ib.*, pp. 309–310). 'Monarchy', then, is by definition *the arbitrary control of Italy*; it depends on the existence of a unitarian State in Central Italy and on the expulsion of the barbarians, which is necessary in order that every source of unrest may be removed. It entails *hegemony, not absolute union*; and such hegemony is made possible only by the setting up of a strong central régime, and by the expulsion of 'foreign potentates'. Machiavelli's conception is no different. Notice also, in particular, how the two writers agree as regards Valentino and his yearning for power.

On the notion of Italian freedom current during those years cf. F. Nitti, *Leone X e la sua politica*, Florence, 1892, pp. 35 *sqq.* Almost all could repeat the words of Coluccio Salutati, 'Sum denique gente italicus, patria florentinus' (*Epistolario*, ed. Novati, Rome, II, 1893, p. 254, Book VII, 3), even if some subsequently referred to 'una Urbs' and 'Itala gens una' (cf. A. Medin, *Caratteri e forme della poesia storico-politica sino a tutto il secolo XVI*, Padua, 1897, p. 35).

[1] Who aspired 'to the domination of Tuscany, as being nearer and more suitable to form a kingdom together with the other States which he controls, (*Del modo di trattare i popoli della Val di Chiana ribellati*).

dium of counsels and practical principles rapidly assembled in a single volume – I would almost call it an unsolicited memorandum submitted by a subject to his Seigneur. In short, it is little different from the various despatches and reports written by Machiavelli and others on the subject of the city's re-organization, nor is it unduly dissimilar in purpose to that *Discorso sul riformare lo Stato di Firenze* which he later wrote for Leo X at the instigation of Cardinal Ginlio de' Medici.[1] He needed to create a world of the mind in which he could move about and discourse freely in his own fashion; he almost took a delight in contemplating a clear pattern of thought, gradually brought to completion as the years went by and crystallized both by his desire to indicate the sure ways of government to those who were preparing for a loftier destiny and by his determination to return to the world of affairs. It is in the interplay of all these varied emotions that the little book has its genesis; and in the excitement of creation the author no longer perceives them in clear outline.

But *The Prince* is not a literary exercise! Machiavelli is too far from being a victim of the wretched habit, long the fundamental weakness of the Italians, of using style and literary artifice as a sop to conscience and will. He does not even write the title on the first page of the little work; and he calls it a treatise *De Principatibus*, *Of Principates* or *The Prince*[2] indiscriminately, as if its worth derives not from its formal dress or its stylistic configuration, but from the gravity that informs it and underlies its precepts and counsels.

---

[1] On this point cf. Tommasini, *op. cit.*, II, pp. 200–7; Villari, *op. cit.*, III, pp. 54 *sqq.* [Ridolfi, *op. cit.*, pp. 275–277, and n. 28, pp. 450–451.] Here, however, there emerges a Machiavelli in whose thought we can detect a return to the democratic outlook of the period of Savonarola – a 'civic' Machiavelli.

[2] The work is entitled *De Principatibus* in a number of MSS. (Tommasini *op. cit.*, II, Appendix, pp. 1016 *sqq.*) [As well as in the celebrated letter to Vettori of 10 December, 1513]. In the *Discorsi* it is called *Of Principates* (II, i) and also *The Prince* (III, xlii).

[In the *Italia* edition of 1813 the allusion in *Discorsi*, III, xlii, reads: 'I have argued at length in my treatise on the Prince.' On the other hand, in the Mazzoni-Casella, the Panella, and the Flora-Cordié editions the title is given in Latin: 'I have argued at length in my treatise De Principe.']

But this time practical necessity and immediacy of purpose, which to an undue extent inspire the writing of the *Discorso sul riformare lo Stato di Firenze*, are transformed by the author's creative fervour into a wholly subjective need of a self-enlightenment, of an act of organic creation, that will justify his solitary musings; and so, happily for us, *The Prince* is different.

Machiavelli, then, bases a political doctrine on a reconsideration of the most recent developments of Italian history, as if his country were still in the most prosperous phase of its life, at the zenith of its organic creativeness, and integrates that vision of reconstruction with a creative act of his own, namely the theory of the State as the possessor of its own militia. But now his doctrinal system is swept away in a flood of emotion that can no longer be contained and is, in short, completely untrammelled by any diplomatic reserve. The analytical method, necessary for the determination of single eventualities and for the gradual construction of the new road along which the chosen *condottiere* will have to advance, is forgotten in the final exhortation, which assembles all the parts and subordinates them to the higher goal that is their only *raison d'être*. In the last chapter of *The Prince* the author gives vent to his ill-suppressed emotion and, having traced out the logical pattern, in a fresh impulse of creation transfuses it into the flood-tide of his desire. Having previously regarded it as something rational, whose realization is a possibility, he now translates it into terms of hope and faith.[1]

---

[1] Instead of confuting at length the well-known assertion of Baumgarten, subsequently echoed by Pastor, that the last chapter is almost an *hors-d'oeuvre*, an irrelevant addition, we may content ourselves with observing that Chapters XXIV, XXV and XXVI are even more closely interlinked than those which precede: the first sets out the causes of Italy's ruin, the second establishes the abstract possibility of a resurgence, the last specifically demands it. The chapter on Fortune especially is only introduced so as to make the final exhortation logical and to provide it with a sure basis in reason (cf. Chapter I, pp. 21–23). The practical and historical significance of the work is fully confirmed in the last three chapters.

IV. THE NATURE AND LIMITS OF
MACHIAVELLI'S THOUGHT

Machiavelli Considered Against the Background of His Time

Basing his doctrine, then, on the present state of Italian history, which he expounds with unwonted clarity, Machiavelli also accepts its premises. In creating the Principate, regarded as the expression of an individual virtue that is extraneous to the life of the masses, he confirms the death-sentence pronounced on contemporary society, which, viewed as a political force capable of revival, is dissociated from the reconstruction of the State. Everything is dependent on the shrewdness and energy of the lonely *condottiere*.

This lack of confidence in the people, this grievous condemnation of contemporary society is implicit in the very creation of the Prince. We find the author breaking off in the middle of a passionate, hitherto uninterrupted evaluation of the energies of a people that discovers the springs of its greatness within itself (this evaluation is marked by sudden slight hesitations, which leave the writer at times incapable, after his initial act of faith in the virtue of the people, of deciding between the mob and the individual, and lead him to interrupt his eulogy of the people's struggle against the patricians with an examination of the ways in which the Prince can avoid the vice of ingratitude). We find him suddenly returning to motifs adumbrated earlier, making them the basis of a lengthy discourse and investing them with an unsuspected vitality. We find him abandoning his comprehensive survey of the past and carrying out a minute and subtle analysis whose purpose is to determine a new social system. These procedures would suffice in themselves to reveal Niccolò's state of mind when, having laid aside his curial robes, he finds himself confronted again and again with the obtrusive problem of the reorganization of present-day life – a problem which had already tormented him dur-

G

ing his years of public service, and which is now aggravated by considerations of a practical nature.

As he contemplates the Italy of his day Machiavelli is filled with a profound sense of grief. At times this becomes crystallized, and finds an outlet now in invective, now in sarcasm, now in the sudden cry of distress,[1] while at other times the sad-eyed writer indulges in vain regrets.[2] At intervals he becomes impatient of the chains that bind him and wants to burst them, dragging with him his fellow-citizens, but he soon relapses into his former state, surveying them with a sad irony in which there is all the disillusionment of the man who yearns for action and is forced to confine himself exclusively to flights of fancy.

To him Florence is an object of pity, so much so that at times his old affection for his native city seems almost to have deserted him. The much-discussed epigram about Pier Soderini is merely the concrete expression of an attitude of mind. This was formerly characterized by passion and indignation but now these give way to a mocking irony, which, however, is tempered with a note of grief when he comes to recognize the futility of his anguish.[3]

Here in Florence there has never been any organized political life. The Republic of Soderini, even though the

---

[1] '. . . but he who was born in Italy or Greece, and has not become, in Italy a Transalpine, in Greece a Turk, has cause to denounce his age and to extol the past. For there are many things about the past that make it marvellous; but as to the present, there is nothing that redeems it from every extremity of wretchedness, infamy and shame. There is no observance of religion or law, there is no military consciousness. Instead, it is defiled by every species of abomination' (*Discorsi*, Preface to Book II). 'As for the union of the other Italians, you make me laugh – first, because no union will ever be able to do any good . . . secondly, because the head and the tail are not co-ordinated; nor will this generation ever move a step, for whatever cause . . .' (*Lettere Familiari*, CXXXI, dated 10 August, 1513).

[2] '. . . say this in justification of him who strives by such vain thoughts to lessen the sadness of his days, that he has nowhere else to turn his head . . .' (*Mandragola*, Prologue).

[3] On Machiavelli's attitude to Soderini cf. Benoist, *Le gonfalonière perpetuel Pier Soderini*, in *Revue des Deux Mondes*, 1 May 1924, pp. 120 and 135 *sqq.*

writer had no small stake in it, is deemed weak and inept, because the Florentine *bourgeoisie*, the raw material of the State, is as corrupt as all the rest of Italian society.[1] The barely perceptible, sarcastic smile of pity which Machiavelli cannot keep from his lips and eyes when he speaks of Savonarola (to him, as to Commynes,[2] Savonarola is a *bon homme*, except that for the somewhat bewildered sincerity of the Frenchman Machiavelli substitutes the slyness and subtlety of a Florentine) reveals to us without need of comment the true impression which this crumbling society makes upon the Secretary.

Not even Venice, dear though she is to the hearts of the Republicans of Florence,[3] offers him any grounds for hope. There, indeed, he sees not the resplendent glory of the lion of St. Mark but the profound weakness of a State which, living in isolation within the narrow circle of a mercantile oligarchy, cannot achieve internal security, and, when it desires to widen the boundaries of its domain, going outside its natural small field of political expansion, is faced with certain ruin. The marvellous economic power of the Venetian Republic does not suffice to create political virtue. Machiavelli, who has little regard for the one, looks in vain for the other; and he bitterly castigates Venice for her efforts to achieve hegemony, efforts that still reverberate in the

---

[1] *Discorsi*, I, xxxviii, xlix; II, xii ('. . . such valour did they [the Florentines] display in the wars of long ago, and such cowardice in those of recent times'), xv, xxi ('And without doubt, if the Florentines, either by the formation of leagues or by offers of help, had tried to civilize their neighbours instead of provoking them, at this hour they would be the masters of Tuscany'), xxiii, xxx ('On the other hand we shall see, in the case of weak States, beginning with our own State of Florence . . .'); III, xxvii and xxx (on Soderini); *Florentine Histories*, III, i ('she became ever lowlier and more abject . . .'); VIII, xxii: 'Florence, a city passionately fond of talking, who bases her judgments on events, not on advice . . .'); *Decennale* I and II, *Asino d'Oro*, V ('And now that she has expanded her power, and is become great and vast, she fears everyone, and not merely the mighty').

[2] *Mémoires*, VIII, iii.

[3] G. Toffanin, *Machiavelli e il 'Tacitismo'* (*La 'Politica storica' al tempo della Controriforma*), Padua, 1921, pp. 9 *sqq.*

memories of Florentine politicians, stunned by the un-expected disaster of Vailate.[1]

Milan and Naples are rotten to the core;[2] Genoa is worth-less;[3] and Italy, taken as a whole, is the most corrupt of nations.[4] Niccolò is quite convinced of it!

But what prompts this harsh, categorical verdict of politi-cal weakness, which as a statement of fact is only partly true?

Sometimes Machiavelli has a clear vision of some of the chief reasons for the failure of the Communal system.[5] In a

[1] *Discorsi*, I, vi; II, x, xix, xxx; III, xi, xxxi (in which we find the harshest reference to the Republic of St. Mark); *Florentine Histories*, I, xxix ('in one day they were deprived of that State which they had acquired during the course of many years at infinite cost. And although in recent times they have recovered part of it, having recovered neither their reputation nor their strength they, like all the other Italian princes, lie at the mercy of others'); *Decennale* I ('Mark, full of fear and full of thirst'), II; *Asino d'Oro*, V; *Lettere Familiari*, CXXXIV. Cf. Vettori's judgment. '. . . they are wasting away and, as we say, are dying of consumption . . . and being sick with this fever, as they have been for the past three years, they are heading for death' (*Lettere Familiari*, CXXIII).

[2] *Discorsi*, I, xvii, lv, and *Florentine Histories*, VI, xxiii. '. . . it was hardly sensible to believe that the Milanese could retain their freedom, because the quality of the citizenry, their way of life, and the outmoded sects which existed in that city were unfavourable to any form of civil government'.

[3] 'The Genoese, being at one moment free, at the next slaves either of the Kings of France or of the Visconti, lived without honour, and were numbered among the lesser powers' (*Florentine Histories*, I, xxxix).

[4] *Discorsi*, I, lv.

[5] *Discorsi*, II, xix: '. . . and he who acquires authority without power is bound to meet with disaster . . . like the Venetians and the Florentines, who were far weaker when the former ruled Lombardy and the latter Tuscany than they were when Venice was content with the sea and Florence with a frontier six miles long. For all that has happened is due to the fact that they wanted to expand and did not know how to set about it. . . .' And the method is '. . . to increase the population of one's city, to acquire allies and not subjects, to send colonists to guard the territories that have been acquired, to make capital out of the spoils of war, to subdue the enemy by means of raids and pitched battles, not sieges, to keep the State wealthy and the private citizen poor, and to display the utmost zeal in the practice of the military art . . .' (*ibid.*). This, moreover, was the Roman method: see *Discorsi*, II, iv, in which we also read: 'We see again that that procedure of acquiring subjects has always been ineffective and has brought little advantage; and when it has been carried too far disaster has quickly followed. And if this procedure of acquiring subjects is useless in armed republics, it is worse than useless in those that are unarmed, as the republics of Italy have been in our day.' So in *Discorsi*, II, iii: 'However, a

wonderful passage in the *Florentine Histories* he succeeds to a great extent in solving the mystery of that civilization's evolution, indicating one of the points at which it was rotten,[1] and at other times themes of astonishing amplitude

small republic cannot occupy cities or kingdoms that are stronger or larger than itself; and if it does so it undergoes the same experience as a tree whose branch is thicker than its trunk: the tree supports the branch with difficulty and is made weaker by every gust of wind, as we see happened to Sparta. . . .' And Sparta is like Venice, 'because expansion is the bane of such republics, and those who govern them should use every possible means to prevent them from acquiring new territories, because such territories, being dependent upon a weak republic, are the cause of its complete ruin, as in the cases of Sparta and Venice' (*ibid.*, I, vi). Elsewhere, alluding to colonies: 'This custom having now died out, thanks to the bad ways of Republics and princes, the result is that the provinces are weakened and ruined, because this system is the only one that makes Empires more secure. . . .' (*Florentine Histories*, II, i).

[1] 'The bitter and natural enmities that exist between the masses and the nobles . . . are the cause of all the evils that arise in cities; for from this diversity of humours spring all the other things that disturb the peace of Republics. This kept Rome disunited, this – if it is permissible to compare small things with great – has kept Florence divided, although in the two cities the results were different. For the enmities that originally sprang up in Rome between the people and the nobility were dispelled by discussion, whereas the Florentines settled their differences by fighting. . . . In Rome these enmities were always an incentive to military virtue, in Florence they completely destroyed it. In Rome they changed the relationship between the citizens from one of equality to one of extreme inequality: in Florence they have changed it from one of inequality to one of marvellous equality. . . . The desire of the people of Florence was wrongful and unjust, so that the nobility prepared to defend itself by superior strength; hence, there was bloodshed among the citizens, and some were sent into exile. And those laws which were afterwards framed were not designed to benefit the community as a whole but were all in favour of the conqueror. . . . But in Florence, the people being left victorious, the nobles found themselves deprived of their magisterial offices; and if they wished to regain them they had . . . not only to be, but to look, like common folk . . . consequently, the military virtue and magnanimity of the nobles became things of the past; they could not re-appear among the people, for the people did not possess them; and so it was that Florence became ever lowlier and more abject' (*Florentine Histories*, III, i). This passage, in spite of errors of detail, bespeaks a conceptive faculty that is truly vast and potent. On the party struggle and Machiavelli's historical vision cf. Moriz Ritter, *Studien über die Entwicklung der Geschichtswissenschaft*, in *Historische Zeitschrift*, 1912, pp. 272 *sqq.* Most interesting, too, are Dyer's observations on the linking of these Florentine factions with Roman history (*Machiavelli and the Modern State*, Boston, 1904, pp. 87 *sqq.*).

and profundity enter into his historical vision.[1] But these are sudden flashes of insight that come to the author in the midst of his rapt meditations, which range over the whole vast course of history. When he has to condescend to a more specific judgment on this or that Italian State – and above all when the regenerative purpose that proceeds from his will seeks to reconcile itself with the creative act of his spirit, and Niccolò no longer moves about amid the quiet of his peaceful and secluded study, but ventures forth into the living world of his time – then it is that his thought loses this breadth of vision. From the consideration of social problems, from the unhealthy party feuds and fruitless struggles between people and nobles his mind turns to the infamies of the mercenary troops, the inertia of the princes, and the weakness of republics that lack armies of their own. To his mind the principal cause of Italy's misfortune is her lack of a national militia. Forgetting the more intimate processes of popular feeling, he concentrates entirely on the visible acts of violence perpetrated by the base and contemptible mercenaries and on the folly of rulers who do not even know how to control their forces.[2] In all his writings he constantly bewails and denounces the indolence of leaders and soldiers, the cause of Italy's present woes; and he never ceases to execrate in turn the bad military organization of the republics and the mean outlook of the hired troops. The militia is not only the foundation of the new structure that Niccolò desires to raise:[3] it becomes in its turn a criterion of history.[4]

[1] E.g. in Chapter XII of Book I of the *Discorsi*, and also to some extent in Chapter LV.

[2] 'Accordingly, my history will be full of tales of these idle princes and these utterly despicable armies....' (*Florentine Histories*, I, xxxix).

[3] The middle Chapters (XII, XIII) of *The Prince* are in fact those which deal with the question of armies, and not only from the point of view of material description. Good laws are themselves conditioned by good armies.

[4] *Discorsi*, I, xxi; II, xviii, xxx; *The Prince*, XII, XIII, XXVI; *Arte della Guerra*, I and VII; and instead of quoting the well-known general assertions we may content ourselves with an examination of his verdict on the downfall of a few individual States: 'The Venetians ... when it came to the point that they had to wage war on land ... engaged as their captain the Marquis of Mantua. It was this inauspicious course of action that ruined their chances of reaching

The Errors in Machiavelli's Assessment of History

This was the most formidable error of which Machiavelli was ever guilty. His reasoning was based on an undeniable fact – the inferiority, military and otherwise, of the Italian States since the last decades of the fifteenth century. But instead of seeking out and thoroughly investigating the ulti-mate causes – the economic and political causes as well as those connected with warlike organization – of this enfeeble-ment, which followed what had been by no means a black period for the arms and the soldiers of the peninsula, he con-fines himself to superficialities, conforming to the outlook of the men of his time, in whom terror suddenly gives way to hope and tranquillity to uneasiness, as they see the worldly fortunes of a State being decided in a single day on the battle-fields.[1]

the stars and expanding their territory' (*Arte della Guerra*, I); 'In 1508 the Venetians . . . not having valorous armies such as would have enabled them to keep the enemy at bay . . . met with disaster' (*Discorsi*, III, xi); 'Because of their pusillanimity, which was due to the incompetence of their war admini-stration, they lost their realm and their nerve at one and the same time (after Vailate)' (*ibid.*, III, xxxi); '. . . I thought little of the Venetians, even when they were at the peak of their greatness, because to me it always seemed a far greater miracle that they had acquired that empire and that they maintained it, than it would have been if they had lost it. . . . What struck me was their way of managing without captains or soldiers of their own' (*Lettere Familiari*, CXXXIV). And so far as Florence is concerned it will suffice to recall the close of *Decennale* I: 'But the journey would be easy and short if you were to re-open the temple of Mars.'

[1] As a result they become somewhat bewildered: 'In this way the fortunes of the Venetian Republic declined at a tremendous, almost a bewildering rate' (Guicciardini, *Storia d'Italia*, VIII, vii); and Commynes, confronted with Charles VIII's lightning conquest, can only say: 'Tout cedict voyaige fut vray mistere de Dieu' (*Mémoires*, VIII, iii). Later, Paruta speaks of 'the sudden arrival in Italy of the French, who introduced into that country a terrifying and unaccustomed method of waging war' (*Historia Vinetiana*, Venice, 1605, Book I, p. 5). It was natural that such an attitude of mind should lead to a wholesale condemnation of the wickedness and corruption of the soldiers and their captains – a condemnation that is even echoed by Montaigne: 'Quand nostre roy Charles huictiesme, quasi sans tirer l'espee du fourreau, se veit maistre du royaume de Naples et d'une bonne partie de la Toscane, les seigneurs de sa suitte attribuerent cette inesperee facilité de conqueste, à ce que les princes et la noblesse d'Italie s'amusoient plus à se rendre ingenieux et sçavants, que vigoreux et guerriers' (*Essais*, l. 1, Chapter XXIV.)

The diplomatic and military incident, instead of being regarded as the visible expression of a more intimate process that is unceasingly at work throughout the social and political fabric of the nation, is isolated and confined within the bounds of its immediate reality. Such are the limits now imposed on the investigations of the Florentine Secretary, who, in his commentary on ancient history, had looked for the origins of a nation's glory in the strength of the people and the uninhibited strife of parties.

It might almost be said that the author is so accustomed to palace politics, so familiar with the recurring outbreaks of armed violence and the sudden warlike convulsions of the time, that when he comes to discuss his age he is oblivious of all other voices. On the other hand, the bitterness of his memories, his indignation, long repressed by the enforced discipline of public affairs, above all his implacable hatred – a legacy from his ancestors – of those ferocious, infamous and profane mercenaries who have so often struck terror into the hearts of the citizens assembled in council and have, moreover, caused him, the chancellor of the Ten and the Nine, prolonged agonies of mind – all these things, it might almost be said, rise up before him now, so that his consideration of history is dominated by the passions which they arouse within him.[1] The author seeks a clearly-defined target for all the hatred and despair that fill his heart, and at this point his error of criticism assumes what is essentially an emotional character. Thrown off his balance by his secret sorrow, he conceives a loathing for 'mercenarism' which remains with him for ever.

He does not ask himself if, and how, Italy's military inferiority is the result of changes that have taken place in the formation of tactical units, in discipline, and in the technique of war.[2] Nor does he pause to consider in what way

[1] Sometimes, indeed, Machiavelli's attitude to soldiers seems to be that of the civil servant. Cf. Hobohm, *Machiavellis Renaissance der Kriegskunst,* Berlin, 1913, II, p. 281.

[2] So far as his observations on infantry are concerned Machiavelli's judgment is sound. But it does not automatically imply the renunciation of

this inferiority is bound up with the complete redistribution of political and economic forces and the profound change that has taken place in the fighting capacity of the various European States. Instead, he condemns outright all the long military experience of the armies of Italy, without perceiving that until recent times this had been not merely necessary, but, indeed, not without its moments of glory.[1] He lumps together in a single context just observations and gratuitous assertions. He apportions blame indiscriminately and in the end bitterly castigates those very Italian régimes which deserve his contempt perhaps least of all.[2]

Nor does he even try to find out in what respects Italian 'mercenarism' differed from that of other nations. He does not inquire, for example, into the reasons why it was in Italy that 'condottierism' achieved its maximum success. (The existence of that system is not to be confused with the mere

'mercenarism'; indeed, the new tactical requirements and the methods of warfare that had now come into use actually made the existence of powerful cadres of professional soldiers a necessity. Equally, it should not have entailed the unreserved condemnation of previous methods of warfare, which had in their turn been both necessary and useful. The truth is that Machiavelli advocates the use of infantry above all because he believes that that is the way to get rid of 'mercenarism'. This also explains why, having established his point, he does not subsequently worry his head unduly about certain other new and important factors in the military art, e.g. artillery.

[1] The charges which not only Machiavelli but also Guicciardini and Giovio level against the *condottieri* are false (Delbrück, *Geschichte der Kriegskunst*, IV, Berlin, 1920, p. 21). Indeed, until the fifteenth century was well advanced the Italians enjoyed a good reputation as warriors. Italian *condottieri*, who were regarded as the authentic trainers of cavalry, were used, for example, by Charles the Bold (A. Spont, *La milice des francs-archers*, in *Revue des Questions Historiques*, LXI, 1897, p. 461). Machiavelli, however, passes a contemptuous judgment on everything. The results of his attitude may be seen in the fact that in the *Florentine Histories* he falsifies (that is the word) his sources simply in order to show up the *condottieri* and the mercenaries in a poor light – so much so that he earns a just reproof from Ammirato. See Villari, *op. cit.*, III, pp. 257–8, 270–1, 279 (Battles of Zagonara, Anghiari and Molinella). For other inaccurate statements about Sforza and Fortebracci, *ib.*, p. 268, first footnote.

[2] Thus, his judgment on Venice and her military organization is mistaken (Hobohm, *op. cit.*, II, p. 25; Fueter, *Geschichte des Europäischen Staatensystems von 1492–1559*, Munich and Berlin, 1919, p. 161).

fact that Italy harboured an element of hired troops, who were the real cause of her disasters and of the changes in her general set-up.) To raise such a problem would have been to get to the very heart of the matter – to reveal the hetero-geneous course of Italian history, not only in the military but in the political sphere, to probe the inmost secrets of fifteenth-century life, and to disclose the organic weaknesses in the constitution of the principates and republics of the peninsula.[1]

But Machiavelli does not realize this. He confuses 'mer-cenarism' with 'condottierism'.[2] Moreover, because of his instinctive need to generalize he extends the scope of his argument with an assurance that is amazing, condemning at a single stroke the *unarmed* nations, Italy, France and Spain, and blaming indiscriminately the Sforza and the King of France.

And he did not realize that just at this period the employ-ment of mercenaries was becoming an absolute necessity for monarchs who were devoting themselves to the laborious task of creating national States. He could not understand how, if it was desired to give them the means to triumph over feudal resistance and the individualism of provinces and cities and at the same time to make possible the initiation of a genuine, large-scale European policy of expansion, it was necessary to place under the orders of the Head of the cen-tral government an army which would depend on him alone

[1] See Hobohm's excellent observations in *op. cit.*, II, pp. 266 *sqq.*, 279 *sqq.* This able scholar has put the matter in its true perspective. Moreover, he has in this essential work clearly exposed all the many serious fallacies in Machia-velli's views on military theory and practice. (For a general criticism of the Florentine Secretary's military thought see also Delbrück, *op. cit.*, pp. 117–33).

[2] See, for instance, how in Chapter XII of *The Prince* he suddenly switches from the subject of mercenary troops to that of *condottieri*: 'I want to indicate the disadvantages of such troops more clearly. Mercenary captains. . . .' He confuses two questions which should be treated separately. It was possible to have an army of mercenaries, in reality dominated by the political ruler in person, as in France (Hobohm, *op. cit.*, II, pp. 266, 279, 324–5). 'Condot-tierism' (if I may be forgiven the ugly word) could only flourish given certain clearly-defined political conditions – those which in fact applied to the Italian principates. He should have insisted on this point, asking himself why the princes themselves had neglected *their own special province*, the militia.

— on him and his exchequer[1] — and which through long habituation to active service would acquire the discipline and fighting technique necessary for victory.

A stable army, thoroughly inured to war — in other words, the sort of army which at that time could only be provided by professional soldiers, indigenous or foreign — was the prerequisite of the internal strengthening and the external aggrandizement of the States of Western Europe.[2] National militias might fill the rôle of territorials, never of regulars. They could not be used for wars of conquest, still less to ensure the absolute internal supremacy of the central authority.[3]

Machiavelli did not grasp this point, and blamed the Kings of France for abolishing those infantry-formations known as *Francs-Archers* which, having been ignominiously routed at Guinegate, had in the course of their inglorious existence spread disorder wherever they went, like the mercenaries, and had in addition excited the ridicule of their own

[1] It is therefore superfluous to emphasize the fallacy in Machiavelli's assertion that monetary resources do not constitute the sinews of war. The experience of these years was proving that quite the reverse was the case.

[2] The case of France illustrates this point clearly enough. The interest of the King, which incidentally coincided with the fundamental and general interest of French policy, was to have available a permanent army dependent on himself alone — in other words a powerful group of mercenary militias. This also accorded with the wishes of the French *bourgeoisie*, who had little desire to bear arms, especially when long and hazardous wars were involved. It is, moreover, extremely interesting to note that when the States General met at Tours in 1484, many years before Machiavelli advocated his Florentine reforms, there was a demand for the dismissal of all mercenaries and the establishment of a national army; indeed, hired troops were the object of a number of hostile speeches. But those who would have benefited from the reform were the feudatories, i.e. the most powerful disruptive element in the land and the prime obstacle to the achievement of national unity. The establishment of national armies would have meant that arms would to a large extent have fallen into the hands of those elements which the monarchy had to oppose in order to reconstitute the nation on a radical basis. (Imbart de la Tour, *Les origines de la Réforme*, I, Paris, 1905, pp. 48 and 61 *sqq*. Cf. also Hanotaux, *Histoire du cardinal de Richelieu*, I, Paris, 1893, pp. 267 *sqq*., 283.)

[3] In point of fact, in France the task of defending individual towns often devolved upon the civic militia. On the refusal to recognize the peculiar qualities of the territorial militia during the Renaissance see Hobohm, *op. cit.*, II, p. 142.

fellow-countrymen.[1] But happily the Kings of France understood their interests better than did their uninformed foreign
adviser. They continued to enlist Swiss, Lansquenets, Gas-
cons and Picards, and with the aid of these mercenaries won
the victories which ensured their country's greatness.[2]

Now this criterion represents a full-scale attempt at a
reconstruction of history, a really notable effort to form a
general picture – for Machiavelli succeeds in ascribing
Italy's woes not merely to a Seigneur's lack of subtlety and
perspicacity as a negotiator, or to the doubts, stupid hesitations and ill-calculated decisions of this or that potentate, but
to a larger, more general cause, which embraces all individual human failings: military decadence. Yet the reason
which he stresses so ostentatiously is not the only one. Above
all, it is not the fundamental one. The grave faults of the
Italian military system, epitomized in the figures of the
condottieri, are themselves due to the basic structure of the
entire social and political organism. Hence, Machiavelli's
reconstruction is here wholly at fault.

And if later on the intrusion of such a preconceived
notion into his historical reflections will lead him into error,
so that he comes to regard the continuance of military dicta-
torships as one of the causes of Roman decadence,[3] for the
moment his habit of representing everything in diplomatic

---

[1] Spont, article cited above, pp. 457 *sqq.*, 472 *sqq.*

[2] On the failure of Louis XII's attempt to organize a corps of infantry,
which survived barely eighteen months, cf. Spont, *Marignan et l'organisation
militaire sous Francois Ier*, in *Revue des Questions Historiques*, LXVI (1899),
p. 60. On the melancholy experience of the legions of Francis I see Delbrück,
op. cit., pp. 18–19.

[3] *Discorsi*, III, xxiv. In fact, he is well aware of the agrarian disputes. But
in consequence of his preconceived notion about military dictatorship he becomes once again the Machiavelli of contemporary Italy: '. . . when a citizen
commanded an army for a long time he won its affection and partisan support,
because in time it would forget the Senate and would recognize him as its
chief.' In other words, says Machiavelli, one of the causes of Roman decadence
is, again, 'condottierism'. And yet, 'so long as she was well ordered, as she was
up to the time of the Gracchi, Rome possessed not a single soldier who adopted
military service as a profession. . . .' (*Arte della Guerra*, I). Cf. Hobohm, *op.
cit.*, II, pp. 105 *sqq.*

and military terms, and the obsessional character of his antagonism towards the men whom he holds responsible for all the disasters of the age, prevent him from seeking out the less obvious causes of Italy's corruption and the prime sources, if any still remain, of powerful 'remedies'.

But the adoption of such a narrowly-based criterion has another consequence besides. Certainly, Machiavelli succeeds in discerning the disunion and brittleness of the territories dominated by republics such as Venice and Florence, which have acquired authority without power. Sharing the feeling common to all the men of his time, he reproaches these republics for having gained subjects and not allies, in contrast with the States that are ruled by princes. But he does not ask himself whether their weakness is due to the failure of the various elements to achieve unity, or to some grave defect inherent in the actual constitution of the State, or, again, simply to an inability to oppose successfully the actions of greater, stronger, and wealthier powers. Machiavelli contemplates the princes and their indolence, dwells on their military cowardice, expatiates on their softness, without trying to find out whether, in addition to these particular human causes, there is not some other graver reason that may explain their deep fears, their sudden headlong retreats, their prodigious reverses. Sometimes he perceives the corruptness of the nobles, but he does not pursue the matter. Indeed, he recommends the establishment of principates in cities in which there is great inequality,[1] as if the hand of royalty were omnipotent and must at once succeed in accomplishing miracles. And he always ends by thrusting into the foreground the figure of the Prince, the cause of all evil. Military doctrinairism[2] and the habit of forming *ad hoc* judgments exert too great an influence on the writer's thought, the scope of which, moreover, is restricted still further by other defects.

There is, for example, that indifference to economic values

[1] *Discorsi*, I, lv.
[2] As Fester calls it (*op. cit.*, p. 179).

which is itself a consequence of Niccolò's militaristic outlook, which leads him to regard wealth and private ownership as breeding-grounds not of strength but of corruption,
as causes of enfeeblement and aversion to military service.
But this is not all. He also displays a persistent spirit of
municipalism, which is in evidence whenever his thoughts
turn to the rural population.[1] Machiavelli would not re-
habilitate that scattered, disordered mob, forced by the
policy of the Communes to labour under a harsh yoke and
excluded not only from public activity but even from the
spiritual and moral life of the city. At best he would grant it
the rôle of a tyrants' satellite.[2]

And indeed the time will come when he has to appeal to
the country folk, so long despised by the urban *bourgeoisie*,
and solicit their direct participation in the life of the State.
But even then, when all the barriers seems to have been
broken down, the townsman appears once again. Cautious
and mistrustful, afraid of losing his supremacy, he op-
presses his fellow-citizens, subjecting them to a leader from
whom they are divided by long-standing parochial feuds.[3]

[1] Mayer, *op. cit.*, p. 100. On the other hand, Tangorra's essay, *Il pensiero
economico di Niccolò Machiavelli* (in *Saggi critici di economia politica*, Turin,
1900, pp. 121–59), and the observations of Gebhart (*Les historiens florentins
de la Renaissance et les commencements de l'économie politique et sociale*, Paris,
1875, pp. 38 *sqq.*) are of little value.

[2] The rural population should be called to arms by the tyrant so that it may
discharge 'that function which devolves upon the common people' when they
resist him (*Discorsi*, I, xl). The same task may be fulfilled either by foreign
satellites or by powerful neighbours with whom the Prince is on friendly terms.
In other words, when Machiavelli addresses himself to tyrants and returns to
his own times the rural population is excluded from the inner life of the State
– even though he is conscious at the same time that his model preaches a
different lesson, 'Rome and its rural suburbs being one and the same thing.'

[3] Extremely significant in its bearing on this aspect of Machiavelli's character is the *Relazione sulla istituzione della nuova Milizia*, reproduced by
Villari, *op. cit.*, I, pp. 637–42. The final pieces of advice on the method of
ensuring that the men under arms do no 'harm' reveal all the mistrust of the
townsman – a mistrust that has existed for three centuries past; and if in his
dissertations Machiavelli condemns republics that have acquired subjects and
not allies, in practice he too is unable to eschew the political custom that he
deplores. This is clearly seen in his advice on the subject of the rural suburbs of
towns.

Here the author's love of his native city continues to stir up in his heart sentiments appropriate to the age of the Communes!

Machiavelli and Religion

All these motifs bespeak a spiritual narrowness that is accentuated by a basic trend in Machiavelli's thought. As a result of this trend he shows little response to any spiritual movement that is not subordinate to a purely political idea; he is ignorant not only of the eternal and the transcendent[1] but also of the moral doubt and the tormenting anxiety that beset a conscience turned in upon itself;[2] and he accordingly cannot help ascribing both to the human and to the mystical elements of a faith an entirely political significance, subordinated to the laws and ordinances of the State. Religion may well constitute, together with good laws and the militia, the foundation of national life;[3] but what comes to light here is not the sentiment in itself, not its indispensability to the very soul of the man who finds in it a palliative for his natural inquietude, but its incidental practical value as a check on corruption and a contributory factor to the orderly conduct of community life. Religion is identified with its outward form, as revealed in its institutions;[4] and the moral influence which it exerts on the lives of nations is that of a coercive force proceeding from above, subjecting men's minds to a wise discipline and assisting them in the fulfilment of their duties as citizens.

Accordingly, every religious movement loses its funda-

[1] Fester, *op. cit.*, p. 146.

[2] I am therefore quite unable to believe, with Tommasini (*op. cit.*, I, pp. 699 *sqq.*), in Machiavelli's religious susceptibility. His desire to see the Church of Rome reformed was prompted by motives quite different from those that inspired the dissenters and reformers of the time (whereas Tommasini puts them all in the same category, *ib.*, p. 738). Cf. on the other hand, the just remarks of Meinecke, *Die Idee der Staatsräson* (already cited), pp. 38 and 44.

[3] Note, however, that in *The Prince* far less importance is attached even to the political significance of religion than in the *Discorsi*. More will be said on this point later.

[4] Mayer, *op. cit.*, p. 97. It therefore goes without saying that we cannot describe Machiavelli's ideal State as *secular* in the modern sense.

mental character and is deprived of its mystical content, retaining only those specific political attributes with which it is in every case necessarily invested, and which may also have constituted a most powerful factor in its evolution, though not the only one. And in Savonarola himself Machiavelli sees merely the unarmed prophet, and adopts an attitude of indifference and ironical scepticism towards the belief that the Friar of St. Mark spoke with the voice of God.[1] But he does not notice that he himself has been profoundly influenced by the failure of so tumultuous a ministry, inasmuch as his irritation at the political mistakes of Savonarola the political reformer is transformed without his realizing it into contempt for the ecclesiastic and, superimposing itself on his naturally irreligious outlook, largely determines his bitterness towards the Church. The Dominican Friar's indignation with Alexander VI is echoed by Niccolò, in whom it takes the wider form of a more general hostility towards the papacy, which he regards as the cause of Italy's corruption; and at the same time the extravagance of the Friar's revivalism reinforces his contemptuous incredulity, which in due course culminates in the creation of Friar Timoteo. A momentary aversion to a Pope becomes a continuous and relentless hostility.[2] Such are the lines along which Machiavelli's religious philosophy develops to its maturity. It is a philosophy shaped by theoretical and practical considerations and restricted by the nature of this thought and by his mental training.[3]

[1] '. . . (the Florentine people) were convinced by Friar Girolamo Savonarola that he was speaking with God. I do not wish to express an opinion as to whether or not that was the case, for of so great a man one should speak with reverence. . . .' (*Discorsi*, I, xi). There are some acute observations on Machiavelli's position vis-à-vis Savonarola in Tommasini, *op. cit.*, I, pp. 160 *sqq.* Villari, on the other hand, is less felicitous (*La storia di Gerolamo Savonarola*, 2nd ed., Florence, 1887, I, p. 319, II, p. 107), while Schnitzer's reference to the question is brief and not too well-considered (*Savonarola*, Munich, 1924, I, p. 592. But cf. also II, p. 1075, footnotes 96 and 99).

[2] On Machiavelli's aversion to the papacy cf. Fester, *op. cit.*, pp. 80 *sqq.*

[3] On the influence *a contrario* of Savonarola on Machiavelli see Luchaire, *op. cit.*, p. 282. De Leva also sought a connection between Machiavelli's intellectual training and the ministry of Savonarola (*Storia documentata di Carlo V*, Venice, 1863, I, p. 159).

The New Seigneur and Machiavelli's New Illusion

Thus the intellectual world from which the Prince emerges is entirely political and military in character. The life of the people has ceased to command the writer's attention; and since Court life and martial activity find their expression in the man who presides over them and are epitomized in a specific human figure, it is the princes of Italy who become responsible for their country's ruin.[1]

But since the cause of error is in them, in them will be the remedy. And while Savonarola, who regarded Princes as the fountain of all wickedness and believed that they were sent by God to punish the sins of their subjects, sought to reconstruct his world by expelling them from society, Niccolò focuses his attention upon them to the exclusion of all else.

Thus there emerges the new Seigneur.

On a number of previous occasions Machiavelli had expressed his faith in individual virtue as the power which could lift the masses from their degradation and restore good institutions; already he had believed in it as being the key to the State's salvation.[2] Even when his imagination dwells

---

[1] Among the many examples given cf. the following: '. . . and those who said that this was the result of our sins spoke the truth; but they were not the sins that they thought, but those that I have described; and because they were committed by princes, the latter have likewise paid the penalty for them' (*The Prince*, XII); 'And among the sins of Italian princes, which have made Italy the slave of foreigners . . .' (*Discorsi*, II, xviii); 'Let no prince complain of any sin committed by the people under his sway, for such sins must be due either to his negligence or to the fact that he is defiled by similar transgressions' (*Discorsi*, III, xxix); 'But let us return to the Italians, who, because they have not had wise princes, have not adopted good laws and ordinances, and because they have not been faced with the same necessity as the Spaniards, have not adopted them on their own account, with the result that they remain the scum of the earth. Yet the peoples are not to blame, but their princes, who have been duly punished, and have suffered just penalties for their ignorance. . . .' (*Arte della Guerra*, VII). There is still great virtue in the limbs: the material remains excellent (*The Prince*, Chapter XXVI).

[2] Cf. the exhaustive analyses by Mayer (*op. cit.*, pp. 15 *sqq.*, 83 *sqq.*), Ercole (*Lo Stato nel pensiero di Niccolò Machiavelli*, in *Studi economico-giuridici della R. Università di Cagliari*, VIII, 1916, pp. 8 *sqq.*; *La difesa dello Stato in Machiavelli*, in *Politica*, March–April, 1921, pp. 22–3; and *passim* in all the

upon the complex life of the people of Rome he sees this isolated quality as an organizing force; it nearly[1] always re-appears, and its presence within the fuller and more varied life of the people is re-affirmed. Here Machiavelli is adapting himself to the facts of Italian history and accepting the doc-trine of the Renaissance. In his affirmation of individual virtue Niccolò reveals the same human limitations as Guicciardini.

But at other times the theme of the virtue of the Man alternates with that of good institutions. Regenerative power no longer resides only in the mind of an individual. It is inherent also in the very strength of the laws, that is to say in the vitality of the people, who find within themselves the goodness and the discipline that will enable them to make a fresh start, to recover their greatness.[2] And now the new law-giver does not develop into a tyrant, but is content to recall the city to the paths of righteousness and to restore to it all its ancient institutions.[3]

Sometimes, indeed, Niccolò hesitates. Not that he does not believe in virtue, not that he has lost faith in the ability of the Man to conquer and rule; but this ability seems to him too dependent on the whims of fortune, too closely bound up with the precariousness of human existence.[4] True, this hesi-

other works of Ercole referred to hereafter), and Meinecke (*Die Idee der Staatsräson* (already cited), pp. 40 *sqq.*, *Einführung* (already cited), pp. 21 *sqq.*).

[1] But not quite. Even Rome, who did not have 'a Lycurgus to provide her at the outset with such a constitution that she could look forward to many years of freedom', attained perfection through the disunion of the plebs and Senate. 'That which had not been achieved by a law-giver came about by chance' (*Discorsi*, I, ii). The virtue of the law-giver, then, is not yet com-pletely essential to the prosperity of the State.

[2] *Discorsi*, III, i.

[3] 'The truth is that when it happens . . . that through good fortune there arises in the city a wise, good and powerful citizen who formulates laws by which the animosities of nobles and common people are appeased, or so curbed that they can do no harm, then it is that the city can call itself free, and the State may be deemed stable and secure. For, being founded on good laws and good institutions, it does not, like other States, need the virtue of an individual to maintain it' (*Florentine Histories*, IV, i).

[4] 'Hence, kingdoms which depend entirely on the virtue of an individual are unlikely to survive for long; for that virtue passes away on his death, and it seldom happens that it is renewed in his successor. . . . It is not, therefore,

tation does not yet altogether reflect the new consciousness which enables the thinker to see how vain is individual effort when the foundation is lacking and the *condottiere's* actions do not find an adequate counterpart in the spiritual life of the people; and often his doubt has a particular reason, and is not due to a sudden change of thought, so that he thinks that if human life were longer, or virtue could be handed down together with authority, virtue alone would suffice to maintain a State. But in spite of this Machiavelli still pauses. Perhaps the new man has his origin in this conflict between the citizen of the Renaissance and the thinker, who at certain moments is in advance of his age.

But now his doubts cease. Good institutions are lost from sight, as is the notion of a return to the principle that determines the organization of a republic. The spotlight is focused on the virtue of the Prince, who must breathe life into his inert material through the compelling power of his will. City, people, good institutions, a return to the principles which would make it possible to re-organize society on its original basis – all these things are far from Machiavelli's thoughts. He is concerned with his own age, and seeks to imbue it with a new vigour. In the fever of creation he forgets his conflicts, his intellectual hesitations, his early doubts about the organizing capacity of the Man, who is a product of recent Italian history. This Man re-appears at the last, all alone in his armour – shrewd in diplomatic manoeuvre, fortified with every sort of civic wisdom, purged of every weakness. He is the redeemer, who will atone for the sins

---

salutary for a republic or a kingdom to have a prince who governs prudently while he lives, but one who orders it in such a way that it will still stand after his death' (*Discorsi*, I, xi). '. . . if a city that has fallen into decline through the rottenness of its inhabitants ever happens to rise again, its revival will be due to the virtue of a man who is living at the time, not to the virtue of the masses who maintain the excellence of its institutions; and as soon as that man is dead, the city will return to its former habits . . . the reason is that no man can live long enough to teach good ways to a city that has long followed the paths of evil. And if one very long-lived man or two virtuous men following one after the other do not succeed in restoring it to order . . . it will come to grief' (*ibid.*, xvii).

of former Seigneurs by his glory – the glory of a new Prince.[1]

And Machiavelli did not realize that even such a reconstruction as this was a vain dream, that this was his last and greatest illusion.

All the vital forces of the nation were in process of dissolution, and no new force had so far appeared. The Communal *bourgeoisie* no longer had the energy to support the burden of government, and signs of a new consciousness, of a new class capable of replacing it were lacking. The provinces were still disunited and fragmentary; every day they were being further weakened, politically and economically, by the pressure of the great Western States. Literature and humanism had deprived the people of their sense of moral values and social necessities, though they still retained their individualistic tendencies. To believe that a military leader could revive the declining fortunes of Italy and constitute a State which neither the transcendent vitality of the Communes nor the unitarian resolve of the great Seigneurs of the Trecento had been able to integrate; to imagine that it was enough simply to adopt a new principle of leadership and to re-form the militia, that to this end actions inspired by a single will, the acute insight into events, resourcefulness, and severity of a supreme Seigneur were sufficient to prop up or rather to reconstruct that which was bound to collapse in the nature of things, so that an entire epoch of history should have a fitting climax – this was a beautiful, audacious, formidable dream, but it *was* a dream!

---

[1] Luchaire seems to me to be making a bold assertion when he declares (*op. cit.*, p. 300) that Machiavelli, 'dans ce terrible dilemme, plus de république, ou point d'unité italienne, entrevoit cette solution: accepter la monarchie, qui démolira les vielles barrières, refondra ensuite les formes sociales, fera la nation: le peuple reprendra ensuite ses droits. Il esquissait ainsi l'histoire future des nations européennes'. Here the author seems to me to want to represent Machiavelli as a prophet at all costs, whereas Machiavelli viewed prophets with extreme disfavour. Neither his thought nor his mind is as complicated as that. At the moment when he embraces the idea of the Prince he is not thinking of future trends of events, he does not dream of the republic that will follow the Principate of the Medici.

And the Machiavelli who, intoxicated by the glory of the Roman people, condemns Caesar, errs now when he forecasts miracles to be wrought by the hand of Valentino[1] or one of the Medici; for their efforts, however admirable in point of administrative sagacity, could not have launched Italian society on to paths different from those along which it was naturally travelling with catastrophic speed. If he heeded the advice and warning of Niccolò the Prince would have had to deny the results of two hundred years of history; he would have had to direct the stream of events into different channels from those which it was destined to follow. And if at first his impassioned vision of the people and their healthy strength prompts him to condemn the 'tyrant' (and what a tyrant!), his yearning for an Italy imbued with a new vigour, capacity and freedom subsequently prevents him from accurately assessing the worth of the 'little castle' that he has built amid the tormenting anxiety of his unhappy leisure.

Carried away by the fervour of his feeling and imagination, Machiavelli in the end contradicts himself. His theoretical pessimism suddenly changes into a boundless confidence not only in the statesman but also in the nation that awaits its redeemer and is all ready to follow him. In this way it reveals itself as nothing more than an intellectual attitude, incapable of resisting the impact of emotion.[2] His scepticism is transformed into a heart-cry of hope and faith; and his words of contempt for Man, who is in himself a base creature, become an invocation, which assumes a religious tone and contains an echo from the Scriptures.

[1] 'Machiavel était plein de son idole, le duc de Valentinois. . . .' (Montesquieu, *Esprit des Lois*, XXIX, xix).

[2] And herein lies the difference between the pessimism of Machiavelli and that of Guicciardini. In the former, intensity of feeling often succeeds in making nonsense of the theoretical assertion, so that men whom his intellect despises regain his confidence. In the latter, the theoretical assertion, even if it is less pungent, is perfectly consistent with his emotional indifference; hence Messer Francesco not only speaks of the 'people' as a crazy animal, but, in conformity with his thought, takes good care not to associate with them. He is haughty, as his contemporaries note, whereas Machiavelli is amiable towards his friends and in everyday life just an ordinary man of the people.

But even when the idea of a 'national army' holds his attention Niccolò fails to perceive the absurd errors into which he falls. To make the security of the State the responsibility of all, not only of the city-dwellers but also of the poor inhabitants of the outlying districts, forcing them to share the heaviest task which men can be called upon to shoulder on behalf of the community; to interest all those who live in a territory in its safety and integrity; to look for the foundation of social life in the duty of all when confronted by the enemy – this was to effect a radical change not only in the military system but in the political and moral system too. In other words, it was to step outside the context of history, that history to which even the writer looked for guidance throughout his work of political theorization.

Machiavelli shuts his eyes to this. When he is concerned with the practice of government the necessity of prompt action prevents him from perceiving the connection between the instructions issued to the discontented Communes and his own concept of the militia as the bulwark of the country, while as Secretary of the Nine he sanctions the dismemberment and the essential division of the State and countenances the distrust that exists between one village and another, and between the villages in general and the mother city.[1] But this is not all. Even later, when he reduces his original practical plan to a theoretical form, he is unconscious of the decidedly

---

[1] He informs the Communes which are opposed to the new levy that their men will be left to guard their own city and seeks to allay their ill-humour by promising to let every township keep its sons for its own defence: '. . . great numbers are not called upon to serve this Republic, save for the purpose of guarding your city; for if she wishes to employ them elsewhere she will never call up even a third of those enlisted; and when they have been paid those who wish to do so will go, and no one else' (Letter to the Commune of Modigliana, 24 January 1512, in *Scritti inediti di Niccolò Machiavelli risguardanti la Storia e la Milizia*, ed. G. Canestrini, Florence, 1857, pp. 373–4). Cf. also the letter of the same date to the Commune of Marradi, the tenor of which is similar (*ib.*, p. 369); and as regards the city's distrust of its 'subjects' it will be enough to refer to the *Relazione sulla istituzione della nuova milizia* (already cited). For a splendid analysis of the Florentine militia and the political problems raised by its formation see Hobohm, I (especially pp. 420 *sqq.*).

revolutionary character with which he is investing not only the military system but the whole body politic.

He will speculate at length as to the correct method of 'swearing-in soldiers';[1] and he will endeavour to find out what religion has the power to make men face death with serenity. But meanwhile he bases the new principate on the idea of his own army, without realizing that this idea is the most flagrant and irremediable contradiction that can be imagined of his political programme. It always remains a mystery to him that if the soldiers are to be made to take a proper oath they need a religion which he does not offer them, and that before demanding sacrifices it is necessary to create a social consciousness, at least on a regional basis, and a political spirit deriving from the realization, however confused, that the passions of rulers are indissolubly bound up with the passions of their subjects.[2]

Nor does he ask himself whether it is actually in the interest of the sovereign of a large and powerful State to create a citizen militia, which would need so many months of training to be capable of withstanding effectively the impact of powerful mercenaries that the efficacy and above all the timeliness of the remedy would be open to question; or whether it becomes the absolute head of a State to put weapons into the hands of subjects who might in many cases use them to drive him from his ducal palace.

When his thought takes this turn, when he finds himself faced with this profound spiritual crisis, from which he

---

[1] 'What can I promise them that will make them love or fear me in a reverent manner, when, the war being over, they are no longer in any way obliged to fall in with my wishes? Of what should I make them ashamed, who were born and bred without shame? Why should they respect me, who do not know me? By what God or by what Saints should I make them swear? By those whom they worship, or by those whom they blaspheme?' (*Arte della Guerra*, VII).

[2] Cf. Fester's acute observations, *op. cit.*, p. 88. Moreover, Ferrari (*Machiavelli giudice delle rivoluzioni dei nostri tempi*, Florence, 1921, pp. 60 *sqq.*) has an extremely happy flash of intuition when he momentarily perceives the fundamental ambiguity of *The Prince*, before allowing the dramatic intrigues of his Guelfs and Ghibellines to reclaim his attention.

might emerge perhaps without hope, but with his powers of judgment enhanced, Machiavelli stops in mid-career, and continues to confine himself to the details of the question. He devotes all his energies to technical analysis, without perceiving the connection between this and the general organization of the State.

In constructing his principate he completely discounts the people as a creative force, but he soon recalls them when he has need of their moral support. The general framework and the new prop are not of the same metal, and they do not go well together. But Niccolò does not notice this, and with touching pertinacity he tries to bolster up an edifice that is destined to be brought down by the first violent gust of wind.

The contradiction is inevitable because it is implicit in the premises — because, essentially, Machiavelli wants a national militia inasmuch as he finds that the cause of Italy's ruin lies in her military corruption: once this has been remedied everything will be all right again. And so we find him concentrating on the remedy *per se* to the exclusion of all else, oblivious of the profound changes that it brings about in the material to which it is applied, and of the strength of tissue that is still required if it is not to prove too drastic.

But it is also inevitable because, in demanding that arms should be entrusted to the actual inhabitants of a town, Machiavelli becomes once again a municipalist, a descendant of the old *bourgeoisie* of the free Communes. He is now not a prophet of the future, but simply an anachronistic evoker of a past that must be regarded as dead.[1] He is unaware of the sentiment that prompts him, and believes that he is preach-

---

[1] Those who have looked upon Machiavelli as the herald of the modern age have been guilty of a gross error. The Florentine Secretary's 'armed people' is merely a momentary and futile reincarnation of the old Communal militias (whatever the technical modifications necessarily introduced). Modern compulsory military service, apart from all the variations of detail, which are neither small nor trivial, is based on such a different conception of the internal political constitution of the State that any comparison is impossible. To be the true prophet of our times Machiavelli would have had to modify not only the

ing a new doctrine of salvation, whereas he is in fact repeat-
ing old phrases that have come back into circulation in these
disastrous times;[1] and he himself does not even heed the fact
that in so doing he is reverting to the habits of thought current in the palmy days of Savonarola and, unconsciously or
not, reviving the fundamental ideas of that age.[2] Long study
of the military greatness of republican Rome has renewed
his confidence: we are suddenly confronted once more with
the citizen of Florence, who contradicts the instructor of the
new Prince.[3]

military system but also, theoretically at least, the political system against the
general background of which alone the individual reforms which he proposed
should be considered; but that would be asking too much. Certain it is, however, that he who in his political thought was a man of the Renaissance became
a man of the thirteenth century when he turned his attention to military
matters.

And it is Guicciardini who tells us what was the true nature of the military
reforms: 'During the same period the first steps were taken in the organization
of military units. These had existed formerly in our territory, at the time when
wars were fought not by mercenary and foreign soldiers but by our own
citizens and subjects. For about the last two hundred years the system had
been in suspense; nevertheless, there were occasions previous to 1494 when its
revival had been considered; and after 1494, in the midst of our adversities,
many had said from time to time that it would be a good thing to return to the
former custom. Yet the matter had never been the subject of consultation,
nor had any initial steps been taken or projected. Later, Machiavelli gave
thought to it....' (*Storia Fiorentina*, Chapter XXIX, in *Opere inedite*, III,
p. 324).

[1] The idea was in the air, and literary men, in fact, were beginning to revive
it (Zabughin, *Vergilio nel Rinascimento* (already cited), I, pp. 233–4, 249).
In France, too, almost at the same time as Machiavelli was writing *The Prince*,
Seyssel, albeit with greater prudence and circumspection, was advocating the
establishment of a national militia. Cf. A. Jacquet, *Claude de Seyssel*, in *Revue
des Questions Historiques*, LVII (1895), pp. 433 *sqq*.

[2] In point of fact the question of entrusting arms to citizens had already
been discussed by Domenico Cecchi (Villari, *La storia di Gerolamo Savonarola* (already cited), I, p. 452; Tommasini, *op. cit.*, I, pp. 145 and 343;
Hobohm, *op. cit.*, I, pp. 44 *sqq*.). The military reforms for which Savonarola's
movement stood were, however, more logical than those advocated in *The
Prince*.

[3] Machiavelli is really taking Valentino as his model; but the military
reforms of the Borgian Duke came close to the notion of a permanent army —
in other words, their aim was quite different from, and indeed opposed to,
that of the author (Hobohm, *op. cit.*, II, p. 297).

And so that vague confidence in the people – stronger than any theoretical pessimism – which is essential if they are to be entrusted with arms, remains an ingenuous and obscure sentiment: the writer is not yet capable either of clarifying in his own mind the motives by which he is actuated or of avoiding contradictions. It is true that among Machiavelli's writings *The Art of War* most nearly approaches the *Discorsi* in spirit, and that in *The Prince* itself the chapters that most of all remind us of the great commentary on Livy are precisely those which deal with the military constitution of the new State; yet there is here only a part of the thought of the *Discorsi*, only a facet of the strength with which the Roman world was imbued. When he returns to his own age and assumes the specific rôle of reformer Niccolò thinks that he is making a new and vital contribution but does not succeed in developing it to the full. His experience can suggest to his mind a tentative scheme of political reorganization, but this is still limited to a particular field; and when that experience is confronted with the world of the Renaissance it is inadequate to inform it with all the motifs which it should embrace.

Restricted, then, by limitations of thought which he is unable to overcome, Niccolò creates his Principate without perceiving the uselessness of his labours; and amid the frenzy of his unbridled passion he gives himself up to his creative vision without measuring precisely its concrete worth. *The Prince*, a theoretical picture and epitome of the outcome of Italian history, is also animated by a vain hope: the Seigneurs of Italy have consigned that hope to oblivion.

But this very fact lends a singular importance to the little treatise. We are conscious at every step of a desperate effort to prop up that which must surely collapse, of a tragic attempt to build in a vacuum, of the unleashing of an emotion which ultimately colours the analysis and attains the grandeur of a religious warning. And it is not without a feeling of sadness that we contemplate the formidable labours of a peerless intellect which seeks with passionate faith to arouse the Redeemer and fails to perceive how its very creativeness makes manifest the disintegration of the material which it vainly wishes to imbue with virtue.[1] Other works, at first sight more deceptive, reveal that in the Europe of those days new seeds of life were germinating.[2] This one, on the other hand, so infinitely superior to all others in virtue of its imaginative power and dramatic emphasis, testifies to the passing of a glorious era that has run its course.[3]

Thus *The Prince* is at once a synthesis and a condemnation of two centuries of Italian history; and far more than its supposed immorality, what should have stirred the emotions of the commentators was the thought of the boundless misery which was overtaking our civilization.[4]

[1] And in this connection the judgment of Gregorovius returns to mind: '*The Prince* . . . is also the most tremendous document of the age in which it was written. It is not less tremendous than the historical figure of Caesar Borgia himself' (*Storia della città di Roma nel Medio Evo*, IV, p. 358).

[2] To give a concrete example, Thomas More's *Utopia*, which Croce rightly regards as a criticism of social conditions in England at the time of the collapse of the feudal economy (*Materialismo storico ed economia marxistica*, p. 243. Cf. also Villari, *op. cit.*, II, pp. 409 *sqq.*).

[3] John Addington Symonds (*The Renaissance in Italy*, Vol. I (2nd ed., 1880), p. 338) says that Machiavelli's system does not enlighten us as to the functions of a social organism under normal conditions. He does not ask himself, however, in what way Machiavelli's social organism is abnormal.

[4] The theme of the practical fallaciousness of Machiavelli's thought was examined at length by Ferrari, who derived from it the material for an imaginative picture of the author: 'He sets himself up as the anti-pope of the universe, the true Satan, the master of the world and of the Nations . . . impelled by the petulance of his genius, he creates a political necromancy which distributes crowns at will among the elect of human reason' (*Corso sugli scrittori politici italiani e stranieri*, Milan, 1862, pp. 197–8). Oriani followed Ferrari's lead in his lively criticism of Machiavelli's thought and political theory (in *Fino a Dogali*, Bari, 1918, pp. 145–239, and, more briefly, in *La lotta politica in Italia*, Florence, 1921 (new edition), I, pp. 150–3). His criticism is, however, exaggerated and above all superficial, because it is not founded on a clear recognition of the limitations of Machiavelli's thought. On Oriani's attitude to the Florentine writer cf. Serra's shrewd observations in *Scritti inediti* (Florence, 1923, pp. 205–10).

V. 'POST RES PERDITAS'

Machiavelli's Disillusionment: The Prince *Becomes a Mere Criterion of Historical Interpretation*

In fact, the Prince invoked by Machiavelli was not forthcoming. Indeed, within a short space of years new events occurred which afforded conclusive proof of his miscalculation. The shattering of the hopes of Medicean pre-eminence as a direct result of the struggle for the Duchy of Urbino, which revealed that Lorenzo had anything but the temper of a political reformer; the new French invasion of Lombardy, in consequence of which the Duke Massimiliano Sforza once more took to his heels and became a private citizen, in order to avoid the exertions and hardships of military life; the doubts and the indifference of Leo X; the death of the Prince to whom the treatise was originally dedicated – the only member of the Medici family with whom Niccolò was at all friendly;[1] and above all the mysterious way in which every firm resolve formulated in the minds of rulers came to nothing, as if they were constantly haunted by the distant menace of the foreigner – all these things made Machiavelli fully aware of the emptiness and sterility of his hopes. The collapse of his new world is clearly symbolized in the story about him and Lorenzo – the story of the Prince who prefers his hounds to the printed reminder of the lesson of events.[2]

And the warning is understood. Not that Niccolò appreciates its true, fundamental meaning: that would signify the sudden discovery of all the defects in his earlier reasoning; it

---

[1] Tommasini, *op. cit.*, II, p. 105.

[2] 'Niccolò Machiavelli presented (Lorenzo di) Pier de' Medici with a copy of his book *The Prince*. He happened to do so about the time when he (Lorenzo) was given a pair of hounds, for which he expressed more gratitude, responding in more friendly terms to the man who had given him the hounds than to Machiavelli. Wherefore Machiavelli went away in great indignation, telling his friends that he was not the man to conspire against princes, but that if they persisted in their ways conspiracies would surely occur – as if he meant that his book would provide him with his revenge' (Alvisi, *Introduction* to the *Lettere Familiari*, p. xiv).

would be to go beyond the limits of his thought. Instead, he continues to blame mercenary troops and Princes for the sorrows of Italy; indeed, to his way of thinking the new events that are unfolding before his eyes furnish grounds for a still more bitter and more insistent denunciation.[1] Always his spiritual orientation remains the same. His experience is enriched by fresh happenings, which are co-ordinated with those of the past, without, however, altering the fundamental texture of his thought.

He only notices that reality is against him, without discerning clearly the hidden meaning of this opposition. At the very moment when he is working out the details of *The Prince*, as well as immediately after, he foresees that his voice will not be heeded; but he blames human passion, and that Fortune which makes men blind and prevents them from listening to a salutary warning.[2]

But meanwhile the passionate, confident aspiration is forgotten in the bitterness of remembrance. The incentive de-

[1] In addition to the well-known passages in the *Arte della Guerra*, in which princes are denounced in vehement terms, see also, by way of confirmation, the following extract from the *Florentine Histories*, V, i: 'Consequently, that virtue which in other provinces was usually destroyed by a long period of peace, was destroyed in Italy by those infamous (wars), as the reader will be able to appreciate clearly from my description of the events that unfolded between 1434 and 1494, from which it will be seen how in the end the road was again opened to the barbarians, and the Italians became once more their bondsmen. And if the actions of our princes at home and abroad, unlike those of the Ancients, are not studied by readers who admire them for their virtue and greatness, perhaps those who consider them will feel a proper admiration for their other qualities, when they see how so many noble peoples were subjugated by such weak and ill-led forces.' And again: 'Now I begin to resume my writing, and I give vent to my feelings by accusing our princes, who have all done everything in their power to bring us to our present pass' (*Lettere Familiari*, CXCIX).

[2] 'I know that my opinion is contradicted by a natural defect in men – first, that they like to live from day to day, secondly, that they do not believe in the possibility of what has never been. . . .' (*Lettere Familiari*, CXXXI). Similarly: 'And I am daily conscious of the truth of what you say, of that which was written by Pontano; and when Fortune desires to intervene she confronts us with the prospect either of immediate advantage or of immediate danger, or else of both at once; which two things I believe are the most inimical of all to that opinion which I have defended in my letters' (*ibid.*, CLVI).

generates into a melancholy vision, which seeks its living expression in the past. Hence the Prince, formerly a criterion for the interpretation of events,[1] is now transformed into an ideal, a historical type;[2] and if he continues to dominate the picture, he is nevertheless a remote figure, pale and indistinct.

The treatise *De Principatibus* is followed by the *Arte della Guerra*. Here, the placid tempo of the exordium testifies to this new feeling of relaxation which keeps the author's mind for a while uncertain and turns it in upon itself;[3] while the harsh censure of the Italian potentates at the end of Book VII is punctuated by the mournful ruminations of a man who finds that he is now old and utterly incapable of active work.[4] Then comes the *Vita di Castruccio*, in which Niccolò transports into the past that figure of a ruler which in *The Prince* he sought to impose on the future; but here all faith is lost, and despair is the keynote of the speech in which the dying man, contemplating the ultimate vanity of his work, reaches such heights of gloomy perspicacity that he commends to his successor the arts of peace and acknowledges that Fortune is the arbiter of all human affairs.[5] A few years before, the theme of Machiavelli's preaching had been the pride of conquest and the power of the human will!

[1] Croce, *Teoria e storia della storiografia*, p. 214.

[2] On the stylization of Machiavelli's characters cf. Mayer, *op. cit.*, pp. 31 *sqq.*

[3] '. . . and [Fabrizio], having looked at the trees, and failing to recognize some of them . . . remained in suspense. Perceiving this, Cosimo said: "Perchance you are unfamiliar with some of these trees; but do not wonder at this, for some of them were more celebrated among the Ancients than they ordinarily are to-day." And when he told him their names, and how his grandfather Bernardo had laboured to cultivate them, Fabrizio replied: "I thought it was as you say, and this place and these meditations reminded me of certain princes of the Kingdom, who delight in these ancient plants and shadowy groves." And having paused for a while, as if absorbed in his thoughts . . . '

[4] 'And I grieve when I think of Nature, who either should not have made me aware of this, or should have given me the power to act. Now that I am old, I do not think I can have any further opportunity. . . . But being advanced in years, I am suspicious of what awaits me. . . .'

[5] Cf. also the following passage at the beginning: 'I certainly believe it to be a fact that Fortune, wishing to prove to the world that it is she who makes men great, and not prudence. . . .' We should remember, too, what Machiavelli says in Chapter XXV of *The Prince*.

In the first of these three works the thought that unites them is inspired, as it were, by a surge of indomitable faith; but in the other two its spirit is one of calm resignation in the face of discomfort, save where its tranquillity is disturbed by violent outbursts which reveal the bitterness of the writer's sorrow. This less exalted pattern of thought, to which Niccolò's imagination is led to conform by the teaching of events, finds an echo in the Prologue of *Mandragola*; we feel it reverberating through the first book of the *Histories*, which opens with an unusually grandiose disquisition on the great reign of Theodoric, the Prince who now inspires not a heartfelt faith but a vain regret. And in the course of his reminiscence the author returns to the theme of monarchy, since faith and passion have not sufficed to create the Principate.

More cautious than Machiavelli, the Princes of Italy had not indulged in any wild dreams; instead, they had been content to hold the balance between the barbarians who fought their battles on the plains of the peninsula. Francesco Guicciardini was likewise more cautious. His policy was to offer occasional trivial pieces of advice, skilfully avoiding possible setbacks to his fortunes.

Machiavelli and Guicciardini[1]

This man was a true aristocrat and descendant of aristocrats; therefore he was a diplomat by birth, not, like Niccolò, by chance. He was haughty and reserved, even mean, according to his contemporaries.[2] He eschewed any word or gesture that might bring him into disrepute among men of consequence. His conversation was as discreet as his smile — certainly *he* would never have hung about the house of a woman such as Riccia giving advice that was both useless and unsolicited.[3] It might almost be said that the characteristics of many generations find their epitome in this shrewd and diffi-

---

[1] [But cf. my article *Guicciardini*, cited above (p. 5, note 1).]

[2] Varchi, *Storia fiorentina*, Milan, 1845, I, p. 245.

[3] Machiavelli himself relates this episode (*Lettere Familiari*, CXLII). The woman called him 'the man who clutters up the house', and Donato del Corno 'the man who clutters up the shop'.

cult man. In his thought we seem to see, re-created with a perfection of style that could not be excelled, the thought of those of his forbears whose minds, already polished and refined by their daily preoccupation with banking, had acquired an added subtlety through their experience of diplomatic manoeuvre.

His mind is outstanding for the balance and the masterly coolness of its judgment. No one else, perhaps, has ever attained the cold objectivity of psychological analysis which he reveals in certain chapters of the *Storia d'Italia* and in many of the *Ricordi*. But his limitation is that he views all things, at all times, through the eyes of a diplomat. And if in Machiavelli recent history is nearly always reduced to political and military terms, in Messer Francesco its basis of interpretation is even narrower, so that it becomes a mere reflection of a personal skill, a pure creation of a mind that knows how to control itself and to develop its own purposes with subtlety. Only occasionally are we given a comprehensive picture; and even then, with his obstinate passion for clarity, the author concentrates on the passions of rulers.[1] Niccolò, by a powerful imaginative *tour de force*, succeeds in reviving the notion of a vast struggle which would lead to the liberation of Italy and the establishment of a strong State. Guicciardini continues placidly to live in the intellectual climate of the late Quattrocento. His only concern is to reconstruct contemporary history within his own acute mind, prompted by an intellectual desire to unravel the various strands which make up the fabric of events. Nor does he dream of breaking fresh ground, of creating something new, because he lacks the primary incentive – an intensely, fundamentally passionate consciousness capable of being translated into faith and action. And while, as we shall see, Machiavelli, in summarizing and amplifying the outcome of Italian history, lays the foundations of a new intellectual outlook, Guicciardini simply mirrors the elegant splendour of the Renais-

[1] As in the *Storia d'Italia*, I, i, where, however, the narrative hinges once again upon some clearly-defined figure, e.g. Lorenzo de' Medici.

sance style – which in his writings attains its ultimate perfection – and is not concerned to look too far ahead. In this he is a true representative of an age of which his serenity with its faint tinge of bitterness is the epitome. Certainly, he too presages something new; but even this – the society of which he is the precursor – is adequately portrayed in his normal measured and somewhat coldly correct prose. In Messer Francesco's shrewd and circumspect thought, as in his style, which is precise, fluent and clear, we can already discern the orderliness and monotony which characterized the future Grand Duchy of Florence.[1]

Certainly, it cannot have been easy for two men of such widely differing temperaments and habits to reach an understanding. In truth, they did not share that emotional intimacy which is based first and foremost on a similarity of thought and feeling. We see this clearly in the letters, in which Niccolò reveals, especially in the early stages, a reserve and a hesitancy which lead him to desist from his usual political castle-building and to talk of humbler things, of concrete, transient scenes from daily life, of questions of immediate interest. Whereas the correspondence with Vettori is often alive with hopes and grandiose plans, and in a certain sense constitutes a running commentary on Italian affairs,[2] in the correspondence with Guicciardini there is very rarely a place for any such reconstruction of events. Political allusions become frequent – and then of necessity – only in 1525 and 1526; yet they are more restricted, more circumspect and less general than those which we find in Machiavelli's letters to his friend, the Ambassador to Leo X. Nearly

[1] The judgment of De Sanctis is therefore not quite correct. 'He (Machiavelli) represents a starting-point in history, the beginning of an era; the other (Guicciardini) is like a beautiful picture, perfect and self-contained' (*Storia della Letteratura Italiana*, Bari, 1912, II, p. 112). The starting-point for the immediate history of Italy is rather Guicciardini; hence, his very style often has a modern air that provides food for thought. On the other hand, the road opened up by Machiavelli was destined to be followed by other peoples.

[2] On the relations between Machiavelli and Vettori cf. L. Passy, *Un ami de Machiavel, François Vettori; sa vie et ses oeuvres*, Paris, 1914, I, pp. 38–113.

always the conversation is confined to jests or agreeable witticisms about the trivialities of day-to-day existence, or to a discussion on *Mandragola*,[1] or else to the question – a serious one for Messer Francesco – of the marriage of his daughters.[2]

From time to time the Lieutenant of the Holy Roman Church, with his equable, precise, calm and aristocratic manner, decorously amuses himself at the expense of his friend and urges him to widen the field of his speculations to include the Republic of the Friars of Carpi, which he likens to 'one of those models of yours'.[3] But Niccolò replies with only a brief, playful allusion to the matter, and does not stop to defend himself, as he would have done had he been dealing with Vettori.[4]

In fact, Machiavelli's sudden outbursts of passion, which distort the dignified and imperturbable features of the diplomat, and disturb a composure so shrewdly cultivated; his all-powerful imagination, which places facts in new and hitherto unseen perspectives; and his very faith in the prospect of a redeemer – all these things must have surprised, disconcerted and even in some degree shocked the objective, well-ordered mind of the counsellor of Clement VII, who had his full share of the gravity and phlegm necessary to one who plays the ephemeral game of diplomacy. And meanwhile Niccolò must have felt a trifle dismayed in face of such an imperturbable serenity, which concealed within itself every imaginable emotional impulse.

Hence he experiences a feeling of distrust, almost of suspicion. As a rule this is barely perceptible in his unwontedly playful and humble manner; yet it is always fundamentally active, and calculated to intimidate Niccolò, who accordingly treats 'Mr. President' with the utmost deference, until the latter tells him to refrain from employing empty titles.[5]

---

[1] *Lettere Familiari*, CXCVI, CXCVIII.

[2] *Ib.*, CXCIX.   [3] *Ib.*, CLXXXI.   [4] *Ib.*, CLXXXIII.

[5] *Ib.*, CXCIII ('if we continue to address one another by these titles ... in the end we shall all find ourselves ... with our hands full of flies').

And how, too, could the heroic grandeur of Machiavelli's passion and his tragic belief in the strong State be intelligible to one who attributed Italy's former happiness to her lack of a monarchy, and who in this way fully endorsed the concept of the balance of power and the Italic *foederatio*?[1] As he read *The Prince* probably Messer Francesco in his heart desired his friend to ponder matters before discussing them, just as on another occasion he was to advise him to reflect carefully on the story of Romulus;[2] and an ironical smile must have lit up his hard, angular features as he considered the plans of a man 'who always takes an excessive delight in extraordinary and violent remedies'.[3]

The difference between the two men is profound – not merely intellectually, but psychologically. In the midst of his analysis of the disasters of his age Guicciardini confesses his regret at his inability to dance and to acquit himself with skill and grace in the field of sport, since this is part of the equipment of the complete statesman,[4] while Machiavelli indulges in melancholy regrets even in the prologue of his comedy, unable completely to forget his one-time faith despite his many disappointments. The one sees that, since it is impossible to drive the barbarians from Italy, it is even advantageous to have at any rate two of them in the country so that the various cities may somehow be able to survive and to save their own possessions;[5] while the other has visions of impossible agreements and alliances aimed simply at driving out the Transalpine hordes. There is too great a contrast of sentiments and aspirations for the correspondence of the two minds to be full and entire.

They are alike in some respects – for example, in their ability to seize upon changing thoughts and emotions and to

---

[1] *Considerazioni sui discorsi del Machiavelli* (Book I, Chapter xii), in *Opere inedite*, Florence, 1857, I, pp. 26 *sqq.*
[2] *Ib.*, Book I, Chapter ix, p. 22.
[3] *Ib.*, Book I, Chapter xxvi, p. 40.
[4] *Ricordi politici e civili*, CLXXIX.
[5] *Discorsi politici*, VIII (in *Opere inedite*, I, p. 264).

subject them to exhaustive analysis. But whereas Niccolò
transforms this analysis into a quest for general, albeit human
axioms, in Guicciardini it takes the form of a shrewd and
lordly irony, it is reflected in the barely perceptible smile that
lurks in the grey depths of his half-closed eyes, it survives
serenely in all its detail. They are alike, too, in the disdain
which they feel for contemporary life.[1] But the disdain of
Machiavelli gives birth to a new faith, which persists in the
form of sorrowful regret, whereas the disdain of Guicciardini, if it emerges at all, is quelled by the composure and
circumspection of a mind that seeks to ignore troublesome
distractions.

And so, however much esteem his great fellow-citizen
may have professed |him,[2] Machiavelli always refrained
from entering into an unduly intimate relationship with
him; nor did he attain that pitch of affection which
would have made possible a full spiritual correspon-

---

[1] E.g. Guicciardini, *Ricordi politici e civili*, XXVIII, LIX (warning to
Clement VII; cf. CXCIV), LXVIII, CXL, CLXXI, CLXXVII, CCV,
CCXXXI, CCXXXIII, CCXXXVI, CCXLI, CCCXXIII, and Machia-
velli, *Lettere Familiari*, CXCIII, CCI (from Guicciardini to Machiavelli).
'I have never known anyone who, when he saw an evil hour approaching, did
not try in some way to shield himself – except ourselves, who are willing to
wait for it in the middle of the street, without taking shelter. Therefore, if
anything untoward happens we shall not be able to say that we have been
deprived of our initiative, but that we basely allowed it to slip from our hands.'
The difference between the temperaments of the two men is summed up by
Messer Francesco himself: 'The temperaments of men vary. In some, hope
burns so bright that they take for granted that which they have not. Others are
so fearful that they never hope for anything until it is in their hands. I am
closer to the second group than to the first, and he who is of this temperament
deludes himself less, but endures greater mental torment' (*Ricordi politici e
civili*, LXI; but cf. CCXCIX). But he succeeds in mitigating his torment with
the aid of his 'style' and his intellectual curiosity, which, originally regarded
as an escape from the misery of life, takes such a hold on the writer that it often
makes him completely oblivious of his erstwhile 'despair'.

[2] E.g. *Lettere Familiari*, CLXXXI. In the eulogies with which the letter
opens there is, however, a faint suggestion of irony, which accords well with
the style of the rest of the communication, just as in Letter CLXXX we may
detect a politely bantering tone: 'I wrote yesterday to Messer Gismondo, saying that you were a rare personage. . . . Take advantage of this reputation while
there is time: *non semper pauperos habebitis vobiscum.*'

dence.[1] He merely kept building his dreams, fostering them with hope, until he saw them dissolve before his eyes.

VI. THE VITALITY OF *THE PRINCE*

But amid the ruins of Machiavelli's intellectual creation something significant and vital remained, something which, in spite of all his errors of detail and the vanity of his illusion, imbued *The Prince* with an exuberant vitality. Hence, instead of meeting with a disastrous fate and a condemnation later to be justified by events, like its author's immediate purpose, instead of disappearing into the grey mists which swallow up the dead things of the past, the little work was destined to attract the attention of posterity and, indeed, to acquire with the passing of the years an increasingly evident importance.

Truth to tell, the principal thesis propounded by the Florentine Secretary was not itself destined to find an echo in the hearts of men; and if his historically determined purpose, the desire to see Italy no longer overrun by the barbarians, had constituted the dominant and most truly impassioned theme of his solitary meditation, that refrain, even though taken up again at various times,[2] was fated to be

---

[1] Only at the end of his life did the relationship become really affectionate: 'I love Messer Francesco Guicciardini . . .' (*Lettere Familiari*, CCXXV). But this emotional reaction was provoked by the practical conduct of the Lieutenant of the Church (*ib.*, CCXXIII), who appeared to Niccolò at that moment as, in a sense, the defender of Florence, his native city, so that his love embraced both his friend and the birthplace which he loved 'more than his soul'.

[2] Voices were later raised emphasizing Italy's need to be independent of the foreigner (cf. Di Tocco, *Un progetto di confederazione italiana nella seconda metà del Cinquecento*, in *Arch. Storico Ital.*, 1924, Part II, pp. 17 and 25–6 of the excerpt). At a certain stage, indeed, Charles Emmanuel I himself is seen to be the redeemer invoked by Machiavelli. 'El duque de Saboya ha tomado por sì la eshortacion lisonjera que Nicolas Maquiavelo hace al fin del libro del tirano, que el llama Principe: para librar à Italia de los barbaros, hàse dado por entendido de las sutilezas del Bocalino, y de las malicias y suposiciones de la Pietra del Paragone; y determinò edificarse libertador de Italia, titulo dificil cuanto magnifico' (Francesco Quevedo, *Lince de Italia*, in *Obras*, Madrid, 1880 (Biblioteca de Autores españoles), p. 237). Cf. G. Rua, *Per la libertà d'Italia*, Turin, 1905, p. 236.

overshadowed, almost obscured by the moral, European in its implication, which in those days could be discerned in *The Prince*. The *leitmotiv* of Machiavelli's posthumous life was his great assertion as a thinker, representing his true and essential contribution to the history of human thought, namely, the clear recognition of the autonomy and the necessity of politics, 'which lies outside the realm of what is morally good or evil'.[1] Machiavelli thereby rejected the mediaeval concept of 'unity' and became one of the pioneers of the modern spirit.

However, in the generations that immediately followed the Florentine Secretary's death such a motif of spiritual enrichment could not be revived, developed and perfected. Amid the vacillation and the uncertainty of thought and feeling which characterizes all periods of transition it remained as a guide-post and no more, above all to the prevalence of bitter and inconclusive controversies which could have no new or concrete result.

But it did remain; and – albeit almost surreptitiously, without appearing in all its theoretical potency – it also upheld the historical value of the work, and by its clarity made it possible for the European significance of the composition to emerge.

For Machiavelli accepted the political challenge in its entirety; he swept aside every criterion of action not suggested by the concept of *raison d'état*, i.e. by the exact evaluation of the historical moment and the constructive forces which the Prince must employ in order to achieve his aim; and he held that the activities of rulers were limited only by their capacity and energy. Hence, he paved the way for absolute governments, which theoretically were completely untrammelled, both in their home and in their foreign policies.

If this was made possible by the Florentine Secretary's recognition of the autonomy of politics, it depended, conversely, on his own peculiar conception of the State, which

[1] Croce, *Elementi di politca*, Bari 1925, p. 60.

he identified with the government, or rather with its personal Head.[1] Accordingly, in *The Prince* all his attention was riveted on the human figure of the man who held the reins of government and so epitomized in his person the whole of public life. Such a conception, determined directly by the historical experience which Machiavelli possessed in such outstanding measure and presupposing a sustained effort on the part of the central government, was essential to the success and pre-eminence of his doctrine.

[1] Cf. Mayer, *op. cit.*, pp. 41, 88, 112; Meinecke, *Die Idee der Staatsräson* (cited above), p. 72; E. Grassi, *Il pensiero di Machiavelli e l'origine del concetto di Stato*, in *Rassegna Nazionale*, June, 1924, p. 201. As for the abstract or universal State, 'as it must have shone forth in the profound mind of Machiavelli', I fear that in recent times scholars have tended to force the writer's thought in order to endow it with a logical rigidity and a schematic continuity which it did not possess. Such systematism seems to me somewhat inconsistent not only with Machiavelli's nature and his character, which was in the highest degree opposed to dogmatic and abstract research, but also with his very thought, which was anything but systematic, and very often even disconnected, as in the *Discorsi*. Ercole (*Lo Stato nel pensiero di Niccolò Machiavelli*, cited above, p. 93) notes, apropos of the republican State, the uncertainty and the continual variation of the terminology. Furthermore, scholars have been tempted to regard Machiavelli's thought as developing continuously and harmoniously in a single direction, whereas it is so bound up with the man's life, so rich in motifs, so varied and so dominated by the events of the day, that one can discern in his works the successive emotional transitions of a writer whose 'mind' is not always and everywhere the same. At one time the Machiavelli of *The Prince* was grotesquely opposed to the Machiavelli of the *Discorsi*. To-day, chiefly through the influence of juridical studies, critics are too often led to minimize the differences that arise from his varying emotional outlook. In saying this I am thinking especially of the essays of Ercole (*Lo Stato nel pensiero di Niccolò Machiavelli*, in *Studi economici e giuridici della R. Università di Cagliari*, VIII, 1916, pp. 40–232, IX, 1917, pp. 1–83; *Lo Stato in Machiavelli*, in *Politica*, June, 1919, pp. 334–55; *L'Etica di Machiavelli*, *ibid.*, September, 1919, pp. 1–37; *La difesa dello Stato in Machiavelli*, *ibid.*, March–April, 1921, pp. 1–36; *Dante e Machiavelli*, *ibid.*, July–August, 1921, pp. 127–74, reprinted in the *Quaderni* of *Politica*). Cf. the opinions of Gentile (*Studi sul Rinascimento*, Florence, 1923, pp. 107 *sqq.*), Solmi (in *Arch. Stor. Ital.*, 1918, pp. 234–6) and Carli (in *Giornale Storico della Letteratura Italiana*, LXXII, 1918, pp. 313 *sqq.*). Precisely because these essays are among the very few contributions of real value that Italian critics have made to the study of Machiavelli I have thought fit to express my disagreement with the general tendency. This does not mean that their work does not abound in weighty and acute observations. Ercole, with his usual shrewdness, has illuminated many aspects of Machiavelli's thought in a truly remarkable way.

This was a turning-point in the history of the Christian world. The minds of political theorists were no longer trammelled by Catholic dogma. The structure of the State was not yet threatened in other directions by any revolt of the individual conscience. An entire moral world, if it was not eclipsed, had at any rate receded into the shadows, nor was any other at once forthcoming to take its place and to inspire a new fervour of religious belief; hence, political thought could express itself without being confused by considerations of a different character. It was an era in which unitarian States were being created amid the ruins of the social and political order of the Middle Ages, an era in which it was necessary to place all the weapons of resistance in the hands of those who had still to combat the forces of feudalism and particularism. It was, in short, an era in which it was essential that the freedom and grandeur of political action and the strength and authority of central government should be clearly affirmed. Only thus was it possible to obliterate once and for all the traces of the past and to offer to the society of the future, in the guise of a precept, the weapons which would preserve the life of the united nation in face of disruptive elements old and new.

This was the great achievement of Niccolò Machiavelli, who accordingly became the legitimate representative of politics and government, the man who was at once admired and hated, followed and opposed, throughout two centuries of European history; and it was on him that the eyes of men were to be fixed, because only he, a poor, weary citizen of a city divided against itself, had proclaimed with an eloquence that was now muted the nature of the arms which the sovereign authority must employ in order to achieve victory.

To obtain such a result it was essential that the writer should ignore everything save the figure of the man who presided at the nerve-centre of the State. He must seek no other virtue, no other political system;[1] he must concentrate

---

[1] Notice, for example, how even the religious problem is presented in *The Prince*. In the *Discorsi* religion is one of the bastions of the State: cf. Ercole's

on one system alone, bringing to bear upon it all his clarity of thought and all his strength of will. In order to recognize fully the value and autonomy of political activity,[1] and on this unshakable theoretical foundation to assert, in the midst of European history, the basic principle which moulded it and was destined for a long time yet to inspire it, he had first to embrace a philosophy of extremism and simplification. It was necessary for him to focus his attention exclusively on the central power, the government, which must be concentrated in a clearly specified individual. In this way the latter's course of action would acquire a remarkable definition – a necessity if he was to survive amid the conflicts that surrounded him. All the errors and defects of historical evaluation which had determined the creation and the practical ineffectiveness of *The Prince* thus became the chief source of its immense vitality:[2] if Machiavelli had judged the events of his time in a truly critical spirit he would not have written his treatise. Instead, it was necessary for the critic to become confused and to make a succession of mistakes in order that the creator might attain his full stature; and the creator, seizing upon two hundred years of Italian history, made them his own and synthesized them with the hand of a master. The serene curiosity of the man who wishes only to observe and judge had to give place to the vehement, reckless passion of the man who wishes to create something new.

excellent analysis, *Lo Stato nel pensiero di Niccolò Machiavelli* (especially pp. 161 *sqq.*), which is perhaps the best thing that has yet been written on the subject. Here, it becomes simply a political instrument of the Head of the State, who has to use it as he uses piety, faith and integrity, only more so (Chapter XVIII). In short, it is simply a part of the *condottiere's* 'virtue'.

[1] Cf. Meinecke, *op. cit.*, p. 127.

[2] Thus in military matters too Machiavelli, even if he committed errors of evaluation, suggesting a particular solution that was neither practicable nor even consistent with the essential spirit of contemporary political life, nevertheless affirmed, with wonderful vigour and efficacy, one of the basic principles of the modern State, viz. the necessity of a strong military organization, which alone would enable a nation to survive and to initiate a 'power' policy. Machiavelli's illusions, ambiguities and errors soon became apparent; but his fundamental concept continued to hold good; moreover, it predetermined one of the salient features of modern civilization.

Had he been a shrewd and profound historian Machiavelli would merely have written a masterpiece. As it was, he was a very bad historian, and he thereby became a universal influence.[1]

Certainly, this European significance was intimately bound up with the particular historical circumstances of the time. When, slowly, the structure of political life changed and, with the final achievement and consolidation of internal unity, its centre of gravity was shifted, then, also slowly, there came about a diminution of the *historical* significance of *The Prince*, which in the end ceased to speak in this sense to the modern age. Instead, the work gradually cast off the slough of its immediate implications, and its lasting significance as an intellectual affirmation became fully apparent. Then Machiavelli remained, as he remains still, a universal influence in a new and ampler guise; but for a very long time *The Prince* had an assured importance as a compendium of the evolution of European political life, which Niccolò

---

[1] Cf. Max Kemmerich, *Machiavelli*, Vienna and Leipzig, 1925, p. 171. It might now be asked whether Machiavelli was truly aware of the enormous significance of his work; but the question would be futile. He was fully conscious of his great theoretical assertion, viz. of the autonomy of politics, and he was also conscious of the process of centralization and unification which was taking place in Western Europe (*Ritratto di cose di Francia*; cf. Schmidt, *Niccolò Machiavelli und die allgemeine Staatslehre der Gegenwart*, Karlsruhe, 1907, pp. 84 *sqq.*). But to infer from this that Machiavelli in turn envisaged the political unification of Italy is a mistake. It is tantamount to identifying his judgment of history with an act of will and faith, which may even not correspond in every respect to that same judgment. On the other hand, it is quite fair to say that Machiavelli, profiting from the lessons of the present, desired a centralized and unified State (cf. also K. Heyer, *Der Machiavellismus*, Berlin, 1918, p. 31), such as might subsequently be extended. In this he was in truth both a very great political theorist and a great historian – as great in his swift conspectus of Europe's evolution as he had been incompetent in his analysis of the situation of Italy. But in creating *The Prince* in order to satisfy a passionate desire and to fulfil an immediate purpose Machiavelli cannot have suspected that he was thus delivering up to Europe the blueprint of two hundred years of her history. Certainly, he gave to posterity far more than he directly intended (Meinecke, *op. cit.*, p. 187). Anyone who thinks that this represents an unduly serious diminution of Machiavelli's genius should consider whether, in history, the effect of men's thoughts and actions is not always seen to go beyond the intention that inspired them.

Machiavelli continued to dominate, openly or surreptitiously, through the agency of the very men who wished to oppose him.[1]

Thus by its unadorned and axiomatic pronouncements Machiavelli's work contributed to keep alive the memory of the greatness which Italy had achieved before the peninsula was obliged to submit to foreign sovereignty. The Seigneurs and the Princes had failed in their purpose; and in the end, overwhelmed by Powers that were wealthier, stronger, and more deeply versed in the arts of war and politics, they had

---

[1] There was only one sense in which monarchs could not subscribe to the doctrine of *The Prince*, and that was the military sense. Here the author, suddenly becoming once again a citizen of the Commune of Florence, had wished to call forth the virtue of the people. In this he was contradicting the general political trend of his treatise, but psychologically the contradiction is easily explained. In this matter European history assumed the task of proving that the Secretary of the Nine was in error. In so far, however, as the problem he raises is a political one Machiavelli paves the way for absolutism. He aims in his thinking at the undisputed dominion of the central power, which will crush every other social and political force. The rules of conduct laid down in Chapter IX—namely, that the Prince should make sure of the friendship of the people in order to bring down the aristocracy – are precisely those which had long been observed by monarchs and ministers (however different the meaning and significance that may subsequently have been attached to the word 'friendship'). Meinecke (*op. cit.*, p. 55) notes that the aims of the egalitarian absolutism of later days are not formulated by Machiavelli. Certain it is that absolutism developed far beyond the Machiavellian position and that even the absolute monarchy of the seventeenth century was vastly different from Machiavelli's Principate. With him we are only at the beginning. His thought is still obscured by the confusions and uncertainties of the age of transition (typical in this respect is his military outlook), while the State had not yet acquired its 'inherent nobility' (Meinecke, *op. cit.*, p. 114). As we trace the formative process of the absolute monarchy we ought to recall to mind a whole series of motifs which are absent from the writings of Machiavelli, and also, for example, the vast influence exerted by the thought and work of Luther (cf. the acute observations of Figgis, *Studies of Political Thought from Gerson to Grotius*, Cambridge, 1907, pp. 62 *sqq.* and, with special reference to Machiavelli, pp. 82 *sqq.*). On the other hand, Machiavelli *does* expound the basic *method*, i.e. the realization of the absolute supremacy of the central government, and this explains the enormous success of *The Prince*, which set forth this concept in the fullest possible detail. The *Discorsi*, Machiavelli's great theoretical work, if it was not 'consigned to everlasting oblivion', as Paruta put it (*Discorsi Politici*, Book II, disc. 1, ed. Venice, 1629, p. 244), was certainly completely overshadowed, and its function became chiefly a polemical one.

had to yield, either taking to flight or resigning themselves
to the idea of leaving the conduct of Italian life to others. Yet
in the course of an effort twice repeated within a hundred
years they had created something which was not destined to
perish, even if it was only completely and successfully developed abroad. The wisdom and administrative ability which
had enabled them gradually to establish their power; the
clarity and preciseness of political vision which had led them
to adopt a vigorous unitarian policy, at any rate within the
borders of their domains; their stubborn fight to ensure the
absolute supremacy of the sovereign authority and to unite
the various elements of the State – all these things established
a tradition of civic wisdom and political energy which was
destined to survive even when it was left to others to bring
about its ultimate triumph.[1]

This was the course on which Western Europe had em-
barked. It was the unique good fortune of the Italian tradition to be seized upon and epitomized in a few pages by

[1] Cognasso very properly takes note of this fact (*Ricerche per la Storia dello
Stato Visconteo*, in *Boll. Soc. Pavese Storia Patria*, XXII, 1922, p. 18 of the
excerpt). It would be a pity, however, if in recognizing the vital achievements
of the Seigniories we were to forget the real catastrophe which occurred –
namely, the failure of our Princes to carry that policy to the conclusion to
which, thanks *entirely* to their efforts, it had been leading. And the very fact
that *The Prince* epitomized Italian history so forcefully was, in view of
Machiavelli's ultimate aim – the salvation of Italy – a terrible condemnation.
The basic rules of conduct which the author lays down had long been observed
by Italian Princes. Mistakes had been made on isolated occasions, but the
treatise certainly could not anticipate those which, in certain fresh circumstances, might be perpetrated in the future. No precept could prevent them,
since no one was in a position to foresee exactly the various conditions under
which decisions would have to be taken. Here *discretion* was needed: *The
Prince* was to be a general treatise, expounding a method. Now, Machiavelli
suggested only one remedy that was really new – the remedy of his own army.
But in the most favourable eventuality this would be quite insufficient to
remove the complex causes of Italian decadence. If, then, at the moment when
it became clear that our grand policy was in no sense an answer to the situation,
a man of genius, who was anxiously seeking the road to recovery, could think
of nothing better than to propose the re-adoption of those same rules of conduct which had not sufficed to avert the final collapse, it was necessary to admit
that the time had come for the Italian Princes to surrender their mandate,
handing over control of the peninsula's affairs to others.

Machiavelli, so that it became a model for Europe. The ultimate consequences of what had been, historically, a slow, gradual process, often confused and always carried through with the adaptability and shrewdness demanded by the changing tempo of events and by the varied circumstances in which the successive political manoeuvres of the Seigneurs had to be conducted, were expounded in his work with an impressive sense of proportion. The contradictions and the moments of delay and hesitation were eliminated, the leisurely, circumspect procedures of the statesman now gave way to the awe-inspiring clear-sightedness and method of one who was well aware of all the forces and aspirations which were involved.[1] A historical development whose various aspects might at times even appear unrelated was clarified by Machiavelli with certainty and theoretical precision.

To be sure, Italian history lacked something, particularly by comparison with the history of the other Western States. It was possible, and indeed necessary, for absolute power itself to be built on broader and deeper foundations – political, social and spiritual – than those on which the Seigniories of Italy had been established. As a result, the State which emerged from *The Prince* lacked the vital elements and the strength that were essential if its greatness and unity were to be real, and not merely apparent. European history could and in effect did give a different stamp to the actions of that central power, which nevertheless acquired a universal dominance.[2]

---

[1] For example, Machiavelli is no longer conscious of the subordination – admittedly formal – of the Princes to the Empire. He makes them truly sovereign.

[2] The accusation which was levelled against Machiavelli by Treitschke (*La Politica*, translated by E. Ruta, Bari, 1918, p. 87), and later by Heyer (*Der Machiavellismus*, already cited, p. 30), that his concept of power lacks definition, derives from an abstract way of thinking. In Machiavelli's day the acquisition and the maintenance of power were the basic necessities of national life. They made possible that unity and internal cohesion which were likewise the prerequisites of economic welfare and – for example, in France – of *bourgeois* prosperity. Because of the necessity of this power, which created and

Thus, the development of these features, which are not to be found in Italian history or in Machiavelli, involved a change in the very character of absolute government. But *The Prince* continued to embody the broad lines of the question; hence, it rightly became a subject of the most acute controversy and the Koran of the rulers of nations.

Later, this second lease of life which Machiavelli's work had enjoyed drew to a close; and to-day, in this respect, Machiavelli belongs to the past. The historical problems of nineteenth- and twentieth-century Europe are no longer those of the Europe of the Cinquecento.[1] But, freed from these specific shackles, dissociated from all that serves to connect him with the actual course of human affairs, Machiavelli shines forth all the more brightly in his glory as a thinker, to whom we owe due acknowledgement.

And there is yet another consideration, perhaps more closely bound up with Italian life alone, which, as it were, isolates *The Prince* and makes us re-read it not without a vague, secret emotion.

Machiavelli's re-affirmation of the importance of open

protected States, and so enabled civilization to flourish in all its forms, Machiavelli conceded full powers to his ideal government, which was placed, as it were, on a throne of Absolutism. On the other hand, it may be said that the social and spiritual basis of Machiavelli's State is unduly narrow. But in order to pursue this question we should have to piece together the history of the Italian Renaissance, comparing it with the different course of events in other great States, above all in France.

[1] To be sure, certain specific features of Machiavelli's work exerted a great influence even during the nineteenth century. Thus, in connection with the problem of the national State and – owing to an arbitrary distortion of fact, for here Machiavelli's position is quite different from the modern one – the problem of the relations between State and Church politicians have often referred to his work, seeking in it suggestions and rules of conduct. This process has depended on the particular historical conditions by which, at a given moment, a country or a group of men has been confronted. One need only think of the conditions that prevailed in Germany towards the end of the eighteenth century and of the correspondingly more powerful influence which on that account Machiavelli exerted on Hegel. But it cannot be said that since the seventeenth century *The Prince* has remained the blueprint of *European* history.

resistance, which requires austerity of mind as well as an un-troubled conscience; his condemnation of laziness, complac-ency and 'style', whose counterparts are hard work, danger and ceaseless struggle; his transformation of a life that is a precise and bitter duty into faith and passion – these things betokened a profundity and an asceticism which became for Italians a lesson in life.[1]

Too often the Renaissance means the conversation of Bembo, the urbanity of Castiglione, the harmonious grace of Ariosto, and also the somewhat contemptuous perspicacity of Guicciardini. To this world Machiavelli opposes his own, which is hard, bitter, narrow, ignorant of literature and shunning discretion. He sees before him cowardly Princes, and he chastises them; finding himself surrounded by a people without a conscience, he proclaims his faith, which is no longer a religious faith; he moves among diplomats who are hypnotized by their own formality, and affirms his passion; he is confronted by Guicciardini, who shows him the error of his ways; he passes on, and again falls into error, but he does so in order to re-affirm his own strength of mind. The stupendously dramatic quality of the emphasis and the animation of the language and style match the dramatic intensity and the forceful exposition of the lesson that emerges.

We have here a first attempt to reform the individual man; and in the very fact that the call to political action drowns every other voice, human or divine, there is such a painful, tragic grandeur that the State may well demand the sacrifice of every passion and require the absolute renunciation of every other sentiment in those who wish to control it. It is essential that someone should sacrifice his soul for his faith, whatever that faith may be.

In this recognition of the austere, dramatic importance of our actions consists the human grandeur of Niccolò Machia-velli as a representative figure of the Italian Renaissance.

[1] The credit for emphasizing this point is due to Francesco De Sanctis.

III

MACHIAVELLI'S METHOD AND STYLE

URING the summer and autumn of 1500 Niccolò Machiavelli was at the Court of France, undergoing his first great experience of European politics. Together with Francesco della Casa, he had been sent by the Government of Florence on a mission to Louis XII, 'the master of the shop', in other words the contemporary arbiter of Italian affairs, his object being to try to solve the disastrous problem of Pisa. As a first 'lesson' of this experience Machiavelli was forced to take due account of the miseries of an indequate salary, inferior 'beyond all reason, human or divine', to Della Casa's. At the very outset he had to draw upon his capital to the extent of forty ducats, so that he was left 'without a halfpenny'. As a result he threatened to return home at once, since it was better to lie 'at the mercy of fortune' in Italy than in France.

Henceforth, in fact, he had to think and act amid daily difficulties and privations. Yet he was by nature an open-handed man, incapable of 'doing anything without spending money' – a sociable man, fated nevertheless 'to lead a life of hardship rather than one of gaiety'. Later on, in the far harsher circumstances of 1513, he would be forced to 'turn his face to fortune', to seek relief from 'the malignity of fate' by gambling at the inn near his house at S. Andrea in Percussina, squabbling over a farthing, brawling and arguing with the landlord, the butcher or the miller, and finding an outlet in letters to friends for his desire to do something, if only to 'roll a stone' because by continuing as at present 'I am wearing myself out, and if I go on like this for long my poverty will make me an object of contempt'.

And yet, in the evenings of those summer and autumn days of 1513, Machiavelli would take off his every-day attire, 'steeped in mud and filth', and, putting on 'regal and curial robes', would enter the 'ancient courts of the men of old, where, being received with solicitude, I nourish myself with that food which is mine alone, and which I was born to eat . . . and for four hours I am conscious of no boredom, I forget all my troubles, I cease to fear poverty, I have no terror of death. I give myself up entirely to them'. These were the days during which, with a single sustained effort, he composed *The Prince*.

Now, in the summer and autumn of 1500, at the time of his first great political experience, just as he was already deploring his privations and troubles, so too he suddenly succeeded in translating himself to another, loftier world – the world of political understanding. And if the great reflections and the powerful pages of *The Prince* were as yet a thing of the future, his thoughts, his notes, even his literary style already presaged his masterpiece.

For the letters which he wrote from the Court of France contain opinions later repeated and fully elaborated in his great works—as when he advises Cardinal Georges d'Amboise about the policy which Louis XII should pursue in Italy—namely, to follow 'the method of those who have in the past sought to acquire a foreign province, which is to diminish the numbers of the strong, to cajole the subject population, to keep one's friends, and to fight shy of would-be 'colleagues', i.e. of those who wish to have equal authority in the region'. Here we have the essence of Chapter III of *The Prince*.

Far more important, the Machiavelli of this period affords us a glimpse of the real Machiavelli, with his characteristic way of looking at political problems, and in particular his dilemmatic technique of invariably putting forward the two extreme and antithetical solutions, disregarding half-meas-

K

ures and compromise solutions, and employing a disjunctive style: for example, the people of Florence think they can no longer hope for anything '*either* because of the malignancy of their fate *or* because they have so many enemies', while the French only respect '*either* those who are strongly armed *or* those who are ready to give'. This method constantly recurs in Machiavelli's prose. He is so rigorous in his use of it that it seems at times too obvious – I would venture to say too ingenuous – as when, in the *Arte della Guerra* (IV) we are confronted with the sentence 'I say, then, that pitched battles are either lost or won'. It is, on the other hand, a perfect formal expression of a mode of thought which is always based upon the precept that 'virtue' in a politician consists entirely in making prompt and firm decisions, and that in public life nothing is more pernicious than obscure or slow and tardy deliberation – a fault which results 'either from weakness of mind and body or from the malevolence of those who have to deliberate' (*Discorsi*, II, xv). Machiavelli is always emphasizing that no State should delude itself that it can always adopt a 'safe course of action; rather should it realize that its policy will always be attended by risk: for we find that, in the nature of things, if we seek to avoid one difficulty we always come up against another; but prudence consists in knowing how to recognize the character of difficulties and preferring to face the one that is least serious' (*The Prince*, Chapter XXI; *Discorsi*, I, vi). He is always resolute in regarding 'half-measures' as ruinous; indeed, they were always avoided by 'his' Romans, who invariably went to 'extremes' (*Discorsi*, II, xxiii). Men adopt ruinous half-measures, says Machiavelli, because they are lazy and incompetent, because they do not know 'either how to be wholly bad or how to be wholly good' (*Discorsi*, I, xxvi).

There are signs that this technique, which is characteristic of Machiavelli in his maturity, was already employed by the author during his early years of political rumination, during the period of the legations.

Most important of all, even at this early stage he is never

satisfied with the mere analysis, however lucid, of a specific political situation. Instead, he is impelled – I would say by instinct – to proceed straight from facts to considerations of a general nature and to regard the concrete episode as one of the innumerable changing manifestations of something which does not change, because it is perennial – the struggle for power, in other words politics. In the reflections of this by no means front-rank civil servant about the events of the day, and in his official reports to his Government, we can already see the mighty Machiavellian 'imagination' at work – the sudden flash of intuition, identical with that of the great poet, who in any single event detects the ever-recurring workings of a universal process that is part and parcel of the human story. Hence the advice imparted to the all-powerful prime minister of Louis XII on the way in which the King ought to conduct himself in Italy, 'following the method of those who have in the past sought to acquire a foreign province'. Here he is already holding up the example of 'his' Romans and recommending the constant study of antiquity. As an assessment of the policy which France should adopt towards Italy it is far more comprehensive than one would expect, coming as it does from a Florentine envoy whose mission was limited to the affairs of Pisa.

Many years later, in 1522, Machiavelli was to offer advice to his friend Raffaello Girolami, who was going to Spain as Ambassador to Charles V. It was useful advice, in which he explained the method by which an envoy should set about winning friends at Court so that he might be well informed concerning matters which it was essential for him to understand and so on. But as for expressing opinions in his reports to Florence, it was better never to speak in the first person. 'To put your opinion into your own mouth would be odious', notes Machiavelli. Let Girolami therefore make use of such devices as this: 'Cautious men here think that the effect is likely to be such-and-such.' Admirably prudent advice for a professional diplomat – a rule for the avoidance of personal embarrassment which might well be termed universal in its application. But when Machiavelli had had to write of 'conjectures' and 'opinions' himself, though sometimes employing such devices, he had often used the first person, openly admonishing his Government: 'I wish to warn you, lest you persuade yourselves that you are likely to be ready every time' (Legation to Valentino, letter dated 9 October 1502); and sometimes he had apologized for having written 'disrespectfully and frankly', at the cost of being proved wrong, because he preferred to injure himself 'by writing and being proved wrong' rather than to harm Florence by not doing so (first Legation to France, letter dated 3 September 1500), or because it seemed to him that he was not exceeding his 'duty' by reporting what he heard at the Court of Louis XII (third Legation to France, letter dated 26 July 1510). But subsequently he had begun once more to offer opinions and advice, and to write 'I consider . . .'. Sometimes he had even ventured to entreat the Dieci di Balià to accept his opinion, 'as they accept the Gospel' (third Legation to France, letter dated 9 August 1510) – his opinion being that, if war broke out between the Pope and the King of France, Florence would have to come out openly on the side of one or other of the contestants: let them therefore think immediately, 'without waiting until the time came', of the advantages that would accrue from an alliance with France; 'and, since opportunities are short-lived, you had better decide quickly' – yes or no, but quickly.

Such was not the procedure which he later recommended to Girolami; nor could he have recommended it to anyone, for this was in truth the food 'which is mine alone', and no one else's. To others he might be generous in his advice regarding what we may call diplomatic technique; but he could not tell them what he felt to be wholly personal, and incommunicable.

Henceforth, then, we find him interspersing his accounts of audiences or his descriptions of certain intrigues with maxims of a general nature. The method is similar to that which he employs in his last great work, the *Florentine*

Histories. Here too, before resuming his discussion of Cosimo de' Medici and Neri Capponi, he says that he desires, 'in accordance with our usual method of exposition, to explain at some length how those who hope that a republic can be unified greatly delude themselves' (VII, i). Again, when describing the conspiracy of the Pazzi he says that he would like 'to follow our custom' and speak of the different kinds of conspiracies and their significance, if he had not already discussed the matter elsewhere or if it were a subject that could be speedily disposed of (VIII, i). Finally, he apologizes if he, a historian of Florentine affairs, has described events in Lombardy and Naples at undue length. The reason is that had he not done so 'our own history would be less intelligible and less agreeable reading' (VII, i), just as, in former days, had he not expressed his opinions and conjectures the Government of Florence would have had a less precise and complete idea of the way in which matters were proceeding in France or in Rome or at the Court of the Emperor Maximilian.

The Machiavelli who emerges from the Legations is a youthful Machiavelli, one who had certainly not yet acquired the comprehensiveness of vision, the incisiveness of phrase, the plasticity of imagination which he was to reveal in the years subsequent to 1512; yet the manner of this Machiavelli is distinctive, precise and confident. We note the frequent intrusion of popular expressions, as when he speaks of his 'horsy' appearance in the presence of Caesar Borgia, of 'tapping sources', 'steering clear' or 'fighting shy' of people or 'giving them a wide berth' in order to pick up information and to avoid compromising himself. We note, too, his way of expressing an opinion by means of a graphic image. And certain syntactical constructions, all subject and verb and therefore concise and vigorous, adumbrate, albeit vaguely, images and syntactical constructions that occur in his most perfect prose, that of *The Prince*.

Moreover, even in these years he contrives in a few writings apart from official reports to express his true nature, which, as he himself said, was that of a man intended by fate to apply his powers of reasoning not to the silk-trade or the wool-trade or to questions of profit and loss, but to politics and politics alone.

In the *Discorso fatto al Magistrato dei Dieci sopra le cose di Pisa*, in the essay *Del modo di trattare i popoli della Val di Chiana ribellati*, as also in the more famous *Descrizione del modo tenuto dal duca Valentino nello ammazzare Vitellozzo Vitelli, Oliverotto da Fermo, il signor Pagolo e il duca di Gravina Orsini* – in other words, in those of Machiavelli's works which were written between 1499 and 1503 – the idiosyncrasies of thought and style already perceptible even in the early Legations naturally emerge far more clearly. Hence, what is most striking about the author's lucid and laconic method of exposition is his unequivocal determination to infer from particular events a lesson in the art of politics, or, as he himself would say, those 'general rules' which are infallible. This determination is clearly expressed in the discussion on the peoples of Val di Chiana, that early, minor work which nevertheless contains the whole essence of Machiavelli and already has the approach and the stamp of a chapter of the *Discorsi*;[1] and it is now justified for the first time by that reference to the immutability of human passions – a theme which will later inspire some famous passages in the *Discorsi sopra la prima deca di Tito Livio* (I, Preface and xi, xxxix; III, xliii): 'I have heard it said that history is the teacher who determines our actions, and above all our principles, and that the world has been inhabited in all ages alike by men who have always been subject to the same passions, and that there have always been those who serve and those who command, those who serve unwillingly and those who serve willingly, and those who rebel and are reconquered. . . . Therefore, if it is true that history is the teacher who determines our actions, it would not have been a bad thing if those whose duty it was to punish and judge the peoples of Valdichiana had modelled themselves upon, and emulated, those

---

[1] Where, moreover, we find the same theme and the same method of development (*Discorsi*, II, xxiii).

who have been masters of the world.' But the Florentines did
not do this: 'And if the judgment of the Romans is worthy of
commendation, yours is equally worthy of blame.' Here too
begins the great polemic which Machiavelli will carry on to
the end of his writings. It is directed against the men of his
time, whom he appraises and judges in the light of the experience of ancient Rome, and rightly so, for every man can
accomplish what others have accomplished in the past, 'because men are born, and live, and die in accordance with an
unvarying order' (*Discorsi*, I, xi). And once again the basic
controversy finds an immediate and highly effective echo in
the style, with the polemical exchanges between Machiavelli
and his imaginary antagonists and the cut-and-thrust – 'And
if you were to say . . . I should say . . .' – which makes the
dilemmatic technique already noticed in the letters from the
Court of France appear even more effective. This has by now
become the typical dialectical method employed by Machiavelli. We shall find an example of it in the polemical denunciation of mercenaries in Chapter XII of *The Prince*: 'I want
to demonstrate more clearly the disadvantage of such troops.
Mercenary captains are either excellent soldiers or not. If
they are, you cannot rely on them, because they will always
seek their own advancement, either by oppressing you, who
are their master, or by oppressing others, contrary to your
intention. But if your captain is without virtue he will generally destroy you. And if the reply is given that anyone who
is put in possession of arms will do this, whether he be a mercenary or not, I would answer that the use of arms should be
controlled either by a prince or by a republic.'

Thus, around the years 1500–1503 Machiavelli's personality was already emerging in ever more emphatic detail,
with its characteristic bias towards politics. And in the
course of these early experiences (as indeed of those which
followed) at Florence or during missions to foreign courts
– as when he returned to France, or when he was accredited
to the Roman Curia and Pope Julius II or to the Emperor

Maximilian – particular thoughts which were later to constitute the ever-recurring theme of his great works steadily
acquired clearer definition. From now on we find him laying
special emphasis on opportunity, which is short-lived, so that
men must understand its nature and know how to put it to
good use; on the small value which can to-day be attached to
'faith', promises and even solemn pledges; or on the tendency of men, and even of princes, to take account of present
advantage without heeding possible eventualities. Again, in-
vocations of 'reason', of what is 'reasonable', alternate in his
disquisitions with appeals to 'nature', i.e. physical nature.
Machiavelli readily falls back on 'nature' when he wants to
pass judgment on the French or the Germans, who are 'by
nature' such-and-such. He also draws a parallel between
nature and incidents of human existence, borrowing from the
language of natural and medical science terms and images
which he applies to political events and to the life of the
community. So we now find him likening the politician to the
doctor who by his skill expels bad 'humours' from the body.
His partiality for this metaphor will later inspire the celebrated image of States that spring up overnight and, 'like
everything else in nature that springs up without warning
and grows quickly, must lack the fibres and the limbs that
are appropriate to them', i.e. cannot have deep roots (*Prince*,
VII).

A continual accumulation of experience and a progressive
strengthening and development of his critical faculty – such
was the fruit of Machiavelli's fifteen years (1498–1512) of
public service. This experience led him more and more to
pass negative judgments on the Italian States of the time and
on the political capacity of their rulers. He became more and
more convinced that Italy's great political crisis, the collapse
of States like Milan and Naples, and the invasion of the
peninsula by 'barbarians' who became 'masters of the shop'
had certain quite definite and recognizable causes. As he says
in the second *Decennale*, these misfortunes were the fault of
arrogant men, 'who possess sceptres and crowns, but have

not an inkling of the future!' They are the fault of princes
who lack not only prudence and virtue but, especially, their
own military forces. 'The road would be short and easy if you
were to re-open the Temple of Mars', he had told the Florentines in the first *Decennale*, written in 1504. But it was above
all in the *Parole da dirle sopra la provisione del danaio* (1503)
that Machiavelli had given expression to what was from that
time forth both the criterion by which he interpreted recent
Italian history and the chief plank in the new political
system of which he dreamed so fondly: '. . . those who have
watched the changes that have come about in kingdoms and
the ruin of provinces and cities have seen that these things
were caused solely by a lack of armed strength or of sagacity.' Without military forces no State can survive, especially as, if the good faith of private citizens is guaranteed by
'laws, written documents and agreements', that of princes is
guaranteed 'solely by force of arms'. Therefore the Prince
must arm or perish; and if he meets with disaster it will be
his own fault, for the gods are neither willing nor able 'to
sustain something that is bound to fail'.

These and similar opinions were the starting-point of
Machiavelli's meditations when the 'ruin' was complete, that
is after 1512. The collapse of the Florentine Republic of
Soderini and the return of the Medici spelt the 'ruin' of a
political experiment in which he had played an active part.
29 August, 1512 saw the 'ruin' at Prato of that military
'formation' (*ordinanza*) which Machiavelli had sponsored
and created and which had represented his own great effort
to give his city 'an army of its own' in place of 'cowardly'
mercenary troops. And he, Messer Niccolò, had now been
completely excluded from public office, confined for a year to
State territory, and even, after Boscoli's conspiracy in
February, 1513, imprisoned and subjected to torture. Eventually, he had taken refuge in his house near San Casciano,
shunning, as he says in a letter to Vettori, the 'conversation'
and the company even of his friends.

And yet it is enough for Vettori to write him a letter, telling him that he would like to be with him so that they could see 'whether we might be able to put this world to rights', and asking him to draft the terms of a peace between the King of France, the King of Spain, the Pope, the Emperor and the Swiss. It is enough, then, for someone to breathe into his ear the word 'politics' ('cose di stato') and he, forgetting his present circumstances and imagining that he is occupied once more 'with those activities on which I have expended so much effort and so much time in vain', plunges once more into political discussion.

In an exchange of letters with his friend Francesco Vettori he discusses the immediate and urgent problem of what is going to happen in Europe and in Italy. It is *to-day*, then, that first demands attention. But *to-day* has never offered sufficient scope for the powerful political imagination of Machiavelli. When he was still a mere civil servant he had sought escape from the present, even when writing his official reports to his Government, in those parentheses and comments which raised an account of certain specific happenings to the level of a general assessment of the political situation. All the more completely does he escape from it now, when he is condemned to official idleness and silence, with no outlet save that of making 'capital' out of his conversation with the 'men of old' and the experience gained during fifteen years 'which I have spent studying the statesman's art' – compelled either to keep quiet or to discourse only upon that which is his special province, to wit, politics and statesmanship. Thus, 'in this verminous atmosphere', he does in truth scrape the 'mould' from his brain. But now it is a brain that comprehends and observes with a lucidity and a discernment worthy of the great moment of creation, which has come at last.

Between *to-day*, i.e. the passing moment with its particular problems, and *the eternal*, i.e. the great and ever-valid laws of politics, there certainly remains a continuing connection, we might even say a reciprocity. For Machiavelli's determination to find a remedy for the present ills of Florence and Italy and his abiding faith in the possibility that such a remedy exists are always bringing him back to these general laws. He derives his faith – that faith which inspires the last chapter of *The Prince* and the exhortation 'ad capessendam Italiam in libertatemque a barbaris vindicandam' – from his diagnosis of the causes of Italy's present woes. As we have already observed, this diagnosis traces the fact that Italy is 'enslaved and reviled' to the political 'sins' of princes, and indicates that the absence of its own army and the cowardice of the Italian *condottieri* are responsible for Italy's having been 'overrun by Charles, plundered by Louis, violated by Ferrando and reviled by the Swiss'.

Hence his abiding faith in the possibility of a revival, brought about through the virtue of a great prince – a faith which induces him to put aside his first notes for the *Discorsi sopra la prima deca di Tito Livio* – a quieter but at the same time a more comprehensive work – and, with a single sustained effort, to throw off *The Prince* between July and December, 1513.

The diagnosis was false. Machiavelli lived at a time when the crisis in Italy's history was at its height, and in reviewing and basing theories upon the outcome of two hundred years of that history he exalted the 'virtue' of an individual, the 'virtue' of a prince, to the dignity of the supreme controlling factor of life. As a result, he attributed Italy's ruin wholly to the 'sins' of her princes. Inevitably, he failed to pin-point the origin and development of that crisis and, in concentrating principally on the 'cowardice' of mercenary troops, he passed outside the realm of truth. He was mistaken, then; his appeal to the prince-redeemer was bound to fall on deaf ears, and it was in the nature of things that the faith which inspires the last chapter of *The Prince* should have given way to the melancholy resignation which characterizes the beginning and end of *L'Arte della Guerra*.

But it was a fortunate mistake, because it prompted Machiavelli once again to admonish rulers and ruled alike and so led him to discontinue his joint commentary with Vettori on the events of the day and to search for those 'general rules' which would enable him at last to open the eyes of the blind and make the true nature of politics intelligible to all. From a polemic directed against the Italian princes he proceeds to a polemic of a more general character whose theme is the contrast between 'my' Romans and all, or nearly all, the men of modern times in whom 'not a vestige of that ancient virtue remains' (*Discorsi*, I, Preface and lv). From the realm of Italian affairs in particular he ascends to the realm of universal history, from advice on how to prevent the Swiss from becoming the arbiters of Italy he proceeds to the enumeration of rules that never fail. In other words, from a simple commentary on events in the Italy and the Europe of his day he proceeds to that great commentary which reveals and proclaims the necessity of regarding politics as an end in itself, i.e. as something beyond the realm of good and evil, unconditioned by any assumptions or aims that are not purely and simply political. In short, his watchwords are 'action' and 'power'.

Now he can give full rein to his political 'imagination', by which is meant the capacity to proceed without hesitation from a point of detail to a problem of a general order, to grasp at once the connection – which is eternal, not contingent – between two political occurrences. For different occurrences are mere moments in the eternal activity of man – in his political activity, which is unvarying in its motives, in its aims, and above all in its fundamental postulate, namely that politics is politics, and must be conceived and practised in the light of purely political criteria, without regard to considerations of a different order, whether moral or religious.

Let us read again those monumental periods in Chapter XV of *The Prince*, in which we are conscious of the writer's full realization that he is throwing open to men the portals of a new world: 'Since it is my purpose to write what may be useful to those who heed it, I have thought it more fitting to concern myself with the effective reality of things than with speculation. And many have imagined republics and principates which have never been seen or known to exist in reality; for there is such a difference between life as it is and life as it ought to be that he who neglects what is done for what ought to be done will ensure his ruin rather than his preservation. For a man who desires to appear good in every respect must surely come to grief among so many who are evil. Wherefore it is essential for a prince, if he wishes to maintain his position, to learn the ways of evil, and to use his knowledge or to refrain from using it as the need arises.'

He is fully aware of the novelty of his ideas, and emphasizes the fact in the Preface to Book I of the *Discorsi*: 'I have resolved to enter upon a road which, not having been trodden by any man before, may lead me into trouble and difficulty, but may also be paved with gold.'

Men are 'wicked', and as a rule 'ungrateful, fickle, prone to simulation and dissimulation, afraid of danger, greedy of gain' (*The Prince*, XVII); and the affairs of the world are 'carried on by men, who are, and always have been, governed by the same passions' (*Discorsi*, III, xliii). Among these passions the two most powerful incentives are love of power, i.e. ambition, and love of 'substance' ('roba'), i.e. greed, because ambition has 'such power over the hearts of men that, no matter to what heights they rise, they never renounce it' (*Discorsi*, I xxxvii), and also 'because a man sooner forgets the death of his father than the loss of his inheritance' (*The Prince*, XVII). Therefore the Prince, whose supreme task it is to maintain and so far as possible to expand his State, cannot possess nor altogether respect the 'good qualities' demanded of private individuals, 'because human conditions do not allow it'. Therefore 'let him not scruple to incur the infamy attaching to those vices without which he can hardly preserve his State; for if we consider the whole matter carefully we shall discover qualities which resemble virtue but which, if he cultivated them, would be the ruin of him, and others which resemble vice but which, if he cultivates them, will ensure his safety and prosperity' (*The Prince*, XV). Men – he will make Cosimo the Old say in the *Florentine Histories* – do not rule States 'with paternosters in their hands' (VII, vi).

Thus Machiavelli came to affirm the principle of 'politics for politics' sake', or, as has justly been said, to recognize the 'autonomy' of politics, regarded as a form of human activity existing *per se* and unconditioned by any assumptions or aims of a theological or moral character.

This, however, is the point on which it is most essential to be definite, especially if we bear in mind certain trends which have become apparent in some of the recent essays on Machiavelli. The writers of these essays strive fruitlessly to saddle Machiavelli with the mentality and the problems of a modern doctrinarian, philosophical or juridical in bias. They try to make him out to be a rigid, over-logical, stereotyped advocate of principles and laws which, being strictly inter-related, conjure up a picture of a State that is 'systematized' down to the smallest detail; or else – and this is an even graver misconception – a prophet of the ethical State in the tradition of Hegel; or, finally, simply the creator of a new moral consciousness.

At the basis of these attempts there is also the supposition that Machiavelli was a pure logician, a logician of an ultra-modern kind, well aware of the various forms of mental activity and therefore concerned to co-ordinate one with another, for example economy with ethics, in a well-ordered 'system'.

All this is quite wrong. Machiavelli knows perfectly well that he exceeds the bounds of ethics – traditional ethics, which in itself he does not question, but indeed accepts; and his reflections sometimes give the impression that it almost pains him to have to disregard moral principles: 'And if all men were good, this precept would not be good; but since they are wicked' the Prince need not keep faith when 'such observance would be to his disadvantage' (*The Prince*,

XVIII). Note the distinction between the acquisition of glory and the acquisition of authority: 'Moreover, it cannot be called virtuous to slay one's fellow-citizens, to betray one's friends, to spurn good faith, pity and religion. Such conduct may help a Prince to acquire authority, but not glory' (*The Prince*, VIII). Note too how he 'blames' Caesar and the founders of tyrannies, and his 'intense longing' for 'good' times (*Discorsi*, I, x); or, again, the emphasis which he lays on men who 'never do anything good except from necessity' – hence, he who establishes a republic must assume that all men are wicked (*Discorsi*, I, iii).

But he has explained his intention. He is entering upon a new road, never trodden by any man, and he will reveal the reality of things – that is to say, the nature of politics – even at the cost of putting moral precepts behind him. He is discussing the actions of princes, not of private individuals. Private life is different from public life; he admits the distinction and, since he is only capable of discussing affairs of State, he will speak to us only about public life. 'And forced promises which concern the public will always be broken when the strength to enforce them is lacking, and this will be no reflection on those who break them.' It is worthy of note that this passage is taken not from the celebrated eighteenth chapter of *The Prince* – the so-called 'tyrants' blue-print' – but from Chapter XLII of the third book of the *Discorsi*.

Nor is it any more true to say that the Machiavellian ethic is embodied in his concept of patriotism; for here too he makes a clear distinction, both when he speaks for himself – 'I love my native city (*patria*) more than my soul' (Letter to Vettori, dated 16 April 1527, *Lettere Familiari*, CCXXV) – or for the Florentines of the Trecento, who 'had a higher regard for their native city (*patria*) than for their souls' (*Florentine Histories*, III, vii), and, especially, when he declares that whenever men are taking thought above all else for the safety of their country, 'they should disregard questions of justice or injustice, of pity or cruelty, of glory or ignominy; rather, setting aside all other considerations, they should follow in everything that party which will preserve their country's existence and maintain its liberty' (*Discorsi*, III, xli). It is only proper that a man should sacrifice his soul for his country; but his country is not synonymous with his soul, that is to say, it cannot take the place of those moral and religious values of which a 'soul' consists. It can and should inspire men to sacrifice even what is just and laudable; but, even when it has been sacrificed in the interest of the safety of the State, *justice* is still *justice*. Nothing is further from Machiavelli's mind than to undermine common morality, replacing it with a new ethic; instead, he says that in public affairs the only thing that counts is the political criterion, by which he abides: let those who wish to remain faithful to the precepts of morality concern themselves with other things, not with politics. In the same way, he does not even think of substituting patriotism for the Christian moral ideal, and thereby creating a new civil ethic.

The truth is that Machiavelli leaves the moral ideal intact, and he does so because it need not concern him. Since he is wholly and exclusively preoccupied with his inner 'demon', his *furor politicus*, his inability to talk of anything but affairs of State – or else he must be silent – and since he is completely absorbed by what is the beginning and end of his inner life, his political fixation, everything else remains outside his range of vision. Above all he possesses *imagination* – that is, an intuition similar to that of the great poet or the great artist, to whom the world presents itself in such and such a light, the only light that he can see. Others see only shapes and colours, and some will say that they *must* express all they feel, that they can only express it, in the form of musical notes. As for him – he frankly admits it – once he has cast off his mud-stained, filthy garments all his thoughts and feelings take on a political character.

He is not, then, primarily a logician, working from principles from which, by a continuous process of reasoning, rigorous and slavish, he deduces a complete 'system'. He is first and foremost a man of imagination, who sees *his* truth in a flash, with blinding clarity, and only afterwards trusts to reason to enable him to comment on that truth. His 'truth' is politics, revealed in all its savage nakedness. Machiavelli bequeathed the problem of co-ordinating this new truth with others previously recognized, and in particular with moral 'truth', to posterity, so that for four hundred years of European thought he has remained in the thick of the bitter and agonizing struggle that has constantly been waged between *kratos* and *ethos*.

Supreme among the political thinkers of all time, Machiavelli, in common with the greatest politicians – who, like him, so resemble the artist in that their logic and their dogma are completely subordinate to their intuition – has what may literally be termed initial inner 'illuminations', immediate, intuitive visions of events and their significance. Only afterwards does he pass on to what we may call 'application by reasoning'. Certainly, in Machiavelli's prose there is frequent repetition of phrases like 'it is reasonable' or 'it is not reasonable that this should be'; but the reasonableness or otherwise consists in the application (it might be termed the 'tactic'), in the particular comment which follows the great moment of intuition and creation and is, comparatively speaking, of secondary importance.

A typical example of the absolute predominance of Machiavelli's intuition, which is concentrated exclusively on the problem in question, first apprehending it, then analysing it and, by a process of reasoning, presenting it in its various aspects, is the way in which he expounds his doctrines. Even at the outset, in the dedications of *The Prince* and the *Discorsi*, he adduces only his 'long experience of modern affairs and . . . (his) continual reading of ancient history'. There is not the faintest suggestion of the excessive logicality which, two centuries later, will prompt another great man, Montesquieu, to make in the *Preface* to *L'Esprit des Lois* another lofty but very different assertion: 'I have stated the principles, and I have observed that particular

L

cases seem to conform to those principles automatically. I have seen that the history of every nation is merely the consequence of this process, and that each individual law is linked to another law or is dependent on a more general law.' Machiavelli, on the other hand, will say that in many cases it is impossible to lay down any 'inflexible rule' because modes of action 'vary according to circumstances'; or else that it is impossible to formulate a 'definite precept without coming down to details'. Therefore he will discuss these cases 'in that general way which is permissible in the nature of things . . .' (*The Prince*, IX and XX; cf. *Discorsi*, I, xviii). Thus, on the one hand we have the general rules that always hold good, on the other those cases for which it is impossible to lay down any definite rule.

When he gets down to his subject in earnest Machiavelli employs a characteristic method, one that is peculiar to himself. He does not enquire, either on his own behalf or on the reader's, as to the nature of the State, its origin and its aims. Hence, we find no hint of the traditional arguments, prevalent both before and since, about the origins of human society and the 'why and wherefore' of the State. He would regard all this as an idle digression. The political activity of man is an eternal reality. The State, in which this activity finds concrete expression, is also a reality. To discuss these things would be like discussing the reasons why a man breathes or why his heart beats. And so he deals straight away with precise and definite problems: 'All those States and Empires which have had, and have, authority over men have been and are either republics or principates. Principates are either hereditary or newly-established.' So begins *The Prince*; and in the first chapter of the first book of the *Discorsi* we read: 'I say that all cities are built either by men who are natives of the district or by foreigners.'

This form of introduction is as clear and incisive as the dilemmatic sentence-structure itself. Think of the *Politics* of Aristotle and the *De Regimine Principum* of St. Thomas, with their preambles on the nature and motivation of society;

think of Locke's lengthy discussions on the state of nature and the origin of the political society, or of the first book of Montesquieu's *L'Esprit des Lois*, or of the early chapters of Rousseau's *Contrat Social* – to cite only a few examples – and you will at once perceive the essential difference between Machiavelli's approach to the problem, which is unique, and that of the other major political thinkers.

But in recognizing the predominance of intuition over pure logic we must also bear in mind not so much the lack of symmetry which is here and there perceptible even in the exposition of the *Discorsi* as certain hesitations and vacillations even in the handling of problems – above all that of the relationship between virtue and fortune – which to Machiavelli are of fundamental importance. It is useless to look for an absolute uniformity of outlook on this question in all his works, from *The Prince* to the *Florentine Histories*, for the simple reason that it is not there. Instead, affirmations of complete confidence in human 'virtue', which is said to be capable even of subduing fortune, alternate with affirmations of the 'power of heaven over human affairs' (*Discorsi*, II, xxix), which reach their climax in the disconsolate assertion (*Vita di Castruccio*): '. . . since Fortune wishes to demonstrate to the world that it is she who makes men great, not prudence.'

Such fluctuations of opinion apart, what greater contrast could there be than that between the pessimistic judgments pronounced by Machiavelli on the Italy of his time, which is 'rotten to the core', and his act of faith in the coming of the Prince who is to be the redeemer of Italy? Again, consider his opinion of men, who in his judgment are for the most part wicked, wholly intent on pursuing their own ends, ready, before the need is urgent, to pledge themselves and their possessions and then, when they find themselves faced with danger and the necessity to fight, forgetful of all their promises and offers (*The Prince*, IX and XVII). Yet in the last chapter of *The Prince* he imagines them waiting with great eagerness for the coming of the Prince-redeemer – waiting

for him 'with what a thirst for vengeance, with what unshakable faith, with what reverence, with what tears of joy!
What gates would not be opened to him? What peoples
would refuse him obedience? What envy would bar his way?
What Italian would not defer to him?' Not a shred remains
here of Machiavelli's pessimistic judgment of mankind.

Exalted by his passion, Machiavelli imagines and can already see almost physically the redeemer of the Italians, a nation
'more servile than the Hebrews, more slavish than the Per-
sians, more scattered than the Athenians, leaderless and un-
organized; a vanquished, despoiled, torn, devastated land'. He
forgets all his past judgments, for he is dazzled by a new
prospect – the prospect of an Italy liberated from the barbarian yoke. And yet the exhortation with which *The Prince*
closes is not a subsequent addition, as has sometimes been
said, nor is it a piece of oratory tacked on as if to justify by
means of a noble invocation the sorry facts affirmed in all
the other chapters of the treatise. It is even in its style an
integral part of the underlying conception of *The Prince*.

For Machiavelli's prose is, in short, a complete expression
of the predominance of imagination over pure logic.

In place of the precise and carefully-weighed opinion we
find, just when a solution seems farthest away, the plastic
image that resolves the doubt through imagination, not
through logic. For example, in Chapter XXV of *The Prince*
we have this necessary premise to the final exhortation to
Italians to open the way to the Prince-redeemer: 'I firmly
believe that it is better to be impetuous than cautious; for
Fortune is a woman, and if you wish to subdue her you must
beat her and chastise her . . . and being a woman, she is
always friendly-disposed towards the young, because they
are fiercer and less cautious, and use bolder methods to keep
her in subjection.'

So we have the plastic image of the woman beaten into
submission, and the powerful climax that dispels all doubts
– by forceful imagery, however, and not by logic. When the
author's enthusiasm runs high the dilemmatic method, the

method of syllogism and disputation gives way, even in the matter of style, to a violent upsurging of emotion in which logic is replaced by imagery. And in the final exhortation at the end of *The Prince* we find the writer suddenly adopting an exalted, Biblical tone and recalling miracles decreed of God: 'The sea has opened; a cloud has accompanied you on your way; water has flowed from a stone; manna has rained down from the heavens.' This is the imagery of one whose emotion is still tempered by faith. At the end of *L'Arte della Guerra* the emotion is that of a man who is disheartened and disappointed: 'Of what can I make them feel ashamed who were born and bred without sense of shame? Why should they heed me who do not know me? By what God or by what saints should I make them swear? By those whom they adore, or by those whom they blaspheme?'

Such, then, is the genius of Machiavelli — a potent genius, peerless in the realm of political thought, consisting entirely of sudden, immediate flashes of insight, coupled with an almost miraculous natural dynamism and the manner and imagery of a great poet. And the miracle of Machiavelli is a miracle that has never been repeated throughout the course of modern history.

During his early years of public life Machiavelli's genius was still kept within bounds, yet it was already clearly perceptible. Becoming fully conscious and certain both of itself and of its novelty and grandeur during the greatest creative period, that of *The Prince* and the *Discorsi*, his political imagination, in other words his political creativeness, remained until the last at once his glory and his torment. Weary, embittered, disappointed both with himself and with others, imbued with a sense of inward disillusionment of which we catch glimpses in the *Vita di Castruccio* and in the *Florentine Histories*, he rediscovered, two months before he died, the old pugnacity which in his youth had prompted him to express even in official letters his scarcely-veiled disapproval of the policy of Florence. Sent on a mission to

Francesco Guicciardini, lieutenant-general of Pope Clement VII, between February and April 1527, he resumed his old habit of offering information and even advice. In one of his last letters, written at Forli on 11 April 1527, he resorts once more to the dilemmatic method: 'Accordingly, matters have come to such a pass that it is necessary either to revive the war or to conclude peace.' On the very eve of the 'utter ruin' which he felt instinctively lay in store for Florence and on the eve of his own death, which he did not anticipate, Niccolò Machiavelli once again adopts his characteristic tone – the imperious, comprehensive tone which typifies all his thought.

THE CONCEPT OF THE RENAISSANCE

The Traditional Concept of the Renaissance

ONE of the most noteworthy features of European historiography in recent decades has been what Dopsch has called 'the problem of continuity'. The attempt has been made to locate the origins of great political and spiritual movements much earlier in time than had formerly been the custom, and to break down the systems whereby the story of humanity had been subdivided into extremely precise and well-defined periods, self-contained and compact as blocks of granite. It has been replaced by a theory of continuous evolution, in which one civilization merges into the next, without violent upheavals or interruptions.

The historians of the enlightened age had devised, or rather perfected, the 'catastrophic' theory concerning the end of the ancient world and the beginning of the Middle Ages, fixing between the two civilizations, classical and mediaeval, an unbridgeable gulf. Present-day thought, on the other hand, reveals, in a much more emphatic degree, the tendency already expressed some seventy years ago by Fustel de Coulanges: it seeks to prove that the barbarian invaders, far from making *tabula rasa* of all the achievements of ancient civilization, accepted, meekly and fully, the legacy of Rome, and that consequently mediaeval civilization, at least in its legal, economic and social aspects, has its essential roots in the rich soil of Roman civilization. For evidence of this tendency we need only recall the well-known works of A. Dopsch and H. Pirenne.

Thus, too, in a narrower field, restricted to Italy and explored only by some Italian historians, an attempt is now being made to prove that the Risorgimento had already begun in the eighteenth century, that its most fruitful and original seeds were already latent then at the courts of reforming princes and within the heterogeneous community of thinkers, writers and poets, from Verri and Parini to Genovesi and Galeani Napione, who evolved conceptions, essentially autochthonous in character, which were destined to be fully developed in the age of Mazzini, Balbo and Cattaneo. The same period, it is alleged, witnessed the birth of the social class which was to consummate the Risorgimento — to wit, the *bourgeoisie*.

In the same way, scholars have emphasized the links that exist between Luther and the mediaeval mystics, between the Reformation and the theological world of the Middle Ages, laying particular stress not on the 'new' but on the 'old' aspects of the Lutheran doctrine. On the other hand, in recent years we have seen Catholic historians endeavouring to establish that a 'Catholic Reformation' was already in progress at the moment when the 'Protestant revolution' broke out, their object being to prove that the triumphant Counter-reformation of the second half of the sixteenth century had its roots in an earlier period. Some of these scholars have, indeed, gone so far as to assert that in the absence of the 'Protestant revolution' the course of the Catholic Reformation would have been swifter and more normal![1] Moreover, they repudiate the very expression 'Counter-Reformation' — which explicitly denotes an event that occurred *after* the Protestant Reformation — and instead speak merely of the 'Catholic Reformation'.[2] And an attempt is being made to bring about an exactly similar revolution in respect of that other 'period' of history, so defined by tradition, which we

[1] [Cf. P. Brezzi, *Le riforme cattoliche dei secoli XV e XVI*, Rome, 1945, pp. 96–7, and cf. p. 88].

[2] [On the disputes that have arisen over the concept of the Counter-Reformation and the expression itself, cf. the admirably-balanced essay of H. Jedin, *Katholische Reformation oder Gegenreformation?*, Lucerne, 1946.]

call the Renaissance. So it is that the motifs and the approach of latter-day Renaissance historiography in particular have been conditioned by a widespread attitude towards the problem of historical continuity which largely characterizes contemporary historiography in general.

Historical thought, then, is based on two distinct premises, each of them fundamental and irrefutable. The one maintains that any movement or event should be considered in itself, as possessed of a precise but limited individuality. (This is what Leopold Ranke called seeing things 'exactly as they have occurred'.) The other recognizes the links between the same movement or event and the movements or events that precede and follow it – in other words, it detects its living and active individuality against the general background of human history. Present-day historians often tend to concede only the second of these premises. Now if we adhere exclusively to the concept of things 'as they have occurred', as though they were self-contained, we may be led to isolate them and to regard the human story as a series of fragments, each one detached from the rest, without connecting links and hence also without meaning; and similarly, if we seek 'continuity' at all costs, forgetting to distinguish very clearly the peculiar and individual characteristics of a given period and engaging exclusively in a search for the connection between ideas and actions of different ages – which, though they may be related and in form almost identical, have nevertheless been felt and 'lived' with varying degrees of emphasis and intensity and are therefore not equivalent – then we shall find ourselves in the long run spreading a grey, uniform veil over the experiences of humanity and robbing history itself of all its meaning. And history, though it is a concatenation of events, also stands for continual change, novelty and differentiation.

The reaction in favour of the 'continuity' theory certainly has its own polemical *raison d'être*, since the traditional concept of the Renaissance was too precise and definite. It represented a clean break, not a gradual one. It was as compact and self-contained as the complementary period known as the 'Middle Ages'.

The two concepts of 'Middle Ages' and 'Renaissance' had in fact come into being simultaneously; and people had been able to speak of the Renaissance as a sudden, brilliant new flowering of all kinds of spiritual activity, just as, by contrast, they had conceived and described the Middle Ages as an epoch of barbarism and darkness during which nearly all intellectual and cultural values had suffered an eclipse.

The tendency to draw this distinction is already clearly perceptible among Italians of the fourteenth and fifteenth centuries, who reveal a lively sense of the difference between the *praesens tempus* and the *media aetas* and, at any rate when they come to speak of literature and the arts, consider the era immediately preceding their own to have been rude, uncultured and puerile.[1]

We find Boccaccio noting the revival of poetry: 'Aevo nostro ampliores a coelo venere viri . . . quibus cum sint ingentes animi, totis viribus pressam [i.e. poetry] relevare et ab exilio in pristinas revocare sedes mens est'; and gaily chanting the Virgilian 'Iam redit et virgo, redeunt Saturnia regna'. We find Coluccio Salutati commenting: 'Emerserunt parumper nostro saeculo studia litterarum.' We find Lorenzo Valla emphasizing how not only painting and sculpture but also literature 'hoc tempore excitentur ac reviviscant' (F. Simone, *La coscienza della rinascita negli umanisti*, in *La*

---

[1] [Cf. W. K. Ferguson's recent work, *La Renaissance dans la pensée historique* (French translation, Paris, 1950), pp. 26 *sqq.*, 63 *sqq.* Ferguson, however, sometimes (pp. 35–6) reveals a tendency which I cannot share, to underestimate the sense of 'liberation' that pervades the literature of the Trecento and Quattrocento.

Yet it is this very consciousness of living in a 'new age' that distinguishes the men of the fourteenth and fifteenth centuries from those of the so-called Carolingian, Ottonian and twelfth-century 'Renaissances'. Cf. the just observations of T. E. Mommsen in *Petrarch's Conception of the 'Dark Ages'*, 'Speculum', XVII (1942), pp. 241–2; also A. Renaudet, *Le problème historique de la renaissance italienne*, 'Bibliothèque d'Humanisme et Renaissance', IX (1947), pp. 23 and 26.]

Rinascita, II, 1939, pp. 847–51); and Flavio Biondo insisting on the fact that 'postquam propitiore nobis deo nostro, meliora habet aetas nostra, et cum caeterarum artium, tum maxime eloquentiae studia revixerunt'. This revival came after long centuries of darkness, after an era of barbarism resulting from the decadence of Rome, of which Leonardo Bruni writes: 'As the city of Rome perished at the hands of perverse and tyrannical Emperors, so did Latin studies and literature undergo similar ruin and diminution . . . And Italy was invaded by the Goths and the Longobards, barbarous, uncouth peoples, who practically extinguished all knowledge of literature' (E. Garin, *Il Rinascimento Italiano*, Milan, 1941, pp. 64 and 77).[1]

But a sense of the 'new' age and an aversion to the recent past, represented as an age of darkness and evil, are revealed in perhaps an even livelier and more pronounced degree by writers on art.

We find Filippo Villani, in his *Liber de civitatis Florentiae famosis civibus*, praising the Florentine painters who 'artem exanguem et pene extinctam suscitaverunt', and exalting Giotto, who 'in pristinam dignitatem nomenque maximum picturam restituit'. Half-way through the fifteenth century we find Lorenzo Ghiberti, in his *Commentarii*, outlining in full detail the system whereby history is divided into periods – a system that was destined to become traditional. The result of the triumph of the Christian faith and of the subversion of idolatry, says Ghiberti, was that 'all statues and paintings were smashed or torn . . . and thus were destroyed not only statues and paintings, but the books and commentaries and handbooks and rules on which men relied for their training in this great and excellent and gentle art . . . and thus the art of sculpture and painting vanished away, together with all teaching relating to that art . . .'. Only after long centuries was there a return to the true art, painting, with the

---

[1] [The importance of Bruni's interpretation has recently been excellently brought out by H. Baron, *The Crisis of the Early Italian Renaissance*, Princetown, 1955, I, pp. 360–364, and II, pp. 620–622.]

advent of Giotto, who 'introduced the new art', abandoning the 'crudity of the Greeks', in other words the Byzantine style (ed. Schlosser, Berlin, 1912, I, p. 35).

This opinion was to be echoed a century later by Giorgio Vasari.[1] The political ruin of ancient Rome involved the ruin of 'the most illustrious Craftsmen, Sculptors, Painters and Architects, who left their arts and themselves buried and submerged beneath the lamentable havoc and destruction of that most famous city'; and even more than by the barbarians, 'infinite loss and harm was inflicted on the aforesaid professions . . . by the fervent zeal of the followers of the new Christian religion, who . . . while they laboured most ardently and with all diligence to remove and to root out utterly every possible cause of error, damaged or demolished not only all the marvellous statues and the sculptures, paintings, mosaics and ornaments of the false Gods of the Gentiles, but also the memories and reputations of countless excellent persons . . .' So it was that the burning zeal of the Christians inflicted 'such ruin on these distinguished professions that they entirely lost their essential character; and so the men of the Middle Ages (finding themselves to be rude and uncultivated, especially in Painting and Sculpture) . . . began to work not in accordance with the rules of the aforesaid Arts, which they did not know, but in accordance with the nature of their abilities. And thus their handiwork was distinguished by those grotesque and ugly features, which are to be seen in old works of art to this day . . .' (*Proemio delle Vite*). This state of affairs continued until the advent of Giotto, who 'alone, though born among incompetent craftsmen, *revived* (resuscitò) with the aid of his divine gifts that which had fallen upon evil days, and restored it to a form that may be called good . . .'. He succeeded in banishing completely 'that ugly Greek style, and revived the modern and excellent art

---

[1] [But cf. Paolo Giovio's classic judgment on 'letters' – 'a multo aevo misere sepultas' – which Petrarch had resurrected 'e Gothicis sepulchris', and after him Boccaccio, Bruni, Valla and others (*Elogia virorum literis illustrium*, ed. Basle, 1577, pp. 12, 13, 19, 25, 41, 46).]

of painting; and he introduced the life-like portrayal of living persons, which for many hundreds of years had been out of fashion' (*Vita di Giotto*). He alone purged art of the 'monstrous conceits (mostruosità) of those Greeks' (*Proemio della II Parte delle Vite*).

We note, too, the passing of the era of Gothic architecture, this 'curse of building . . . which has polluted the world. . . . And may God preserve all lands from the intrusion of such thoughts and such a style of craftsmanship . . .'. The credit for this belongs to Filippo Brunelleschi, 'who . . . was given to us by Heaven that he might endow Architecture with form, which it had lacked for hundreds of years past . . .' (*Vita del Brunelleschi*).

The traditional picture of the antithesis between the Middle Ages and the Renaissance had therefore been fully etched in already by the men of the fifteenth and sixteenth centuries. Thanks to Vasari, it had a decisive influence on all art-criticism until quite recent times.

The collapse of the Roman Empire, the triumph of Christianity in its struggle against the old pagan civilization, the end of the latter, the darkness of the Middle Ages – that is the classical picture, on which Voltaire, in the eighteenth century, was to set the seal of his European reputation. It is true that Ghiberti and Vasari had spoken of the baleful effect which the religious zeal of the Christians had had on art (though they had not ventured to cast any blame upon religion, but had rather maintained that the Christian religion was prompted not by hatred of art 'but only by a feeling of repugnance and a desire to overthrow the Gods of the Gentiles' (Vasari, *Proemio*)). Voltaire, on the other hand, finds a suitable pretext for expressing once more his antipathy to Catholicism. Hence he speaks of the 'guilt' of religion, which he declares to be directly – and deliberately – responsible for mediaeval obscurantism. It is also true that in Voltaire the echo of the words of the artists, art-critics and *littérateurs* of the Renaissance is confused with the echo of those other words, quite different in tone, which had been transmitted to him by the men of the Reformation, whose antipathy to the *media aetas* was above all an antipathy to the era of papal domination and only to a small extent, if at all, an antipathy to the alleged crudeness of mediaeval culture. In the *gothique* of Voltaire and his contemporaries we encounter the legacy of the Renaissance and the legacy of the Reformation – that is to say, the anti-papal *furor* (which afterwards broadened into a general anti-ecclesiastical and anti-theological *furor* directed against all the Churches, including those which had been reformed) and Vasari's contempt for artistic ugliness.

Yet although it is enriched by different motifs, although its tone is more pungent and its polemical aim far wider and more general, the picture painted by Voltaire reproduces the characteristics of its Ghibertian and Vasarian prototypes. In other words, it represents the total collapse of the Roman world, that *grand colosse* which was destroyed by the 'deux fléaux ... les barbares et les disputes de religion ...', by the 'déluges de barbares' and by Christianity, which 'ouvrait le ciel, mais perdait l'empire' (*Essai sur les moeurs*, Chapter XI). It represents too the beginning of the period of desolation: 'Lorsque on passe de l'histoire de l'empire romain à celle des peuples qui l'ont déchiré dans l'Occident, on ressemble à un voyageur qui, au sortir d'une ville superbe, se trouve dans des déserts couverts de ronces ... L'entendement humain s'abrutit dans les superstitions les plus lâches et les plus insensées. Ces superstitions sont portées au point que des moines deviennent seigneurs et princes; ils ont des esclaves, et ces esclaves n'osent même pas se plaindre. L'Europe entière croupit dans cet avilissement jusqu'au XVI siècle' (*ib.*, Chapter XII). And then at last the light reappeared in the Italy of the fourteenth and fifteenth centuries: 'Les beaux arts, qui se tiennent comme par la main, et qui d'ordinaire périssent et renaissent ensemble, sortaient en Italie des ruines de la barbarie. ... On fut redevable de toutes ces belles nouveautés aux Toscans. Ils firent tout renaître par leur seul génie ...' (*ib.*, Chapter LXXXII). That was the moment of Italy's glory, for then she was the scene of one of the four great eras of happiness that are recorded in human history (*Siècle de Louis XIV*, Chapter I).

This was the picture which Michelet and Burckhardt, Spaventa, Dilthey and Gentile were to amplify, in the sense that they translated the originality and the merits of fourteenth- and fifteenth-century Italy from the single field of literature and art to a vaster sphere, stressing above all the philosophical aspect, the general 'conception of the world', through which alone, they averred, the men of that epoch made their so-called 'discovery of man and of nature'. But they kept the picture fixed and rigid not only in its broad chronological lines but also in respect of its absolute independence of the Middle Ages, in which, essentially, they sought no bonds of union. We need only recall Jacob Burckhardt's celebrated work, *Die Cultur der Renaissance in Italien*, a masterpiece from which the Renaissance emerged like a splendid flower that suddenly blooms in the middle of a desert. It seemed that before there was nothing, or practically nothing. No one discerned the links and the points of contact between the new epoch and the civilization of the centuries that had gone before, and the Renaissance remained in splendid isolation.[1]

As in the case of the antithesis between the Renaissance and the Middle Ages, so too as regarded the problem of the connection between classical culture and the Renaissance, the essential elements of the traditional picture had been furnished by the men of the fifteenth and sixteenth centuries.

Had not the rebirth of literature and the arts been due perhaps to the 'imitation' of ancient models? Had not Humanism, which was in actual fact the expression of that imitation, preceded chronologically, and hence also causally, the full flowering of the Renaissance, the golden age – so much so that men distinguished the age of Humanism, which extended from the second half of the fourteenth to the

[1] [However, cf. now W. Kaegi, *Jacob Burckhardt*, III, Basle, 1956, pp. 445–447, and n. 68, 690 *sqq.*]

second half of the fifteenth centuries, from the Renaissance proper, being pin-pointed, so to say, by the great figures of Leonardo, Raphael, Michelangelo, Machiavelli and Ariosto?

Such was the point of view, such the *communis opinio* prevalent in the second half of the nineteenth century; and the fact that the two essential works on the subject, Voigt's *Die Wiederbelebung des classischen Altertums* (1859), and Burckhardt's *Die Cultur der Renaissance* (1860), had seen the light of day within a year of each other may have seemed like a symbolical expression of such a concept.

Here too it was the men of the Renaissance who had provided the raw material of the conclusions now reached. And once again the most explicit views on the subject are expressed by artists and students of art. In Vasari's opinion the Renaissance had its origin on the day when the 'glorious minds that sprang from the soil of Tuscany' like a gift from Heaven succeeded in doing what their predecessors had been unable to do – namely, to turn the ruins of ancient Rome, the 'remains of the arches, colossi, statues, pillars and storied columns', to their advantage, inasmuch as, 'distinguishing very clearly the good from the bad and forsaking the old styles, they began once more to imitate, to the limit of their energies and abilities, the styles affected by the ancients . . .' (*Proemio delle Vite*).

Brunelleschi 'had two mighty visions, one of them being the restoration of good architecture . . .' (*Vita del Brunelleschi*). In order to achieve his aim 'he had spent all his days delving into antiquity for the purpose of making notes and sketches, and besides this he studied continually', so that 'his mind acquired a remarkable capacity for visualizing Rome as she was before her ruin'. Thus architecture 'regained the symmetry and proportion which it had possessed in ancient times' (*Proemio della II Parte*). In sculpture too, Donatello, 'studying the evidence of the ancient style of the excellent Greeks and of the Romans, reproduced it so exactly that he is certainly admired as one of the greatest of geniuses . . .' (*Vita di Donatello*).

The belief that the ancients exercised a direct influence on the rebirth of art and literature became general. Thus in 1590 the Genoese painter G. B. Paggi noted that 'no sooner did men begin to dig up the ancient statues that lay buried beneath the soil of Rome than art likewise was born again, in consequence of the diligence with which the fruits of the excavations were studied and observed'.

The Attitude of Some Recent Critics

Wholly at variance with the traditional picture of the Renaissance are the findings and assertions of a considerable number of recent critics.

It goes without saying that such critics must have come under the increasingly dominant influence of that historiographical *forma mentis* to which reference has already been made – a *forma mentis* characterized by a passionate belief in the theory of 'continuity' and strengthened in its convictions by the results that have followed the deepening of our knowledge of mediaeval life. The last few decades of European scholarship have in fact led to the definite rehabilitation of the life of the Middle Ages, even from the point of view of art and literature (whereas the Romantics' love for the Middle Ages had been confined mainly to the religious and political fields). Indeed, one of the greatest achievements of the art-criticism of recent decades, as Max Dvorák has rightly observed, has been its arrival at a full understanding of the mediaeval art-forms, the mediaeval 'style', previously regarded as crude and barbarous and invariably judged in the light of Vasari's classical schemes, which applied to a type of art whose predominance was complete only towards the end of the fifteenth and at the beginning of the sixteenth centuries.

Scholars have come to see how ancient civilization was not entirely swamped by the tide of the barbarian invasions, how instead it bequeathed to the Middle Ages a legacy of juridical standards, economic customs and, moreover, cultural traditions. They have emphasized how, beneath the apparent

M

'religious' uniformity of the period extending from the sixth to the fourteenth centuries, there existed a world distinguished by the complexity of its sentiments and ideas, which cannot easily be reduced to the single common denominator of other-worldly aspirations. They have discovered periods of intel-lectual and artistic reflorescence even in the centuries that once were known as 'the iron age', and they have spoken of a Carolingian renascence and an Ottonian renascence – that is to say of renascences that occurred even before the French renascence of the twelfth century. Finally, they have learned to understand, to love and to appreciate as a powerful ex-pression of art what Vasari had execrated as 'an accursed jumble of little tabernacles piled one on top of the other, with innumerable pyramids and spires and ornamental leaves' (*Del la Architettura*, Chapter III), or – referring to painting – 'those wild eyes, and bodies poised on tip-toe, and long, tapering hands, and that absence of shadows, and the other monstrous conceits of those Greeks' (*Proemio della II Parte*).

As a result of these new findings the age which preceded the Renaissance no longer appears to have resembled a desert. Instead, it is looked upon as an age rich in variety, stimulated incessantly by multifarious problems, interests and aspirations – a restless age, full of exuberant life. Hence the more positive tone of the question which had already been asked by Émile Gebhart in 1885 (in an article in the *Revue des Deux Mondes* on the French translation of Jacob Burckhardt's work): What in reality are the *points d'attache* between the Renaissance and the Middle Ages – *points d'attache à peine visibles* in *Die Cultur der Renaissance?*

The question is entirely logical and justified. It is obvious that the Renaissance must have inherited, at least in part, some of the tendencies and attitudes of mind of the preced-ing era on to which the Renaissance was grafted. We must therefore seek out and define the connecting-links between these two periods of history, which once were separated in men's minds by so wide and irreducible a gulf.

But here we find that more than one foreign scholar, having drawn what is generally speaking a somewhat superficial parallel between mediaeval patterns of life and thought and their Renaissance counterparts, has used this first and legitimate inference as a direct stepping-stone to the far more radical assertion that the Renaissance created nothing essentially new, that all its observations on man, nature, history, etc., were already present, in embryo at least, in the thought of the twelfth and thirteenth centuries – that, in short, contrary to the belief that has prevailed for centuries, it does not represent an epoch of decisive importance in the history of mankind.

The tendency to extol the Renaissance as an isolated phenomenon, as a first reflorescence of the humane virtues following the dark ages of barbarism, had first been manifested chiefly by artists and art-critics in the field of art; and it was in this field too that the first positive attempt to deny its originality and importance found expression, at the end of the last century, in the thesis advanced by Courajod, who maintained that 'the new art' had been invented by the Flemish artists of the fourteenth century and had originated not, indeed, in Italy but in the Netherlands. Since then, keeping pace with the growing tendency to re-assess the art, thought and culture of the Middle Ages, this tendency to deny the importance of the Renaissance has become steadily more marked. Developing to the utmost limit of possibility a view which had already attained prominence during the last century, the view that it is in twelfth-century France that the real seeds of the Renaissance must be sought (cf. W. Pater, *The Renaissance*), historians speak to-day of a twelfth-century French renascence which, they assert, anticipated all the spiritual achievements of the Italian renascence of the fourteenth and fifteenth centuries. It is asserted that by the thirteenth century European culture was essentially complete, nothing remaining but to exploit what had already been achieved (J. Boulenger, *Le vrai siècle de la Renaissance*, in *Humanisme et Renaissance*, I, 1934, p. 30). And in the opinion of some scholars, of whom Nordström is one, the

most that can be said is that the term 'Renaissance' can in
some measure be justified so far as Italy is concerned, but
that it cannot be accepted as applying to Europe, which had
already perfected its civilization in the course of a century of
evolution north of the Alps (*Moyen Âge et Renaissance*, Paris,
1933, p. 47).

Thus the problem is clearly posed: What should we
understand by the term 'Renaissance'? In its classical form,
in which it is primarily Italian, how far is it original in its
basic motifs, and to what extent does it reveal features of its
own? Are we confronted with something which, by comparison with mediaeval civilization, is essentially new? Or are
we rather confronted merely with a development and a
broadening – notable, if we like, but not very original – of
motifs of which there were already traces in that vast crucible
which was the European civilization of the Middle Ages?

*Preliminary Questions: Facts and Ideas. The Idea of Classical
Antiquity in the Middle Ages and the Renaissance*

To enable ourselves to solve the problem thus formulated we
must first of all purge our minds of a great and gross error
into which scholars are all too prone to fall. This error consists in confusing practical life with the life of the mind, the
day-to-day activities of man with the rational consciousness
which he may or may not have of those activities. It consists
in regarding as a single entity what I would call the 'physical'
life of the individual on the one hand and his thoughts and
ideas on the other.

For example, we find Chamard asserting that the love of
life in its sensuous and more objective form – wine, women
and various kinds of amusement – was in no sense a discovery of the Renaissance. Mediaeval man, far from being
bowed down by remorse for his sins and devoting all his
time to the singing of psalms, was profoundly attached to
worldly life with its many and not always pure pleasures. He
therefore had no need to look to the Italians of the fifteenth
century to initiate him in the delights of love and to imbue

him with a taste for agreeable living. *L'amour intense de la vie, l'esprit gaulois et l'esprit courtois* were a legacy bequeathed to the Renaissance by the Middle Ages (*Les origines de la poésie française de la Renaissance*, Paris, 1920, pp. 47, 181). Again, we find Nordström emphasizing that the 'divine Hildebert', that is to say Hildebert of Le Mans, who lived in the twelfth century, was, like many of his brethren, an ardent worshipper of women and love, a fact which proves him to have been a child of a new age (*op. cit.*, p. 65).[1]

At this point we must make it absolutely clear that when we use the term 'Renaissance' to describe a certain very definite phase of European history we are referring to a mobilization of ideas, an artistic, literary and cultural 'period' which is first and foremost an 'intellectual' reality.

So defined, the Renaissance does not find its expression in practical activity, which is incidental to the existence of the individual – in the gay life of a citizen of Florence, the self-indulgence of a Mantuan gentlewoman, the unrestrained ambition of a *condottiere* or the amorous intrigues of some member of the Court of Naples – but rather in the manner in which human designs and actions conform to an ideal system and are elevated from the plane of mere practical, instinctive activity to the status of a spiritual creed, a programme of life. Ever since the world began men in their everyday life have always obeyed certain instinctive and fundamental passions; and love and ambition, sensuality and the need for amusement, the desire for riches and the yearning for political power are peculiar to men of all ages and countries. Hence, if

---

[1] [Occasionally we find even so excellent a scholar as Gilson falling into the same error, as when, referring to Héloïse and Abélard, he asks himself the question: 'If it is claimed that a Renaissance is only possible in an age of dominating personalities, may we not retort that the age which produced our own hero and heroine is singularly worthy to be so described?' – or, again, when he speaks of a 'drama of passion, peopled with clerics, monks and nuns' that is 'none the less a story of the twelfth century' (*Héloïse et Abélard*, pp. 160 and 178).

Dopsch had earlier maintained that powerful personalities had already existed in the Middle Ages, even going so far as to assert that individualism was one of the chief characteristics of that era (*Wirtschaftsgeist und Individualismus im Früh-Mittelalter*, 'Archiv für Kulturgeschichte', XIX, 1928).]

we had to reconstruct history in the light of such considerations we should be obliged to regard as equal and alike in
their significance all the things that have happened from the
times of the Egyptians and the Babylonians down to the
present day, and history would become a grey blur in which
we could no longer distinguish one epoch from another. But
this is not so; for when we speak of historical 'periods', of the
classical world and the mediaeval world, of the Renaissance,
of the Age of Enlightenment, of Romanticism, to what are
we referring if not to political, moral and cultural ideas and
the institutions in which those ideas have found expression —
ideas and institutions which characterize individual epochs?
The eighteenth-century man loves, studies his personal convenience, is fond of luxury and sings the praises of wine and
women no more and no less than did his predecessor of the
fourteenth century; but the 'manner' in which men sing the
praises of love, extol riches and hanker after political power
has changed, and it is precisely this 'manner' that interests us.

The 'manner' is dictated by contemporary thought, and it
is to this alone that we must direct our attention.

It is obvious, for instance, that the actions of Heads of
States and politicians have always been determined by political interest. A French scholar, Benoist, has seen fit to
examine 'Machiavellism' as it was practised before the age of
Machiavelli in order to prove that even before the time of the
Florentine secretary Heads of States had applied the doctrine which he subsequently formulated in *The Prince* and
the *Discourses on the First Ten Books of Titus Livius*. Even in
the Middle Ages men like Charlemagne, Otto I and Frederick Barbarossa acted, on isolated occasions, in conformity
with the dictates of what were destined to be described after
Machiavelli's death as 'reasons of state' — in conformity, that
is, with the principle that where affairs of state are involved
decisions must be based above all on political criteria. But
this does not make it any the less true that only when
Machiavelli arrives on the scene are we confronted with the
theoretical affirmation — complete, clear and brutal — that

politics are politics, apart from all other considerations; *only then*, in other words, does a practical truth become a theoretical precept, a law explicitly credited with a universal validity. The horror with which such affirmations have filled even those who on the other hand have been not at all shocked when they have come up against the virtual 'Machiavellism' practised from day to day by this or that ruler shows clearly what a profound and real difference there is between a simple fact or practical truth and its postulation as an axiom.

In the same way, it is certain that the Middle Ages were not lacking in human figures of the first magnitude: we do not have to wait for the 'virtuous' Italian princes of the Renaissance to provide us with examples of such figures. Men like Charlemagne, Otto I and Philippe Auguste are 'personalities' who certainly have nothing to fear from comparison with Gian Galeazzo Visconti, Francesco Sforza and Caesar Borgia. But, as we shall shortly see, the respective ways in which these powerful personalities influenced the thought of their contemporaries and shaped their ideas were entirely different. Completely different, too, is the importance ascribed to each of the two groups by historiographers. This, then, is the problem – not whether or not the Middle Ages produced strong personalities (which at this time of day no one could dream of denying), but whether or not in the general conception of the world the personalities of great men had the same importance and the same function in the Middle Ages as in the Renaissance.

In short, that the mediaeval man also loved women, that he liked a good dinner or costly fabrics or artistic ornaments in his house, that he too experienced a swelling of the heart when he contemplated the burnished blue of an April sky – to-day all this is acknowledged, it is outside the realm of discussion. But what we are concerned to know is whether he ever ventured to set up as an ideal, a theoretical standard of life, that emotion which Leon Battista Alberti for his part idealized half-way through the fifteenth century as 'delight in living'. This delight in living, in so far as it is an immediate and instinctive sensation, is experienced by the men of every age. The question rather is whether and to what extent, as a conscious, deliberate affirmation of principle, it characterizes the Renaissance as distinct from the Middle Ages.

Having thus rid our minds of this first, gross and dangerous misconception we now have to see whether the qualities hitherto looked upon as peculiar to and typical of Renaissance civilization are in fact nothing but a reproduction of qualities previously possessed by mediaeval civilization.

Those critics who have seen fit to deny or at any rate to minimize the importance of the Renaissance have adopted the following argument. While, they declare, the disciples of Burckhardt maintained that the 'discovery of man and of nature' (i.e. individualism and realism in art, literature, the sciences, etc.) was an achievement of the Renaissance, it must on the other hand be recognized that the concepts of realism and individualism are already clearly implied in the literature and thought of the Middle Ages; and while it has been maintained for centuries that the rediscovery of classical antiquity (i.e. Humanism) was a typical achievement of the Italian civilization of the fourteenth and fifteenth centuries, it must be realized that classical antiquity had never suffered an eclipse, that its influence had remained strong even during the early Middle Ages, and that, actually even before the era of Italian Humanism there had been a genuine revival of 'Latinity' in twelfth-century France, where we find a species of 'humanism' which anticipates the much-vaunted Humanism of fourteenth- and fifteenth-century Italy. This earlier 'humanism' produced such men as Hildebert of Le Mans, Pierre de Blois – and above all John of Salisbury; it gave the world the Chartres School, and, a little later, the neo-classical carvings which adorn Rheims Cathedral.

However, as soon as we try to probe more deeply into the question we see that the two periods only resemble each other very superficially, while they differ profoundly in their essential character.

Certainly, the influence of classical culture was extremely strong throughout the Middle Ages. This fact has been established following decades of research, and it can no longer be open to question. In literature, as in philosophy and – at any rate from the twelfth century onwards – even in art, there are frequent and abundant examples of the debt which the men of the Middle Ages owed to classical culture.

In the second or third decade of the ninth century Alginard sketched a portrait of Charlemagne; and we find him turning to Suetonius and taking from the *Lives* of Augustus, Tiberius and Claudius a number of distinctive physical characteristics, calculated to lend majesty and a virile beauty to the personage portrayed. We find him assembling them and transforming them into a likeness of the pious Emperor who was crowned by the Pope on Christmas Day in the year 800 A.D. (cf. L. Halphen, *Études critiques sur l'histoire de Charlemagne*, Paris, 1921). This is a single example, but it is enough; and a thorough investigation of the mediaeval chronicles would show that if many of the portraits of eminent personages comply with the *rex iustus* and *rex iniquus* or *tyrannus* formulas of Augustinian and Gregorian memory, in other words with the formulas popularized by the Pseudo-Cyprian in the *De XII abusivis saeculis*, others are based on the models provided by classical historiography, and especially by Suetonius.

It would be superfluous now to allude to the mediaeval cult of Virgil. It would be superfluous to stress how in the *tabulae exemplorum* – those curious books of examples and comparisons, so widely circulated during this period and so necessary to preachers and writers – examples are freely derived not only from the Holy Scriptures but also from the legends of the ancient 'pagans' (cf. T. Welter, *L'exemplum dans la littérature religieuse et didactique du moyen âge*, Paris, 1927, pp. 94 *sqq.*). Finally, it would be superfluous to recall the survival of ancient mythology in the form of poetry.

It is very true also that this cult of classical antiquity finds even more enthusiastic champions in the twelfth century.

Pierre de Blois – one of those who to-day are given the title of 'humanists' born before their time – professes himself to be a devotee of classical Rome, in spite of dogs and pigs; while John of Salisbury in his turn is a declared champion of antiquity. And the artists who, in the thirteenth century, carved what is known as the Visitation group on the main door of Rheims Cathedral were certainly inspired by ancient models, on which they intentionally based their work.

However, as soon as we try to probe more deeply into the so-called 'Latinity' of the Middle Ages we perceive how profoundly it differs from the 'Latinity' of the fifteenth-century humanists.

Let us consider Hildebert of Lavardin (or Le Mans), perhaps one of the most widely-acclaimed of these 'humanists' of the twelfth century; let us read his famous elegy on Rome, which he visited in 1106. Undoubtedly he too was stirred as he contemplated the spectacle of the mighty ruins and the proud remains of the Eternal City; he too was filled with boundless admiration for the men who had been able to create so many and such mighty masterpieces. But his admiration of the past is accompanied by regret for the present. His eulogy is coupled with the assertion that what has been has been and will never return. Hence his cry of desolation:

Vix scio quae fuerim, vix Romae Roma recordor;
vix sinit occasus vel meminisse mei.

It is a beautiful world – but a world that has gone for ever. *Par tibi, Roma, nihil cum sis prope tota ruina.*

Let us now look at the collected letters of Cola di Rienzo, in which we shall read the proud statement, made in July, 1350, that he, Cola, would think he had achieved nothing if he did not imitate his ancient models with the object of making them live again: 'Nichil actum fore putavi, si que legendo didiceram, non aggrederer exercendo' (Cola di Rienzo, *Brief-wechsel*, ed. Burdach, Berlin, 1912, p. 204). And we shall find the lofty statement made to the Emperor Charles IV, also in July, 1350, that he, Cola, having from his earliest years derived his mental nourishment from the study of antiquity, had made up his mind – proud aim! – to reconstitute and revive the Roman Empire: 'Vos etiam allegastis, quod non absque divino miraculo Romanorum imperium reformaretur. Certe totum hoc ad divinum spectat miraculum, si per virum pauperem ac novum ruenti imperio Romano succurritur, sicut alias ruenti Romane Ecclesie per Franciscum' (*ib.*, p. 209). These notions had already been clearly formulated in the famous decree of 1 August 1347, regarding the sovereignty of the Roman people: 'Nos . . . volentes et desiderantes . . . voluntates, benignitates, et liberalitates antiquorum Romanorum principum . . . imitari . . .' (*ib.*, p. 101). *Imitatio*: here we find uttered the all-important word that divides the world of Cola from the world of Hildebert of Le Mans. In place of admiration, mingled with regret, for what can never return, we find a determination to act in scrupulous conformity with the teachings of the Ancients. *Legere* becomes *exercere*. And instead of an elegy we have an exhortation to revive the ancient splendours, the glories of Rome.

After Cola di Rienzo comes Coluccio Salutati: 'Latent in literis documenta virtutum, latent mores, latent omnia quae scire non est satis, nisi et operibus impleantur'; then Leonardo Bruni, with the 'studia quae pertinent ad vitam et mores, quae propterea humanitatis studia nuncupantur, quod hominem perficiunt et exornant'; then, greatest of all, Machiavelli, who never tires of adducing the example of the Romans as a stimulus to better deeds in the present, and makes the 'imitation' of ancient wisdom the keystone of his political and military doctrine. Men must imitate the Ancients 'in matters calling for strength and vigour, not in those which require delicacy and gentleness'; they must 'adopt the true and perfect ways of antiquity, not the false and corrupt' (*The Art of War*, I) – in other words, they must not confine themselves to a purely formal, stylistic and literary imitation, but must revive the 'human' [i.e. manly] virtues of the Ancients, superimposing a new world, deeply imbued with political consciousness, patriotism and human sensibility, on the religious world of the Middle Ages, which is responsible for the present 'weakness'. This is far removed indeed from the nostalgic regrets of Hildebert of Le Mans!

The fact is that the mediaeval spirit, for all its indebtedness to classical authors – poets, historians and philosophers – had never ceased to be dominated essentially by another consideration and by another paramount motif, to wit, the problem of the relationship between God and man and the Christian and Augustinian sense of sin and grace. Hence, classical antiquity had been a mere instrument, a cultural tool placed at the disposal of a spiritual way of life which derived its *raison d'être* from quite a different source. To be sure, we may exploit Virgil, Ovid, Lucan, Statius, Cicero and Quintilian. We may even try to imitate them, superficially. But when all is said and done they are all merely ornaments whose function is to add lustre to a moral and spiritual way of life that is founded on a religious conception of the world and finds active expression in the ecclesiastical and hierarchical organization of society.

Imitation of the classics, then, when it occurs, can only be purely superficial – so much so that even in those writings which most strongly resemble the classics we detect an inspiration profoundly alien from the spirit of the Ancients. Indeed, this is true of the Visitation group at Rheims with its much-vaunted classical form. This group (as has been shrewdly noted by E. Panofsky and F. Saxl, *Classical Mythology in Mediaeval Art*, in 'Metropolitan Museum Studies', New York, IV, 1933, pp. 266 *sqq.*), despite its seemingly classical poses, remains profoundly 'Gothic' in the spirit that informs it and in the sensibility that it expresses.[1]

---

[1] [Such formal qualities are intended to express different ideas and to symbolize Christian themes: 'Les idées païennes se dépouillant graduellement de leur expression plastique, les idées chrétiennes sont venues habiter ces formes désaffectées, tout comme le culte chrétien s'installait dans les temples vides.' And the Renaissance appears as the 'réintégration d'un sujet antique dans une forme antique' (J. Seznec, *La survivance des dieux antiques*, London, 1940, pp. 181–2; and 'il est remarquable . . . que pendant la période la plus radieuse de la Renaissance les types iconographiques 'transmis' et donc altérés, – soient presque partout abandonnés au profit des types 'retrouvés' dans leur pureté première' (*ib.*, p. 289).]

As regards the actual cult of *Roma aeterna*, we must draw a clear distinction between classical and pagan Rome, the Rome of the Scipios and the Caesars, and Christian Rome. Indeed, the concept of Rome has about it a complexity and a magnificence that are sometimes unsuspected. Prudentius, we may recall, in his *Peristephanon* extolled the soil of Rome, declaring that it was hallowed by the bones of the Christian martyrs ('Quam dives urbanum solum – sacris sepulcris floreat': *Hymnus in honorem passionis Laurentii*, vv. 543–4); and St. Augustine, in the *De Civitate Dei*, imparted majesty to the conception of the Roman basilicas, before which even the barbarous Visigoths, when in the summer of the year 410 they sacked the city, halted in awe (Book I, Chapters I and VII). Ever since then – ever since the fifth century, in fact – the concept of pagan Rome, a city made great by her military victories and the splendour of her sons, has been associated with, and often eclipsed by, the concept of another Rome – Christian Rome. This other Rome was great because she was the centre of the Catholic world and the home of the successors of Peter. This was the Rome which, as Pope Leo the Great said mid-way through the fifth century, had become, thanks to Peter and Paul, 'civitas sacerdotalis et regia, *per sanctam beati Petri sedem caput orbis* effecta'. Two ideas, these, which could quite easily be reconciled; and they had indeed been linked together in the imagination of Prudentius. Yet they could also appear as irreconcilable – witness the eleventh-century fragment *De Sancta Romana Ecclesia*, by Cardinal Humbert a Silva Candida who, about 1053, had clearly contrasted, as being diametrically opposed, Rome 'fundata super arenam per Romulum et Remum profana sacerdote et quo nescitur sacrilego editos' and Rome 'hedificata super Christum petram per Petrum et Paulum' (in P. E. Schramm, *Kaiser, Rom und Renovatio*, II, Leipzig, 1929, pp. 129 *sqq.*).

If we bear all this in mind we perceive what is the crucial point of the question: ancient Rome had indeed found favour in the eyes of mediaeval man, but *only* in so far as it was compatible with, or rather 'served the interests of', Christian

Rome. Classical culture had survived merely as a subordinate element. Its function was to provide an aesthetic outlet, a vision of the world, a means by which men might contemplate a life which possessed an organic structure of its own, totally independent of classical influence. Virgil was world-famous in the Middle Ages; but it was not merely Virgil the poet who had prophesied the coming of Christianity: it was Virgil the semi-magician, the Virgil whom Dante himself, who was, all in all, a product of the Middle Ages, chose to guide him on his journey to the after-world. His, then, was a pagan soul in Christian guise; and this is enough to explain the true nature of mediaeval 'classicism'.

Completely different in meaning and importance is the idealization of classical antiquity in the Italy of the Renaissance, even though it did not necessarily amount to a repudiation of Christian Rome: cf. a characteristic passage from Flavio Biondo, in which Prudentius's vision of Rome as great 'sacro martyrum cruore' is reproduced (Garin, *op. cit.*, p. 93). It is not surprising that here too the idealization has sometimes been no more than superficial, assuming an exclusively literary and erudite character, and that in consequence the influence of classical antiquity has become in such cases a liability, to which may be ascribed the Byzantinism of contemporary scholars.

But on the whole, and in its greatest exponents – Cola di Rienzo, Petrarch, Coluccio Salutati and Valla, Ghiberti, Alberti and Machiavelli – the idealization of classical antiquity represented the essential 'myth' of which the Renaissance movement, like all great historical movements, stood in need. This movement – originally political and economic, and later cultural and ideological in character – had rocked and convulsed Italy ever since the age of the Communes. It was the *mot d'ordre*, a programme indicating a common line of action to those whose aspirations after new forms of life, more in keeping with the needs of the times, were still confused. Men fixed their gaze on Ancient Greece and Rome in the manner – to quote Machiavelli – of prudent archers, 'who, considering that their intended objective is too far off, and knowing the range of their bows, aim much higher than their target, hoping, not that their arrows will reach such a height, but that, by aiming so high, they will attain their objective' (*The Prince*, Chapter VI).

In other words, classical antiquity now became the ideal moment of human history, in which the highest aspirations of mankind were realized. It became the supreme moment, in which men must seek clear and sure guidance to loftier achievements, in literature and the arts as well as in politics and war.

If it does not entirely supersede it (and some, Machiavelli for instance, maintain that it does), this supreme moment at least ranks equally with what mediaeval Christendom had regarded as the only supreme moment, namely the moment of Revelation; and in any event, granted that the latter takes precedence in ultramundane matters, it remains the 'only human pattern from which men can draw their inspiration'. This attitude is very different from that of the 'humanists' of the twelfth century.[1]

In the Middle Ages, classical antiquity was purely an ornament, a decorative fringe, a stylistic pattern. Now, it becomes a *pattern* of life. Hence also it is at last identified with the will to probe it, to understand it in itself and for itself in all its forms and aspects, quite apart from the fact that it may act as a useful dispensary of prescriptions or formulas for the use of wroters or preachers who are seeking examples and resounding phrases with which to dignify their writings or sermons. The fact that archaeology and philology in the modern sense date only from the Renaissance is in itself sufficient proof of the difference between the

---

[1] [On this twelfth-century practice of turning to Antiquity for isolated motifs and forms which could be made to serve a present purpose cf. the opinion of Liebeschütz, who asserts that the men of that age, unlike their Renaissance successors, never regarded 'das Ganze der Antike' as a medium of escape from the present, i.e. as an ideal that would inspire them to invent and create new forms of life (H. Liebeschütz, *Das zwölfte Jahrhundert und die Antike*, 'Archiv für Kulturgeschichte', XXXV, 1953, p. 271).]

two ages so far as their attitudes to antiquity are concerned.

It has been pointed out that the question here is one of approach, not one of material divergence (Faral, *Recherches sur les sources latines des contes et romans courtois du moyen âge*, Paris, 1913, p. viii); but in the history of the human spirit what matters is in fact 'how', not 'how much'.

'Realism' and 'Individualism' in the Middle Ages and the Renaissance

Similar considerations must be given to the problem of 'realism', as it is called, and 'individualism'.

We are urged to note that even mediaeval writers and artists observed living and corporeal reality with close attention, that even they, far from being perpetually absorbed in spiritual contemplation of God and the Saints, the Madonna and the Cherubim, knew how to portray, with an accuracy that was sometimes very crude, the incidents of everyday life, subjecting to scrutiny now the human body, whose anatomy they described with a wealth of detail, even if not yet with precision, now various aspects of nature, both smiling and horrible. We are urged to note that even they would willingly pause to describe the figures of the protagonists of history, sometimes, indeed, lingering unduly long over the portrayal of, let us say, Charlemagne or Henry IV.

Here too, indeed, we can readily perceive that the men of the Middle Ages knew how to observe with watchful eyes the reality that surrounded them, and that they loved to portray it in their writings. There are numberless examples of this. Think of the *Fabliaux*; think of the miracle plays themselves, into which realistic — I was about to say 'veristic' — detail is introduced readily and with great frequency; think of the chronicles, which abound in realistic details. See, for instance, how a lively and vivacious chronicler like Liutprand of Cremona describes the death of King Arnulf, whose body is gnawed by countless tiny worms which suddenly appear on every side in teeming multitudes, while the doctor stands impotently by (*Antapodosis*, Book I, Chapter 36). It is immaterial that he is echoing a Biblical story (from the Second Book of Maccabees), because even in this imitation he reveals a taste for the crudely realistic detail. Or consider Acerbo Morena's insistence on the exquisite hands and gleaming white teeth of Frederick Barbarossa and his consort Beatrix (*Historia Friderici I*, ed. Güterbock, p. 170); or the vignettes with which Friar Salimbene da Parma embellishes his chronicle—a beautiful Pisan garden in which graceful youths and girls sing and dance, rare animals from the East, monks who devour with great relish highly-seasoned capons, the strange garb of Friar Benedetto. Or again, to seek examples outside Italy, note how realistically Villehardouin describes the Crusaders' assault on Constantinople, and observe the fidelity of the Sire de Joinville's picture of Louis IX, King of France, dispensing justice in the shade of a great oak, or of his account of the death of his chaplain at Mansourah: 'Quant je vi que il vouloit cheoir, je, qui avoie ma cote vestue, sailli de mon lit tout deschaus....'

It would be hard to imagine anything more scrupulously realistic than the minute, accurate and colourful descriptions of human beings inspired by this material 'curiosity'. Indeed, mediaeval writers and artists often reveal a taste for the horrible and terrifying detail.

But this adherence to sensible reality remains, as always, emotional rather than intellectual in character; it is still instinctive rather than premeditated. Hence it is confined to the detail, the episode. If the detail is 'realistic', the general conception is not, inasmuch as the Prime Mover of life and of human history is located outside the world and the destinies of men are invariably determined by the will of God. The sensibility is 'human' and 'mundane'; but the spirit is nourished by an inner life whose centre lies outside the earthly city and carnal humanity.

A few examples will serve to clarify this statement. In no field, perhaps, is the profound difference between the two forms of 'realism' more immediately and easily perceived than in the field of historiography. The mediaeval chronicler

N

does indeed assemble vast quantities of realistic details, and he likes to paint every scene in vivid, flamboyant colours, delighting in a sort of 'photographic' naturalism. But afterwards, as from his eyrie he surveys the course of human fortunes, he sees the hand of God as the supreme and universal arbiter. The great Florentine historians of the Renaissance are far less inclined to cap their work with realistic flourishes. They prefer to create a comprehensive picture, continually sustained by a sense of human reality, of the will of those single individuals who, through their interests and passions, alone weave the pattern of universal history. Mediaeval realism is naturalistic and purely descriptive; it is made up of bits and pieces and, we may say, it lacks perspective; and the characteristic of the chronicler or of any mediaeval writer is just this accumulation and juxtaposition of minute details. Look, for example, at Acerbo Morena's description of Frederick Barbarossa, in which the writer lists in mechanical succession all the attributes, physical and moral, of the Emperor – his well-proportioned body, his reddish hair, his white teeth, his beautiful hands, his extreme bellicosity, his daring, his speed of movement, his eloquence, his passion for justice, his devotion to the laws. His qualities are listed one after the other, in such a way that we cannot form a clear and reliable opinion of the man as a whole. Note also how all historians ascribe the same qualities, at any rate the same moral qualities, to nearly all kings. Nothing could be more monotonous than an inspection of the gallery of 'portraits' painted by mediaeval historians. It can be subdivided into two distinct categories. On the one hand there are the good kings, conforming to the Augustinian and post-Augustinian pattern and tradition of the king who fears God, reveres the Church, protects the widows and the orphans, etc. On the other, there are the bad kings – violent, cruel, despising God, true personifications of the Antichrist on earth. There are the two types of the *rex iustus* and the *tyrannus*, described, as has been said already, by the Pseudo-Cyprian in the *De XII abusivis saeculis*. If, for instance, we examine the historiography of the age that witnessed the struggle of the Investitures we see how it is based entirely on this a-prioristic system (cf. G. Werdermann, *Heinrich IV, seine Anhänger und seine Gegner im Lichte der augustinischen und eschatologischen Geschichtsauffassung des Mittelalters*, Greifswald, 1918, pp. 9 *sqq.*).

On the other hand, the realism of historians like Machiavelli and Guicciardini is a 'conceptual' realism. It may even ignore the realism of a particular detail, it may be less 'photographic', precisely because the impressionistic clarity of an isolated detail is far less emphatic and important when it forms part of a picture completely dominated by a sense of human reality. It is enough to compare, for example, Eginhard's description of Charlemagne with Guicciardini's description of Clement VII in his *History of Italy*. The one strives to portray his protagonist by picking out one after the other the various aspects of his personality, the physical in particular (the minuteness with which Alginard describes the person and habiliments of Charlemagne is extraordinary!), but at the same time he is incapable of combining his separate observations into an organic whole. The other furnishes a precise, expert, powerful sketch of the Pontiff's personality, concentrating exclusively, be it noted, on his character and his spiritual and moral attributes, whereas the physical details are disregarded. Here, then, in a nutshell, is the historian whose conception of a series of events determined purely by human influences is perfectly expressed and epitomized by analysis of the characters and their motives. On the other hand, the mediaeval chronicler's representation of the physical traits of this or that prince is still purely superficial. It serves merely to adorn, to embellish an edifice that was built by another and far more sublime craftsman.

The realistic description of outward physical detail is undertaken by a Machiavelli or a Guicciardini, if at all, only inasmuch as it serves to complete the moral portrait of the man, in other words only inasmuch as it can furnish the writer with material which will help him to integrate his general assessment of the man's 'personality. Alginard, Liutprand of Cremona and the rest describe physical appearance and moral character without properly connecting the two. Here, on the other hand, is how Machiavelli portrays the Duke of Athens: 'This Duke, as his administration proved, was avaricious and cruel. He was wayward in audience, he was haughty in response. In others he looked for servility, not goodwill; and for this reason he desired to be feared rather than loved. Nor was his presence any less odious than his behaviour; for he was short and dark, with a long, sparse beard: so that, all in all, he deserved to be hated . . .' (*Florentine Histories*, Book II, Chap. XXXVII). Here the reference (a very fleeting one, incidentally) to the Duke's physical appearance – 'short and dark, with a long, sparse beard' – is only inserted inasmuch as, in the historian's opinion, it completes the moral picture of the man, who is, in a word, odious. We are very far from the attention to physical detail which characterizes Acerbo Morena's description of Frederick Barbarossa.

The distance that has been travelled in the period between the fourteenth and the beginning of the sixteenth centuries, in other words the difference between the 'realism' of the high Renaissance and that of a more primitive age, emerges with crystal clarity if we compare Villani's and Machiavelli's explanations of the civil strife in Florence. It should be noted that Machiavelli (in the second book of the *Florentine Histories*) uses Villani as the source from which he derives his information and his facts; but this lends all the more significance to the profound disparity that exists between the comments of the two authors.

It should also be observed that we have selected Villani as a term of comparison – a man, that is to say, who is a typical representative of the Florentine *bourgeoisie*, with his feet firmly planted on the ground; a representative of a calculating, practical *bourgeoisie*, which manages its own affairs with great efficiency, is concerned with harsh realities, eschews vain fancies and dreams, and certainly does not spend its

time singing psalms and beating its breast, a prey to the
terror inspired by its own sins; a man whose incipient
'modernity' has been praised because he bethinks himself in
his chronicles not only of political and military events but
also of economic factors, because he knows how to give due
weight, for example, to the creation of the golden florin, 'that
excellent coin, made of gold twenty-four carats fine'; a
chronicler who describes with great accuracy and much
realistic detail the dress worn by the Florentines in the good
old days: 'And they and their women dressed in thick
clothes, and many of the men wore leather jerkins with no
outer garments, and caps on their heads, and they all wore
long boots. And the Florentine women had shoes without
buckles, and the greatest among them wore very tight petti-
coats of thick scarlet material from Ipro and Camo, fastened
with old-fashioned belts, and minever-lined cloaks sur-
mounted by hoods with which they covered their heads . . .'
(Book VI, Chapter 69).

Yet this man is still so dominated by typically mediaeval
ideas and even superstitions that when he comes to survey
the general course of events his realistic grasp of detail
deserts him and we witness the re-appearance in human
history of God and the devil, who alone pull the strings that
control earthly affairs. Already Buondelmonte de' Buondel-
monti had, *subsidio diaboli*, broken the pledge he had given to
the daughter of the house of Amidei; already he had been
slain at the feet of the graven image of Mars, within whose
precincts the 'enemy of the human generation' was all-
powerful. The subsequent party struggles at Pistoia, like the
great rift between the Bianchi and the Neri in Florence, were
also due to the sins of men and the instigation of the devil:
'In consequence of their excessive wealth and the machinations of the devil, anger and enmity were stirred up among
them' (Book VIII, Chapter 38). 'At the time of which I
speak, when our city of Florence was greater and happier
than it had ever been . . . the sin of ingratitude and the
machinations of the enemy of the human generation trans-

formed the said wealth into a source of pride and corruption, (Book VIII, Chapter 39). As is logical, the writer's contemplation of the course of events culminates in a passionate moral appeal and the historian becomes a preacher: 'And let him who reads this note how, as a punishment for our sins, God caused and allowed our city to be visited ere long by all manner of tribulations – floods, famine, hunger, death, defeats, humiliating failures, loss of wealth and substance, bankruptcies among merchants and financial discredit – and finally has led us from freedom into bondage and subjection to tyrannical masters. And so, with God's aid, beloved citizens, present and future, let us correct our faults and foster in our midst love and charity, that we may please the most high God, and that we may not incur the extreme penalty of his wrath, which he reveals to us most clearly in His visible threats' (Book XII, Chapter 3).

This is the climax to which the mediaeval chronicler's descriptive realism has led him. So, at the decisive moment, when we are awaiting his 'interpretation' of history, that sense of human 'individuality', which had seemed to exist when he was describing the outward appearance of individual men or the idle conversation and multifarious activity of a crowd, comes to nothing.

With Machiavelli, on the other hand, there is no further intervention on the part of God or the devil, the Saints or the 'enemy of the human generation'. Everything is determined by human agencies – by the conflicting appetites of the *Grandi* and the people or, again, by the 'restless spirit' of Messer Corso Donati. Everything is reduced to a purely worldly level. There is no interference from the other world – unless it be a sort of natural, almost mechanical fatality, a note of naturalistic determinism which has nothing to do with the Christian conception of history as expressed by men like St. Augustine and Otto of Freisingen. Note this comment: 'Because of his conduct, or else because it comes *naturally* to the Florentines to dislike any state of being and to be divided by any happening.' (*Florentine Histories*, Book

II, Chapter XXV). Compare this with Villani's lament when he tells 'how, *as a punishment for our sins,* God caused and allowed our city to be visited ere long by all manner of tribulations'. Or again, observe how Machiavelli regards the 'sins' which led to Italy's political ruin not as moral sins, as Friar Gerolamo Savonarola had proclaimed them to be, but as purely political sins, the 'sins' of princes (*The Prince,* Chapter XII), and you will have the exact measure of 'realism' as it was envisaged at the height of the Renaissance.[1]

We shall be led to similar conclusions if we analyse the 'realism' of mediaeval political thought in the light of the realism of a Machiavelli or a Guicciardini. The political writers of the Middle Ages had undoubtedly been concerned to discover and to call attention to rules that were applicable to everyday life, rules that could be put into practice and might prove 'useful'. Note, for instance, how St. Thomas concerns himself with the actual site on which a city should be built, the salubrity of the air, etc. (*De Regimine Principum,* Book II, Chapter 2).

But sensible and practical observations of this kind are quite unrelated to the realism of Machiavelli, who regards politics as something in which considerations of good and evil, of right and wrong, have no part, and does not permit the State to be embarrassed by any preconceptions or aspirations of an ethical or religious character! And just as other literary men and artists of the Renaissance have clearly perceived how utterly different their world is from the world that preceded it, so too Machiavelli is fully aware of its essential, formidable 'novelty'. He says so in the plainest terms in Chapter XV of *The Prince* – a chapter which, as has been justly observed, makes us genuinely feel as if we were entering a new world. 'But since it is my purpose to write

[1] [Cf. the parallel recently drawn between the Chronicles of Utrecht (1481–3) and Machiavelli's *Florentine Histories* by H. Schulte Nordholt, *Het Beeld der Renaissance,* Amsterdam, 1948, pp. 157 *sqq.* A similar comparison might be made between the 'realism' of, for example, Froissart or Chastellain on the one hand and that of a Machiavelli or a Guicciardini on the other.]

what may be useful to those who need it, I have thought it more fitting to concern myself with the effective reality of things than with speculation. For many have imagined republics and principates which have never been seen or known to exist in reality.' The man who seeks to discover this 'effective reality' will confine himself to *living* and *being*, without troubling about 'how one ought to live', that is to say *how things should be*; and his attitude will reflect exactly that of the historian, who, finding that men and their passions condition his life, seeks in them the immediate 'causes' of events and refrains from asking a supernatural Will to explain the ultimate reason for things.

Finally, we are led to precisely the same conclusions when we come to consider art and its manifestations. Here too there is a difference between naturalistic detail and comprehensive inspiration, between the 'sensibility's' adherence to nature and to worldly life and the mystical afflatus from which the 'faith' of the artist springs. The mediaeval craftsman creates for the glory of God and seeks to imbue his work with a moral significance, no more and no less than does the chronicler whose purpose in his writings is to exhort men to despise the uncertain and transient things of the world and to eschew pride, or the poet to whom the true and positive virtue of his work consists in its allegorical meaning. He creates – as we read in the 'title' of a mosaic in the Church of SS. Cosma and Damiano in Rome – to the end that 'the fair house of God may be resplendent with brilliant metals, so that the precious light of faith may shine more brightly'. Here are the rules which Theophilus (twelfth century) prescribes for the artist in his treatise *Schedula diversarum artium*: 'Do not hesitate, my beloved son, believe with a whole faith that the spirit of God has filled thy heart when thou hast adorned His house with so much richness and variety of ornamentation; and that thou mayest not fear, I will show thee with clear proof that whatever thou mayest study, comprehend or contemplate in art is a gift graciously bestowed upon thee by the Spirit in its seven forms. Through the spirit of wisdom, thou knowest that all created things proceed from God, that without Him there is nothing . . . Spurred on by the promise of these virtues, beloved son, thou hast trustingly entered the house of God and hast beauteously adorned it . . . thou hast revealed to the eyes of the faithful a sort of divine paradise, bright with all manner of flowers, verdant with herbs and leaves, wherewith thou hast exalted the spirits of the Saints according to their deserts; and thou hast succeeded in glorifying the Creator in His Creature, in causing God to be admired in His works' (in L. Venturi, *Il gusto dei primitivi*, Bologna, 1926, pp. 50 and 52–3).

The glorification of the Creator – that is the aim of the mediaeval artist; and as for the verdant herbs and the bright flowers, in other words the so-called realistic detail, what purpose have they if not to stir the souls of the faithful by revealing to them a sort of *paradise of God?* This is the theme that reverberates through the writing of St. Francis of Assisi when he glorifies and praises the things of the world, the creature and nature, in which all things bear witness to God and His omnipotence.

On the other hand, the fifteenth-century artist, who is if anything over-conscious of the intrinsic merit of his work, and is convinced that man is capable, unaided, of any miracle, will strive only, according to the precept of Alberti, to ascertain the truth and, on a foundation of precise knowledge, to create a 'beautiful', immortal work that will lead men to glorify his name. Let us specifically compare Alberti with Theophilus. Nothing is further from Alberti's purpose to cause God to be admired in His creatures! 'The object of painting,' he says, is 'to earn favour and goodwill and praise' – in other words, the glorification of the painter, whose function is 'to represent in line and colour, on a given canvas or wall, a likeness of the visible surfaces of some object, in such a way that the same, when viewed at a certain distance and from a certain position, may appear in perspective and closely resemble the original in shape' (*Della Pittura*, Book

II, in *Opere Volgari*, ed. Bonucci, IV, p. 73). In other words, the artist should imitate nature *per se*, not inasmuch as it mirrors the power of God, but inasmuch as it alone can furnish him with happy inspiration. He should imitate it scientifically and exactly – hence he needs to be a man of learning. He must have a perfect knowledge of draughtsmanship. His knowledge of anatomy must be good, his knowledge of perspective very good. We are on the road that leads to Leonardo da Vinci; and we are already witnessing the complete liberation of the artist from every restriction that is not dictated by artistic reason. Henceforth he will be left alone with himself and his dreams; for him the world will become a synthesis of lines and volumes and colours. As has been well said, long before Machiavelli created the hero of politics the world had acclaimed the hero of art, a personage blind to every form of life save that of his own artistic imagination (Venturi, *op. cit.*, p. 101).

And herein lies indeed the essential novelty of the Renaissance. As in art and literature, so in political theory and historiography, its so-called 'realism and individualism', by means of a continuous process initiated by Alberti, carried on by Machiavelli and Ariosto, and brought to its logical conclusion by Galileo, lead to the affirmation of the complete autonomy of art, politics, science and history. In other words, they lead to the abandonment of the typically mediaeval conception of the world according to which no branch of human activity could be considered independently of its relationship to life as a whole. The answer to allegory is the well-known precept of 'art for art's sake'. The two worlds are essentially different.

Art for art's sake, politics for politics' sake, and even, ultimately, science for science's sake – the results of Italian thought might well be summarized in these phrases. Bartolo of Sassoferrato had applied to States the formula *superiorem non recognoscentes* as an indication of their full autonomy; and this formula could very well be applied to forms of cultural activity during the Renaissance. From which it follows that realism, individualism, love of glory and the imitation of ancient culture, which admittedly were sanctioned by the mediaeval world, but only as incidentals serving a loftier purpose, are now freely proposed as ends in themselves.

Lack of Coherence and Symmetry in the Renaissance Conception of the World

This is not intended to imply, however, that the men of the Renaissance made equally original contributions to every sphere of thought, nor that they had an organic, comprehensive conception of the world which could be substituted, immediately and finally, for the previous one.

In certain branches of human activity – for instance, in economic life – definite traces could even now be found of the survival of ancient traditions and ideas. Usually the age of the Renaissance is thought of as that which saw the birth of the capitalist spirit. Yet if the manner in which business was conducted was already seemingly capitalistic, if the financial and commercial structure of Italian economy at least already bore the capitalist stamp, the souls of big business-men continued in fact to be oppressed by cares of a kind unknown to the capitalist of the modern age. It is symptomatic that at a certain moment in their lives, especially – as is logical! – when they were on the point of death, many merchants and financiers were assailed by unexpected qualms of conscience which compelled them to confess their guilt in public and to return, in one form or another, part of their ill-gotten gains. But even more symptomatic is the misgiving which in the second half of the fifteenth century assailed Alessandra Macinghi Strozzi, mother and mother-in-law of merchants and financiers, and hence a woman well-versed in the ways of business, and also Marco Parenti, a silk-merchant who was at the same time a friend of humanists like Cristoforo Landino, Marsilio Ficino, etc. Alessandra Macinghi Strozzi and Marco Parenti (and the year is 1466) consider that it is improper, and indeed *sinful*, to sell Monte di Firenze bonds when their market-price has soared so that they may later redeem them if they happen to depreciate. They regard as *sinful* (and the expression should be noted, for the criticism it implies is no longer economic in character, but purely and simply moral!) what in the modern world has become a normal practice which no one would dream now of condemning! (*Lettere di Alessandra Macinghi Strozzi*, ed. Guasti, Florence, 1877, pp. 573–4.)

Thus in the fifteenth century we are confronted with the survival of a moralistic attitude to economic life which had previously characterized the society depicted by Villani. Villani himself – a merchant and a man of sound practical experience, prompt to celebrate a particular economic event such as the creation of the golden florin – had subsequently been unable, once he had stopped to consider and appraise economic practice in general, to justify his own actions, and had instead allowed himself to be restrained by those very scruples about commerce and finance which the mediaeval mind had fostered as a matter of principle! He who extols Florence, 'worthy daughter and creature of Rome', he who celebrates the creation of the golden florin and the opulence of his city, now condemns the luxurious life of the rich, which breeds 'softness', while 'simple living and poverty' promote 'good faith and goodness among them and within their Commune' (Book VI, Chapter 69). Again, at the very moment when he is saluting with heart-felt satisfaction the greatness of Florence and rejoicing in its mansions and villas, which provide a 'magnificent spectacle', he is newly and unexpectedly assailed, albeit only for an instant, by a sort of remorse, by the pangs of a conscience that has been suddenly recalled to a sense of Christian humility: '. . . there was not a citizen, from the highest to the lowest, who had not built or was not building his own large and palatial country property, a sumptuous habitation with beautiful buildings, better by far than those in the city. And in this all *sinned*, and by reason of their extravagance were deemed mad' (Book XI, Chapter 94).

Sinned – once again we have a moral stricture on life as it is expressed in action. It is the same expression that will recur to the lips of Alessandra Macinghi Strozzi, an expression that makes us think again of the traditional sins – the sensuality, pride and avarice of Augustinian and Dantesque memory – just as we are reminded of the deadly sins of mediaeval imagination by Villani's stricture on the Peruzzi, in whose banking operations he himself had played an active part: 'Lust for gain expressed in a mad scramble for possessions' (Book XI, Chapter 88). In Villani's thinking, as in that of Donna Alessandra, traces persist of a theoretical aversion to all wealth save the fruits of the earth and of husbandry. This aversion was deep-rooted in the Middle Ages. It was based ideally on the Aristotelian precept that money in itself is valueless, and morally on the verse in St. Luke's Gospel: *Mutuum date nihil inde sperantes.*

In the historical and political sphere Machiavelli replaces the God and devil of Villani with man and man alone. But in the sphere of economic thought nothing happens – until the triumph of Calvinism – to change the old attitude, to sweep away men's scruples and perplexities regarding the problem of wealth. And the logical conclusion is reached in 1532, when the Spanish merchants of Antwerp enquired from the Sorbonne whether or not their activities are morally justifiable!

Apart from everything else, this is another very significant example of the profound divergence which, as has already been said, can exist between concrete reality and the life of the mind, between action and its conceptual systematization. The men of the Renaissance, like their mediaeval predecessors, loved wealth, transacted business – and on what a scale! – and built up great concerns on solid foundations. But in their hearts, when they came to consider the great problems of life and death, of earthly activity and the Unknown, they always perceived that there was, to put it mildly, something shady about their conduct. And then they would rush back into the arms of their confessors, seeking forgiveness for that which over so many years had constituted their whole life.

To Alberti's maxim 'art for art's sake', to Machiavelli's theory of 'politics for politics' sake', there is certainly no corresponding affirmation of principle that can be expressed in the phrase 'economic activity for economic activity's sake', or that can be said to contain even the germ of that principle of 'production for production's sake' or 'making for making's sake' which is characteristic of modern capitalism and which has been so explicitly formulated in the writings of Henry Ford.

But this is not all. When the question arises of fusing the various forms of life into a comprehensive organic unity, then it is that the tone becomes far less certain and the thread is lost.

The excellence of man was extolled all through the fifteenth century. Everyone, from Giannozzo Manetti to Pico della Mirandola, had a little to say about the *dignitas hominis*, while the study of the various aspects and laws of nature was being steadily intensified, especially by artists and art-critics, who adhered rigorously to the principle of 'the imitation of nature' (the Ancients were their preceptors, for the precise reason that they had been able to apprehend and reproduce nature). But the more clearly nature is seen in its fullness, as an organic force with its own laws (and not merely as a spectacle rendered agreeable by the greenness of the meadows and the beauties of the house of God), the more pressing becomes the problem of how to reconcile this force with the freedom and excellence of man – and also the problem of how to reconcile man and nature with the divine Will, with the omnipotence of that Providence whose power no one dreams of denying. This latter problem is all the more harassing in that the moral world is always closely bound up with the religious world. Art and politics have at last ceased entirely to serve a supernatural purpose; but ethics have not. The idea of a purely rational ethic, universal in its application and not subject to the dictates of religion – an ethic which (as Hugo Grotius subsequently maintained in the case of natural law) would continue to stand on its solid rational foundation even if, to take an absurd hypothesis, God did not exist – such an idea has not yet been dreamed of. The conception of 'how things ought to be' is always closely bound up with the idea of the beyond and the divine ordinances. Its necessary premises and corollaries are the ideas of sin and eternal punishment or eternal bliss.

In their respective fields Alberti and Machiavelli have treated the question of 'being' with the utmost realism; but the question of 'how things ought to be', even if they consider it at all, is still always bound up with religious precept. The world of morality and the world of religion are one. Ethics finally merges into theology.

Far from having been disposed of, the thorny problem of religion continues to agitate men's minds. Indeed, it reappears in an even more emphatic form at the end of the fifteenth century by reason of the fact that the Italian soul has been plunged into gloom by the tragic happenings of which the peninsula has been the scene. The need to justify the world and existence, nature and creature, will and fortune, and to hold fast to a moral law which seemingly can spring from no other source, brings man back to the idea of God – a transcendent God Who is the Lord of humanity.

How, then, is it possible to reconcile all these divergent forces – man, nature and God? The answer is never clear. Instead, we are confronted with a vacillation between one or the other of the terms of the problem, or with the intrusion of ambiguous notions like that of Fortune (a word that constantly recurs in the writings of the fifteenth and sixteenth centuries). 'Fortune' is very hard to define. At one moment, in conformity with the Christian adaptation of the ancient concept, it appears in the guise of an *ancilla Dei*. At another, it resumes its ancient character of a blind, uncontrollable fate. Now it becomes a magic influence radiating from the stars, now the natural consequence of preceding events, though it always defies precise analysis. And we find phrases and similes of a naturalistic or positively medical character creeping into political treatises and histories. This is notably the case with Machiavelli. In order to describe the State, which he regards as a creation of the human will, he is for ever racking his brains for expressions which liken it to a plant, complete with roots, or for similes in which its development is compared to the development of life in a human body — so much so that he comes to adopt a naturalistic view of the State itself, attributing to it alternative modes of development, birth, growth and death, exactly as if it were one of the phenomena of nature. Down to the last detail the State is 'human', in the sense that it is a progressive, laborious achievement of man's will. It is, in fact, with the object of guiding this will that Machiavelli writes his books. But when seen against the changing background of the years, when viewed from a distance, even this human accomplishment seems to go through a fatal process of petrifaction, which the human will can delay or check, but cannot wholly prevent. And so we have the proem to Book III of the *Discourses on the First Ten Books of Titus Livy* and a rapid description of the changeless course which all States follow.

Thus rational humanity and deterministic naturalism are linked together at every turn; and over them there presides a divine Providence. This Providence is certainly endowed by some thinkers with somewhat novel characteristics. It is different from the Providence of Dante and Petrarch. Already it embodies some of those purely rationalistic conceptions which were developed some two centuries later, albeit in quite a different way, by the English deists; yet in spite of everything it still transcends mortal man. Right at the end of the fifteenth century, beneath the preoccupations of the Florentine neo-Platonists, with their attempts to combine religion with philosophy and their mystical-religious syncretism, we discern once again, more clearly than before, a yearning to escape from the purely mundane sphere. From this point of view the movement initiated by Savonarola is not a mere anachronism; nor should we dismiss as a mere incident either the friendship which Pico della Mirandola, prince of Florentine philosophers and extoller of the 'dignity' of man, conceived for the reformer, or, again, the characteristic last phase of the art of Botticelli.

The moment of transition from the mentality which appraises each aspect of life separately to that which sees life as a whole, to an organically unitarian vision of the world, in short, to a system that can replace, wholly and completely, the disputed theological system of the schoolmen – this is the moment of crisis for Renaissance thought. Each of the aspects of life is self-contained; and the consequence is an unresolved dramatic conflict. It is enough to mention the problem raised by Machiavelli – the problem, that is, of the relationship between politics and ethics. This problem had remained outside the purview of the Florentine secretary, whose life was in very truth motivated by his political feeling, which burst forth with the impetuosity of a force of nature, of an underground spring that suddenly finds an outlet, expressing itself with a directness, a vivacity and, we might say, a natural innocence that have had no parallel in the whole of modern history. But it soon presented itself to his contemporaries and followers – the more obtrusively in that it had been so far from the thoughts of Machiavelli himself. Thus we find them grappling long and painfully with the question implicit in the phrase *raison d'état*, for the precise reason that Renaissance thought, having unlocked the door to various branches of human activity, was subsequently unable to redintegrate them, in spite of the fact that human nature is constantly tormented by its need for a comprehensive vision.

The Ideal of the 'Pattern' and the 'Revival': Its Decline and the End of the Renaissance

But there is yet another observation to be made regarding the 'modernity' of the Renaissance.

As has been said, to the men of the fourteenth and fifteenth centuries classical antiquity was an idea-force, an

o

energizing myth, the myth-exemplar of which they, like every generation of men possessed of lofty aspirations and the vibrant strength of youth, stood in need. They did not wish to 'imitate' antiquity slavishly, in the sense of reproducing it down to the smallest detail. They wanted to 'imitate' it in the sense of following its example and by that means to achieve a fuller life, richer in culture and beauty. But it is in what has been regarded as a typical expression of the Renaissance that the *forma mentis* of the men of the fourteenth and fifteenth centuries reveals one of those essential characteristics which make it resemble the mentality of the Christian Middle Ages. The resemblance is not due to the fact that similar aspirations after a *renovatio Romae* had already found expression in the past — not, that is, to the existence of any supposed precedents of a specific kind, determinable in space and time. It springs from a basic attitude of the human spirit towards history and its processes. Faith in the possibility of a 'revival' (using the term in the same sense as before) in any field, from that of religion to those of politics and art, in fact presupposes a firm conviction that, at a clearly-defined moment in human history, the religious, artistic or political ideal has been achieved, and that Truth has been revealed. Men take what has happened in the past as a pattern only when they are convinced in their inmost hearts that it represents perfection (whether such perfection is absolute or relative to the state of mankind does not now matter). Thus we find ourselves confronted with an attitude that is typical of the religious mentality in general and of the mentality of Christians in particular, to whom Truth had revealed itself at a precise moment in history, which accordingly embodies *in nuce* the whole of human history and all the possibilities of development open to men, both as individuals and in the mass. This attitude constitutes a most notable element of the mediaeval spirit, which was ever tormented by a longing for a 'return' to the primitive Church and for a 'revival' of evangelical poverty and purity. The heretical movements, with their particular brand of radicalism, had sought to impose this ideal on a Church whose dogma had been evolved in the course of centuries. Those movements which had remained within the limits of orthodoxy had confined themselves to proposing it as a pattern of Christian life. In one way or another, however, it had always constituted a guiding principle of religious thought.

It was in this communal Italy, in which the seeds of the Renaissance had been ripening, that an appeal for the revival of the primitive Church by means of a return to moral purity, poverty and humility had been made to the multitude in more vehement and insistent terms than ever before. Milanese Patarians, Arnaldians and Waldensians on the one hand, St. Francis of Assisi on the other, had focused the attention of the masses on the ideal, and a yearning for a religious revival had been one of the essential concomitants of the rise of the free communes (think of Milan in the second half of the eleventh century!). But if the 'myth' subsequently lost its religious character, assuming instead a purely human significance, the tendency to regard the ideal to which mankind aspired as having been realized during a specific period of past history nevertheless remained unaltered. Men retained a firm belief not only in the 'pattern' itself but in their ability to conform to the pattern once more by modifying their principles of life and action, their doctrines and ideas – in short, by rejecting the immediate past, which was regarded by Renaissance *littérateurs* and artists in exactly the same way as it had once been regarded by Cistercian reformers, Patarians, etc. – to wit, as a period of aberration and decadence.[1]

Just as the humanists' almost mystical expectation of the coming of the new *humanitas* reveals a close spiritual affinity with the eschatological expectation of the coming of the Kingdom of God, so belief in the 'pattern' betrays an affinity

---

[1] [On this Renaissance tendency to retrospection, this 'ferveur d'espérance tournée vers le passé', cf. A. Dupront, *Espace et humanisme*, 'Bibliothèque d'Humanisme et Renaissance', VIII (1946), pp. 9 *sqq.*]

with belief in revealed Truth; and the idea of 'making a fresh start' (*ridursi al segno*), of 'reverting to first principles' (*ritorno ai principii*) which Machiavelli advocates as essential for the conduct of States is a principle common to the Renaissance. It is wholly symptomatic that Machiavelli himself, in proclaiming his theory of 'revival', invokes the example 'of our religion, which, if it had not been taken back to its origins by St. Francis and St. Dominic, would be completely extinct . . .' (*Discourses on the First Ten Books of T. Livius*, III, i). Thus he too, most secular of thinkers, reverts to an attitude of mind which a century and a half before, as we have already seen, had conjured up in the fancy of the 'religious' Cola di Rienzo, alongside the image of himself as the saviour of the Empire, the pattern-image of St. Francis as the man who had checked the decline of the Church '. . . sicut alias ruenti Romane Ecclesie per Franciscum . . .' (cf. above, p. 169).

There follows from this, among other things, the logical consequence that the period in question reveals little or no trace of the concept of progress, and that historical and political conceptions continue instead to be based on the axioms that human nature remains constant throughout the centuries, that human history repeats itself in cycles, and that civilizations arise, prosper, become 'corrupt', and are 'revived' thanks to the virtues of reformers and a reversion to first principles.[1]

This constitutes the strongest link between the Renaissance and the Middle Ages, between the 'profane' mentality

---

[1] [Weisinger, in maintaining that the idea of progress is one of the six fundamental ideas of the Renaissance, cites in support of his thesis authors such as Le Roy, who belong to the second half of the Cinquecento, live in an intellectual climate vastly different from that of the fifteenth and early sixteenth centuries, and are already exposed to the influence of the great inventions and geographical discoveries of the period (*Ideas of History during the Renaissance*, 'Journal of the History of Ideas', VI, 1945, pp. 415 *sqq.*). And he himself points out that this idea, together with the controversy to which it gave rise, belongs to the late Renaissance, i.e. to the second half of the sixteenth century. I venture to add that for this very reason it cannot possibly contribute to our understanding of the Italian Renaissance.]

and the 'religious' mentality, just as it constitutes the indissoluble link between the Renaissance and the Reformation. To be sure, the latter seeks to re-establish the reign of God, not the reign of *humanitas* – and in this respect the gulf between them could not be more apparent. But the Renaissance and the Reformation alike represent a belief in the possibility of revival. Each concentrates on a remote pattern in the hope of deriving from it an impulse towards the future, towards the imminent *novus ordo*. Both reflect essentially the same mental attitude – an attitude which, in short, springs from a single source: the mediaeval mentality. If in some figures, both in Italy and elsewhere (Petrarch and Erasmus), the two aspirations – for the revival of *humanitas* and the revival of *christianitas* – are still seen to be closely interconnected, for the most part they have diverged and have come to be identified with two different and even conflicting movements; but underlying everything there is still a mode of thought and intuitive perception which has universal and exceedingly deep roots, and which will disappear only slowly, very slowly. Even the writers of the Enlightened Age – who initiate the dissolution by repudiating the myth of the ancient pattern – with their concept of limited progress and their joyous eagerness to reach the threshold of the Kingdom (no longer the Kingdom of God, but the Kingdom of Reason), still remain faithful to the eschatological mentality, which had been handed down through sixteen centuries of history and was destined to survive until the advent of nineteenth-century historicism.

Yet even as this spiritual attitude is being newly affirmed in the religious field through the Reformation, it is disappearing during the last phase of the Renaissance in Italy, where a definite reaction is setting in against the acceptance of 'antiquity' as a pattern and a standard. This reaction is far more fundamental and continuous than the sporadic protests, which can be discerned even in the fifteenth century, against the excessive idolization of the Ancients (see, for example, Benedetto Accolti's defence of the 'moderns' in Garin, *op. cit.*, pp. 85 *sqq.*; and cf. also Alberti's eulogy of the moderns in the dedication to Brunelleschi which prefaces his treatise *Della Pittura*).

The contrast between the two mentalities – that which still believes in the possibility of 'revival' and yet concentrates on classical or, to be specific, Roman antiquity as representing the perfect moment of human history, and that which, by contrast, rejects the idea of 'patterns', and simply postulates a knowledge of present reality, which is self-contained, differs from the historical realities of the past, and therefore cannot be disciplined and controlled in the light of their example – finds its chief expression at this time in the contrast between Machiavelli and Guicciardini. The latter, in denying the significance of the historical 'example' and declaring that those who at every step adduce the example of the Romans are deceiving themselves, illustrates the passing not only of the humanistic mentality – in the restricted sense of the epithet – but of the Renaissance mentality itself. In this, more than in anything else, lies the great historical importance of the contrast between the two figures, of whom the one is fascinated by the mirage of ancient Rome, while the other is concerned solely with the reality of the present, and does not look back at what has been and will never return.

The answer to the *Discourses on the First Ten Books of Titus Livius* is provided by the *Reflections on the Discourses of Machiavelli* and the *Ricordi*. Throughout the remaining years of the century political writers emphasize the parallel between Rome and Venice – in other words, the political parallel between the Ancients and the Moderns. And the result is certainly not to the disadvantage of the latter.

This trend is intimately bound up with a marked decline in creative power, with the evaporation of great hopes and of the will to action – in short, with that enfeeblement of the Italian spirit which characterizes the post-Machiavellian era and the moral crisis which besets the Italy of the first half

of the sixteenth century. As proof of this it is enough to compare Machiavelli, who used the example of the Romans as a
means of continually reviving his enthusiasms and his
dreams of the redintegration of Italian political life, with
Guicciardini, who, if he preached 'discretion' and attached
little importance to example, at the same time renounced his
fellow-citizen's grandiose dreams and shut himself up in his
ivory tower of disillusionment and bitterness. The 'myth' of
the Romans died simultaneously with the complementary
myth of a revival, of a new golden age; and this, incidentally,
suffices to show how, in the Italy of the fourteenth and fifteenth centuries, the myth of classical antiquity had been the
expression of a vigorous inner life, and not a mere excre-
scence, not the hobby-horse of a clique of scholars.

At the start, then, this eclipse of the ancient ideal is intimately bound up with a moral decline in the generations
which find themselves faced with the collapse of the political
power of the Italian States and see in prospect certainly not
an Augustan age but a 'wretched and unhappy era' (Varchi,
Storia Fiorentina, Book XVI, Milan, 1845, II, p. 423), a
'century of iron', in which men can only bewail 'the heart-
lessness of the times' (Giovio, *Istorie*, translated by Domeni-
chi, Venice, 1564, II, p. 269, Book XXXI); outside Italy,
moreover, the reaction against the doctrine of the perfection and superiority of the Ancients is fostered by the
reaction of self-conscious nationalism against the Italian
humanists, who usually regard other peoples with contempt.
Subsequently, however, with the dawning of the baroque
age, factors of a more general nature play their part in estab-
lishing on a firmer footing the parallel between the Ancients
and the Moderns and in exploding the myth of former days.

There is, on the one hand, the admiration aroused by the
new inventions, above all printing, and by the use of artillery.
There is the influence which is beginning to be exerted on
the *forma mentis* of mankind by the sciences, in which reliance
on Pliny and the other authorities is beginning to be superseded, especially in the field of everyday, unacademic science,

by reliance on 'experience', the mother of knowledge. Above all, there is the influence of an event whose impact on economic life has been the subject of much study and discussion, but whose repercussions in the spiritual sphere have received too little notice. I refer to the discovery of America and the new lands, which one writer does not hesitate to describe as the 'mayor cosa después de la creación del mundo' (F. López de Gómara, *Historia general de las Indias*, in *Historiadores primitivos de India* (*Bibl. de Aut. Españoles*), I, Madrid, 1874, p. 156), the 'greatest and most wonderful' event since the preaching of the Apostles (Botero, *Relazioni Universali*, Part IV, Book II). The vast expansion of the physical horizon, which gives the men of the sixteenth century the proud distinction of knowing more than any of their predecessors; 'the infinite marvels not known to the Ancients' (Varchi, *Lezioni sul Dante e prose varie*, I, Florence, 1841, p. 145), which invalidate many opinions bequeathed by antiquity and hitherto accepted as gospel truth – all these things shatter the doctrine of the superiority of the Ancients and instead spread the conviction that if the latter excelled in art, literature and philosophy, the Moderns can nevertheless lay claim to a superiority of their own, no less effective and no less conspicuous.

Nor are Europeans alone in their ability to stand comparison with the Ancients. Indeed, people are beginning to mention in the same breath the great public works of the Romans and the roads built by the Incas of Peru, the Pantheon and other Roman edifices and the temples which are to be found in India and on the coast of East Africa, even the laws and ordinances of the Romans and those of the newly-discovered peoples; sometimes, indeed, the comparison is unfavourable to Rome. If the two great roads built by the Incas of Peru are to be 'preferred to those of Egypt and of Rome' (Botero, *Relazioni Universali*, Part I, Vol. II, Book III), the laws of the Incas concerning the distribution of land seem 'far' superior both to 'the territorial dispensations of Lycurgus and the agrarian laws of the Romans' (*id.*, *ib.*, Part II, Book IV), while the language of the peoples of Mechoacan seems preferable (what an assertion!) to Latin (*id.*, *ib.*, Part I, Vol. II, Book II). The 'myth' concerning China, so dear to eighteenth-century enlightenment, begins to take shape – China, that paragon of organization, than which 'no kingdom or dominion, ancient or modern, has ever been better ordered' (*id.*, *ib.*, Part II, Book II). This leads to the complete transformation of one of the most characteristic concepts of the Renaissance, which in this matter had completely embraced the Greco-Roman tradition. I refer to the concept of 'barbarian'. In the fourteenth and fifteenth centuries this term had been used to indicate those who lived outside the bounds of a clearly-defined civilization, that of Italy and the Humanists. Now, on the other hand, it is used to designate only those who live outside the realm of 'right reason'; hence it is invested with a purely rational significance, no longer determined and established on a historical basis (Botero, *Relazioni Universali*, Part IV, Book III).[1]

This fundamental change of attitude finds its supreme expression outside Italy, to wit, in the writings of Montaigne, who not only ridicules the traditional distinction between 'barbarian' and 'non-barbarian' ('chacun appelle barbarie ce qui n'est pas de son usage', *Essais*, I, 31), but even goes so far as to place the so-called 'savage' races on a higher plane than those normally regarded as 'civilized' (*ib.*), asserting that the former are closer to 'nature' and that 'ce que nous voyons par experience en ces nations là [i.e. the peoples of America], surpasse, non seulement toutes les peintures dequoy la poësie a embelly l'age doré . . . mais encore la conception et le desir mesme de la philosophie' (*ib.*).

But even in Italy itself this revolutionary doctrine has its adherents. Thus, Campanella refers to the greatness of 'this

[1] [The first four parts of the *Relazioni Universali* were published in Rome between 1591 and 1596. The fifth part remained unpublished till 1895. Quotations are from the Turin edition of 1601. Cf. my *Giovanni Botero*, Rome, 1934, pp. 74-80.]

age of ours, which has more history in a hundred years than the world had in four thousand'.[1] Such ideas undermine the concept of the 'pattern' and 'revival' and pave the way for the ultimate triumph of the Moderns – a triumph which, however, will only be confirmed in the eighteenth century, after the *querelle*, and will determine the realization of the concept of progress. This represents a profound revolution in the mentality both of the Renaissance and of the Reformation, facilitated in the last analysis, to some extent at least, by the Catholic Counter-Reformation, which upholds the value of tradition, in other words of history, as against the bibliolatry of the reformers, that is, against the myth of 'the single moment of Truth'.

[1] [In the Italian text of this article, I referred at this point to Giordano Bruno, and to the interpretation of a passage from the *Cena delle ceneri* given by Gentile, *Il pensiero italiano del Rinascimento*, 3rd ed., Florence, 1940, p. 337 *sqq.* But against the thesis of Gentile, see now E. Garin, *Medioevo e Rinascimento*, Bari, 1954, p. 195 *sqq.*]

BIBLIOGRAPHY

The following list does not purport to be a complete bibliography even of the most recent studies of the Renaissance. It should be regarded, more simply, as a preliminary, short guide firstly to the discussions that have taken place in recent decades about the actual concept and the so-called 'problem' of the Renaissance, and secondly to the multifarious writings and researches specifically devoted to the latter's most noteworthy aspects.

I would, however, warn the reader that, just as the theme of the preceding essay is the Renaissance as manifested in the country of its origin, so too this bibliography is confined to works and discussions on the subject of *Italian* Humanism and the *Italian* Renaissance, except in certain cases where the very nature of the discussion calls for an appraisal of non-Italian problems and trends of thought.

I

I

The history of the concept of the Renaissance, of its formation and its evolution under the influence of successive schools of thought, has been the subject of particularly intensive study during the first half of the present century. Indeed, it forms an important chapter of historiography, one that is to-day of vital interest to all who propose to make a special study of this or that aspect of the Renaissance.

The question was first examined by German scholars in the following essays: W. GOETZ, *Mittelalter und Renaissance*, 'Historische Zeitschrift', XCVIII (1907), reproduced in *Italien im Mittelalter*, Leipzig, 1942, II; K. BRANDI, *Das*

Werden der Renaissance, Göttingen, 1908 (2nd ed., 1910; now in BRANDI, *Ausgewählte Aufsätze*, Oldenburg-Berlin, 1938); A. PHILIPPI, *Der Begriff der Renaissance*, Leipzig, 1912; W. WEISBACH, *Renaissance als Stilbegriff*, 'Historische Zeitschrift', CXX (1919); and, most important of all, K. BORINSKI, *Die Weltwiedergeburtsidee in den neueren Zeiten*, I, *Der Streit um die Renaissance und die Entstehungsgeschichte der historischen Beziehungsbegriffe Renaissance und Mittelalter*, 'Sitzungsberichte der bayerischen Akademie der Wissenschaften, Phil.-phil. u. hist. Klasse', 1919.

Since then hundreds of articles and essays have appeared, having as their theme the 'problem' of the Renaissance, but necessarily touching also upon the question of the historical origin and evolution of the 'concept' of the Renaissance. Here too I shall content myself with mentioning those which are more specifically devoted to the history of the movement, viz. the excellent essay of D. CANTIMORI, *Sulla storia del concetto di Rinascimento*, 'Annali della R. Scuola Normale Superiore di Pisa', 2nd series, I (1932), and the same author's recent *De Sanctis e il Rinascimento*, 'Società', IX (1953); F. ERNST, *Der Anteil der Schweiz an der Entdeckung der italienischen Renaissance*, in the volume *Die Schweiz als geistige Mittlerin*, Zürich, 1932; the very important work (one of the most notable on the subject) of F. SIMONE, *La coscienza della Rinascita negli umanisti francesi*, Rome, 1949; L. FEBVRE, *Comment Jules Michelet inventa la Renaissance*, 'Studi in onore di Gino Luzzatto', III, Milan, 1950 (also L. REFORT, *Michelet et la Renaissance*, 'Mélanges d'histoire littéraire de la Renaissance offerts à Henri Chamard', Paris, 1951); C. ANGELERI, *Il problema religioso del Rinascimento. Storia della critica e bibliografia*, Florence, 1952.

This line of research to-day finds its epitome in some important works of a general character – above all, in W. K. FERGUSON's *The Renaissance in Historical Thought. Five Centuries of Interpretation*, Boston, 1948 (French translation, Paris, 1950). This work, which traces the various evolutionary phases of the concept of the Renaissance and the different attitudes to the question adopted by artists, scholars and men of letters from the fourteenth and fifteenth centuries to the present day, constitutes the most exhaustive survey of the problem yet published. Apropos, cf. H. BARON, *The First History of the Historical Concept of the Renaissance*, 'Journal of the History of Ideas', XI (1950); D. C. PHILLIPS, *Ferguson on the Renaissance, ib.*, XIII (1952); J. H. HEXTER, *The Renaissance Again – and Again*, 'The Journal of Modern History', XXIII (1951).

See also FERGUSON's *The Interpretation of the Renaissance: Suggestions for a Synthesis* ('Journal of the History of Ideas', XII, 1951) and *The Church in a Changing World: A Contribution to the Interpretation of the Renaissance* ('The American Historical Review', LIX, 1953).

To be read in conjunction with Ferguson's thesis are two other notable contributions to the subject, in each of which, however, the historical inquiry is also the prelude to the author's personal interpretation and *prise de position*. Although, historically speaking, H. SCHULTE NORDHOLT's *Het Beeld der Renaissance* (Amsterdam, 1948) deals solely with writings published and questions debated since the appearance of BURCKHARDT's *Die Cultur der Renaissance*, it is nevertheless a valuable and exhaustive work, while the extremely well-informed treatise of H. BAEYENS, *Begrip en Probleem van de Renaissance*, Louvain, 1952 (Université de Louvain, Recueil de travaux d'histoire et de philologie, 3e série, 48e fasc.) which is concerned mainly with the problem of Renaissance art, takes its start from Vasari.

Finally, for the discussions in England (in addition to the writings, cited below in paragraph 2, of H. Weisinger, who has much occupied himself with the problem in general) see now J. R. HALE, *England and the Italian Renaissance. The Growth of Interest in its History and Art*, London, 1954.

2

In addition to the above-mentioned writings, the student who seeks to obtain a clear idea of the present state of the

debate on the Renaissance will need to refer to a large number of other essays and articles (as well as critical bibliographical reviews), including the following:

C. Neumann, *Byzantinische Kultur und Renaissance Kultur*,
'Historische Zeitschrift', XCI (1903) (but cf. G. Volpe's
forceful essay, *La Rinascenza in Italia e le sue origini*, 'La
Critica', II (1904), reproduced in *Momenti di storia italiana*,
Florence, 2nd ed., 1952, in which Neumann's arguments are
convincingly refuted); W. Goetz, *Renaissance und Antike*,
'Historische Zeitschrift', CXIII (1914), reproduced in
Italien im Mittelalter (cited above), II; P. Joachimsen, *Vom
Mittelalter zur Reformation*, 'Historische Vierteljahrschrift',
XX (1920–1921); E. Troeltsch, *Renaissance und Reforma-
tion*, 'Gesammelte Schriften', IV, Tübingen, 1924; C. de
Lollis, *La marcia francese verso la Rinascenza*, 'La Cultura',
IV (1925); J. Huizinga, *Das Problem der Renaissance* and
Renaissance und Realismus (German translation in *Wege der
Kulturgeschichte*, Munich, 1930. Two very important essays);
H. Hefele, *Zum Begriff der Renaissance*, 'Historisches
Jahrbuch', XLIX (1929); W. Rehm, *Das Werden des
Renaissancebildes in der deutschen Dichtung vom Rational-
ismus bis zum Realismus*, Munich, 1924, and *Der Renaissance-
Kultum und seine Überwindung*, 'Zeitschrift für deutsche
Philologie', LIV (1929); E. F. Jacob, *Changing Views of the
Renaissance*, 'History', New Series, XVI (1931–1932), to-
gether with another article by A. S. Turberville published
under a similar title in the same volume of the same review;
R. Kaufmann, *Der Renaissancebegriff in der deutschen Kunst-
geschichtschreibung*, 'Schweizerische Beiträge zur Kunstgeschichte', I, Winterthur, 1932; A. Haseloff, *Begriff und
Wesen der Renaissancekunst*, 'Mitteilungen des Kunst-
historischen Instituts in Florenz', III (1931); F. Chabod, *Il
Rinascimento nelle recenti interpretazioni*, 'Bulletin of the International Committee of Historical Sciences', XIX (1933),
and the same author's *Il Rinascimento*, 'Enciclopedia Italiana
Treccani', XIX (1936), *Momenti e forme del Rinascimento*,
'Romana', V (1941), and *Gli studi di storia del Rinascimento*,

'Cinquant'anni di vita intellettuale italiana 1896–1946. Scritti in onore di B. Croce', Naples, 1950, I; N. NELSON, *Individualism as a Criterion of the Renaissance*, 'Journal of English and Germanic Philology', XXXII (1933); H. W. EPPELSHEIMER, *Das Renaissance-Problem*, 'Deutsche Vierteljahrschrift für Literaturwissenschaft und Geistesgeschichte', XI (1933); R. STADELMANN, *Zum Problem der Renaissance*, 'Neue Jahrbücher für Wissenschaft und Jugendbildung', X (1934); C. NEUMANN, *Ende des Mittelalters? Legende von der Ablösung des Mittelalters durch die Renaissance*, 'Deutsche Vierteljahrschrift für Literaturwissenschaft und Geistesgeschichte', XII (1934); A. JANNER, *Individualismus und Religiösität in der Renaissance*, 'Deutsche Vierteljahrschrift für Literaturwissenschaft und Geistesgeschichte', XIII (1935); F. NERI, *La rinascita medievale*, in the volume *Storia e poesia*, Turin, 1936; A. BUCK, *Das Problem der italienischen Renaissance in der neuesten Forschung*, 'Italienische Kulturberichte', II, Leipzig, 1937; E. ANAGNINE, *Il problema del Rinascimento*, 'Nuova Rivista Storica', XVIII (1934), and *Concetto del Rinascimento. Roma, renovatio, rinascita*, 'Rivista Storica Italiana', 5th series, V (1940); R. H. BAINTON, *Changing Ideas and Ideals in the Sixteenth Century*, 'Journal of Modern History', VIII (1936); R. MORGHEN, *Rinascita romanica e Rinascimento*, now in *Medioevo cristiano*, Bari, 1951; B. CROCE, *La crisi italiana del Cinquecento e il legame del Rinascimento col Risorgimento*, 'La Critica', XXXVII (1939), reproduced in *Poeti e scrittori del pieno e del tardo Rinascimento*, Bari, 1945, I (but cf. in this connection the first chapter of CROCE's *Storia della età barocca in Italia*, Bari, 1929, 2nd edition 1946); L. RUSSO, *Umanesimo, Rinascimento, Controriforma e la storiografia contemporanea*, reprinted in *Problemi di metodo critico*, 2nd edition, Bari, 1950; the articles by D. DURAND and H. BARON and the relative discussions by E. CASSIRER, F. JOHNSON, P. O. KRISTELLER, D. LOCKWOOD and L. THORNDIKE (A 'Symposium' on the Renaissance) in 'Journal of the History of Ideas', IV (1943); E. PANOFSKY, *Renaissance and Renascences*, 'The Kenyon Review', 1944;

H. Baron, *Articulation and Unity in the Italian Renaissance
and in the Modern West,* 'Annual Report of the American
Historical Association for 1942', III (1944); H. Weisinger,
Renaissance Theories of the Revival of the Fine Arts, 'Italica',
XX (1943), *Who began the Revival of Learning? The Renaissance Point of View,* 'Papers of the Michigan Academy',
XXX (1944), *The Renaissance Theory of the Reaction Against
the Middle Ages as a Cause of the Renaissance,* 'Speculum', XX
(1945), *English Attitudes Toward the Relationship between the
Renaissance and the Reformation,* 'Church History', XIV
(1945), *Renaissance Accounts of the Revival of Learning,*
'Studies in Philology', XLV (1948), and *The English Origins
of the Sociological Interpretation of the Renaissance,* 'Journal of
the History of Ideas', XI (1950); A. Renaudet, *Autour d'une
définition de l'Humanisme,* 'Bibliothèque d'Humanisme et
Renaissance', VI (1945), and *Le problème historique de la
Renaissance italienne, ib.,* IX (1947); K. M. Setton,
Some Recent Views of the Italian Renaissance, 'Report of the
Canadian Historical Association', 1947; E. H. Wilkins,
On the Nature and Extent of the Italian Renaissance, 'Italica',
XXVII (1950); B. L. Ullman, *Renaissance – the Word and
the Underlying Concept,* 'Studies in Philology', XLIX (1952),
now in *Studies in the Italian Renaissance,* Rome, 1955; T.
Gregory, *Gli studi italiani sul pensiero del Rinascimento (1949–
1952),* I, *La polemica sul Rinascimento,* 'Rassegna di filosofia',
I (1952); the contributions of E. Panofsky, G. Sarton,
R. H. Bainton, L. Bradner, W. K. Ferguson, R. S. Lopez,
on general problems concerning the art, science, religion,
etc., of the Renaissance, in the Symposium held at the Metropolitan Museum of Art in New York in February, 1952
('Renaissance News', V, 1952, ns. 1, 2, 3, and *The Renaissance. A Symposium,* New York, 1953); and C. Vasoli, *La
civiltà dell'umanesimo e il problema del Rinascimento,* 'Itinerari',
IV (1956).

The Third International Convention on the Renaissance,
held in Florence from September 25th to 28th, 1952, under
the aegis of the 'Istituto Nazionale di Studi sul Rinasci-

mento', had the avowed object of 'defining ... the conceptual limits within which the Renaissance finds expression'. The proceedings included lectures on Renaissance literature (U. Bosco), philosophic and scientific thought (G. Saitta), art (M. Salmi), the economic problem (A. Sapori), the political problem (B. Barbadoro), and the religious problem (A. Pincherle). The lectures and discussions, which were attended by a considerable number of scholars, both Italian and foreign, are published in *Il Rinascimento. Significato e limiti*, Florence, 1953.

For such lectures and discussions during congresses and conventions on Humanism and the Renaissance, of which there have been many in recent years, cf. the essays (not all of which, it should be added, are of equal merit) published in *Sodalitas Erasmiana*, I, *Il valore universale dell'Umanesimo*, Naples, 1950; *Pensée humaniste et tradition chrétienne au XVe et XVIe siècle*, Paris, 1950; *Umanesimo e scienza politica*, Milan, 1951; *Cristianesimo e ragion di stato. L'Umanesimo e il demoniaco nell'arte*, Milan, 1953; *Retorica e Barocco*, Milan, 1955. V. also *Umanesimo e Machiavellismo*, a miscellaneous collection of essays published by the 'Archivio di Filosofia', Padua, 1949. Important, too, are the contributions of D. Cantimori and E. F. Jacob, *La periodizzazione dell'età del Rinascimento nella storia d'Italia e in quella d'Europa*, X Congresso Internazionale di Scienze Storiche, Rome, 4–11 September, 1955, *Relazioni*, IV (Florence, 1955).

3

For the actual expressions 'Renaissance', 'Humanism' and 'humanist' v. E. Heyfelder, *Die Ausdrücke 'Renaissance' und 'Humanismus'*, 'Deutsche Literaturzeitung', XXXIV (6 September 1913); H. Philippart, *Essai sur le mot et la notion d'humanisme*, 'Revue de synthèse historique', 1931; J. Trier, *Zur Vorgeschichte des Renaissance-Begriffes*, 'Archiv für Kulturgeschichte', XXXIII (1950); and above all A. Campana, *The Origin of the Word 'Humanist'*, 'Journal of the Warburg and Courtauld Institutes', IX (1946).

P

But for indications of the close relationship between the problem of the Renaissance and that of the Middle Ages the student should refer also to the principal writings of recent decades whose object has been to illustrate the origin and evolution of historiographical tradition about the Middle Ages. V. especially G. FALCO, *La polemica sul Medioevo*, Turin, 1933, and the chapter entitled 'Il significato del Medio Evo' in the same author's *Albori d'Europa*, Rome, 1947; also P. LEHMANN, *Vom Mittelalter und von der lateinischen Philologie des Mittelalters*, Munich, 1914, and *Erforschung des Mittelalters*, Leipzig, 1941; A. DOVE, *Der Streit um das Mittelalter*, 'Historische Zeitschrift', CXVI (1916); K. HEUSSI, *Altertum, Mittelalter und Neuzeit in der Kirchengeschichte*, Tübingen, 1921; H. SPANGENBERG, *Die Perioden der Weltgeschichte*, 'Historische Zeitschrift', CXXVII (1922); G. GORDON, *Medium Aevum and the Middle Ages*, Oxford, 1925; A. MONTEVERDI, *Medioevo*, 'La Cultura', VI (1927); L. SORRENTO, *Medioevo: il termine e il concetto*, 'Annuario della Università Cattolica del Sacro Cuore', Milan, 1930–1931; L. VARGA, *Das Schlagwort vom 'finsteren Mittelalter'*, Vienna, 1932; N. EDELMAN, *The Early Uses of Medium Aevum, Moyen Age, Middle Ages*, 'Romanic Review', XXX (1938 and 1939); A. SCHREIBER, *Das Mittelalter, universalhistorisches Problem vor der Romantik*, 'Archiv für Kulturgeschichte', XXXI (1942); T. E. MOMMSEN, *Petrarch's Conception of the 'Dark Ages'*, 'Speculum', XVII, 1942; E. S. DE BEER, *Gothic: Origin and Diffusion of the Term; The Idea of Style in Architecture*, 'Journal of the Warburg and Courtauld Institutes', XI (1948).

For this 'periodic' conception of history see also A. ELKAN, *Entstehung und Entwicklung des Begriffs 'Gegenreformation'*, 'Historische Zeitschrift', CXII (1914); and especially H. JEDIN, *Katholische Reformation oder Gegenreformation? Ein Versuch zur Klärung der Begriffe nebst einer Jubiläumsbetrachtung über das Trienter Konzil*, Lucerne, 1946, and the observations of CROCE in his *Storia della età barocca in Italia* (cited above), Introduction and final note.

II

I

The broad lines of contemporary research on the Renaissance frequently do not accord with the classical picture painted by Burckhardt. Nevertheless, the latter's *Die Cultur der Renaissance in Italien*, Basle, 1860 (now available in *Jacob Burckhardt Gesamtausgabe*, Stuttgart-Basle, V, 1930), has not yet been superseded by any other comprehensive work and remains to this day the essential starting-point of any discussion. (On the composition of the work, see now W. KAEGI, *Jacob Burckhardt*, III, Basle-Stuttgart, 1956.)

Still to be consulted is W. DILTHEY's *Auffassung und Analyse des Menschen im* 15. *und* 16. *Jahrhundert*, 1891–1892 (reprinted in *Gesammelte Schriften*, 2nd edition, Leipzig, 1921), which from a philosophical standpoint represents an amplification of Burckhardt's vision.

In this sense – i.e. in virtue of the fact that they contain valuable appreciations of the philosophical ideas of the fifteenth and sixteenth centuries regarded as the fountain-head of modern thought – some of the most important and significant studies on the Renaissance were published during the first half of our century. On the one hand, we have E. CASSIRER's *Das Erkenntnisproblem in der Philosophie und Wissenschaft der neueren Zeit* (I, 3rd edn., Berlin, 1922) and especially *Individuum und Kosmos in der Philosophie der Renaissance* (Leipzig, 1927); on the other, the series of works by G. GENTILE, viz. *I problemi della Scolastica e il pensiero italiano* (Bari, 1913; 2nd edition, 1923), *Il pensiero italiano del Rinascimento* (3rd edition, Florence, 1940), *Studi sul Rinascimento* (2nd edition, Florence, 1936), and also *La filosofia italiana dalla fine della Scolastica agli inizî dell'Umanesimo* (Milan, 1915).

Reverting to the Hegelian interpretation, [which in Italy had already inspired the treatises of B. SPAVENTA (*Rinasci-*

mento, Riforma, Controriforma, Venice, 1928, being a reprint of essays written for the most part between 1854 and 1856 and published in 1867; and *La filosofia italiana nelle sue relazioni con la filosofia europea*, last edition, Florence, 1937, likewise a reprint of an inaugural lecture delivered in 1861) and F. FIORENTINO (*Pietro Pomponazzi*, Florence, 1868; *Bernardino Telesio*, two vols., Florence, 1872–1874; *Il risorgimento filosofico nel Quattrocento*, Naples, 1885; and *Studi e ritratti della Rinascenza*, Bari, 1911)], Gentile has persisted in stressing – no doubt somewhat unduly – the 'modernness' of fifteenth- and sixteenth-century Italian thought.

G. SAITTA's *La filosofia di Marsilio Ficino* (Messina, 1923), *Filosofia italiana e umanesimo* (Venice, 1928), and *Il pensiero italiano nell'Umanesimo e nel Rinascimento* (three vols., Bologna, 1949–1951) are clearly inspired by the theories of Gentile.

The Crocian school of historians has also held firm to the opinion that the Renaissance was a great spiritual movement which, along with the Reformation, lies at the root of modern civilization. The most complete exposition of this interpretation is furnished by G. DE RUGGIERO in his *Storia della filosofia* (Part III: *Rinascimento, Riforma e Controriforma*, two vols., Bari, 1930; 4th ed., 1947). Here, Gentile's exaggerated emphasis on 'modernness' is largely tempered by a recognition of the complexity and occasional inconsistency of the thought of two centuries, characterized by the intermingling of elements both old and new; and the author reaches the balanced conclusion that the philosophy of the Renaissance contains some of the essential elements of modern thought, but that, since it did not deal with the problem of method, which remained outside its compass, its 'fresh intuitions constitute a rhapsody of sudden and ephemeral flashes of insight rather than the fruit of a methodical and logical process of reasoning'.

2

Very different, however, is the attitude of G. TOFFANIN, as expressed in his various writings: *Che cosa fu l'Umanesimo*

(Florence, 1929); *Storia dell'Umanesimo dal XIII al XVI secolo* (3rd edition, Bologna, 1943; Engl. transl., *History of Humanism*, New York, 1954); *Il secolo senza Roma (Il Rinascimento del secolo XIII)* (Bologna, 1942); *La fine del Logos* (Bologna, 1948) (these three works have recently been reprinted under the general title of *Storia dell'umanesimo*, three vols., Bologna, 1950); *G. Pontano tra l'uomo e la natura* (Bologna, 1938); *Montaigne e l'idea classica* (2nd edition, Bologna, 1942); *La religione degli umanisti* (Bologna, 1950); and *L'Umanesimo al Concilio di Trento* (Bologna 1955). (See also *La fine dell'Umanesimo*, Turin, 1920, and *Il Cinquecento*, Milan, last edn. 1954.)

In Toffanin's view, the triumph of the spirit of liberty occurred in the thirteenth century. So far as culture was concerned, it signified the triumph of scientific, Averroistic and heretical thought. Humanism, on the other hand, signified the triumphant revival of Catholic traditionalism, allied to classical traditionalism, as a counter to thirteenth-century heresy. It signified, too, the reaffirmation of the spirit of authority and of the Catholic conservative mentality, opposed to the spirit of innovation and revolt. Thus Humanism paves the way for the Counter-reformation, whereas the 'modern' spirit reaches its culminating point in the Reformation.

The fourteenth, fifteenth and sixteenth centuries accordingly witnessed a schism, a fundamental clash between Humanism on the one hand and Averroism on the other, between the science of Man and the science of Nature.

Toffanin's thesis, which is often paradoxically polemical, is expounded with a remarkable crudity of antithesis and based on interpretations which often leave the reader feeling extremely dubious. Indeed, it appears quite unacceptable, at least so far as its more extreme assumptions are concerned.

However, this separation of two ideas (Humanism and Renaissance) which in the eyes of Burckhardt and his followers had always been one and indivisible, is no longer the contention of one lonely scholar.

As long ago as 1914 and 1920 E. WALSER insisted that Catholic and religious values had continued to be respected throughout the period of the Renaissance (*Christentum und Antike in der Auffassung der italienischen Frührenaissance* and *Studien zur Weltanschauung der Renaissance*, now available in *Gesammelte Studien zur Geistesgeschichte der Renaissance*, Basle, 1932; cf. also P. WERNLE, *Die Renaissance des Christentums im 16. Jahrhundert*, Tübingen, 1904). His conclusion was that in considering the Renaissance it is not possible to speak of general indifference or religious scepticism.

But for those who wish to get a general idea of present trends in Renaissance studies there is much significance in the fact that certain scholars stress the difference between Humanism and other expressions of the Renaissance. This difference is brought out, albeit from quite another point of view, by L. OLSCHKI (*Geschichte der neusprachlichen wissenschaftlichen Literatur*, three volumes, Heidelberg-Leipzig-Halle, 1919–1927; cf. also *Machiavelli the Scientist*, Berkeley, Cal., 1945), who sees the great revival of learning as the achievement not of the humanistic 'clique', who are remote from reality, but of practical men – master craftsmen, engineers and artists. The Italian Renaissance is a truly stupendous *popular* movement, an intellectual revolution whose reality only those who conceive it exclusively in terms of books, texts, schools of thought and erudition can deny. It is a spiritual fellowship, whose bounds extend far beyond the closed circle of the humanists; and its true creators are not to be found in the accepted literary *milieux*.

More recently, Olschki has given us a comprehensive picture of the spiritual life of Italy between 1300 and 1500 in *The Genius of Italy* (New York, 1949; London, 1950). Humanism is not the plaything of a few scholars, it is not the invention of a 'school' or an erudite literary fashion. It is, on the contrary, a movement supported by the majority of Italian lay society, a spiritual force that invigorates the entire life and civilization of Italy. It is both the essential expression of the new Italian civilization and the first secular movement of the Christian era. When, however, Olschki comes to assess the several aspects of this movement we perceive that his criteria vary from one moment to the next. Sometimes the Papacy is said to hold the reins of Italian lay civilization and the Church to succeed in canalizing and absorbing a powerful intellectual trend that originated outside itself (for it finds that the humanistic conception is far less of a menace to its security than the Averroistic doctrine). Humanism would thus appear to be the moral and intellectual counterpart of Christianity. At other times, however, Olschki stresses the immanentist theory of life and the world, formulated by the humanists.

In the recent work of H. HAYDN, *The Counter-Renaissance* (New York, 1950), we likewise find a distinction between the classical, humanistic and fundamentally Christian 'Renaissance', which is not an open revolt against mediaeval conceptions, and the 'Counter-Renaissance', personified by such men as Luther and Machiavelli, Calvin and Giordano Bruno, Pico and Bacon, and which rejects the classical-Christian-Renaissance ideals of measure, harmony and hierarchy.

This 'Counter-Renaissance' is a movement which exists, chronologically speaking, within the Renaissance itself. Here again we find Burckhardt's unitarian theory in dispute.

Also based on the contrast between 'naturalism' and humanistic ideals is the picture of the Renaissance presented by the art-historian G. WEISE (who here largely supports Toffanin's thesis) in a series of essays, including *Der doppelte Begriff der Renaissance* ('Deutsche Vierteljahrsschrift für Literaturwissenschaft und Geistesgeschichte', XI, 1933); *Italien und das heroische Lebensgefühl der Renaissance* ('Germanisch-Romanische Monatsschrift', 1934); *Vom Menschenideal und von den Modewörtern der Gothik und der Renaissance* ('Deutsche Vierteljahrsschrift für Literaturwissenschaft und Geistesgeschichte', XIV, 1936); *Der Realismus des 15. Jahrhunderts und seine geistigen Voraussetzungen und*

Parallelen ('Die Welt als Geschichte', VIII, 1942); *Machia-velli und Philippe de Commynes. Neuzeitlicher Wirklichkeitssinn und das Fortleben mittelalterlicher Bindungen in der Geschichts-betrachtung am Übergang vom Mittelalter zur Renaissance* ('Universitas', I, 1946); *Renaissance und Antike* (Tübingen, 1953); and *Dürer und die ideale der Humanisten* (Tübingen, 1953). Weise, who has, incidentally, examined the question of Italian Gothic in *Die geistige Welt der Gotik und ihre Be-deutung für Italien* (Halle, 1939) and *Italien und die Welt der Gotik* (Mainz, 1947), will publish shortly a comprehensive work on 'the heroic ideality of the Renaissance and its hu-manistic premises'. Meanwhile, see his article, *Il duplice con-cetto di Rinascimento* ('Rivista Storica Italiana', LXVIII, 1956).

In Weise's view, then, there are two phases, which even in a chronological sense are clearly differentiated. These are the 'naturalistic' or 'realistic' phase, which dominates much of the fifteenth century yet in itself represents nothing new, particularly so far as northern and central Europe is con-cerned; and the 'classical', 'heroic' phase of the High Re-naissance (i.e. from 1480 onwards), which is characterized by the eclipse of naturalism and the creation of a style, an ideal, classical-heroic 'type'. This 'type' is the true and original creation of the Italian Renaissance, as a result of which Italy exerts a profound influence over European cul-ture. It continues to flourish both in Italy and France in the form of the baroque ideal and is not superseded until the eighteenth century, when the bourgeois-scientific spirit makes its triumphant appearance.

3

There is another respect – and a most important one – in which Burckhardt's conception has in recent decades been generally revised and modified.

According to Burckhardt, the Renaissance was a sudden isolated phenomenon, comparable to a flower that blooms in the desert. That is to say, in his view it had no links with an earlier age. The attempt to trace such links, to discern the bond of union between the fourteenth and fifteenth centuries on the one hand and the thirteenth century on the other, has been made in a series of studies, of which the following by K. BURDACH are the most notable: *Vom Mittelalter zur Reformation* (Halle, 1893); *Reformation, Renaissance, Humanismus* (Berlin, 1918; 2nd edition, 1926); *Rienzo und die geistige Wandlung seiner Zeit* ('Vom Mittelalter zur Reformation, Forschungen zur Geschichte der deutschen Bildung', II, *Briefwechsel des Cola di Rienzo*, 1, Berlin, 1913–1928, two vols.). Also to be consulted are the same writer's *Deutsche Renaissance. Betrachtungen über unsere künftige Bildung* (Berlin, 1916; 2nd edition, 1920); *Dante und das Problem der Renaissance* ('Deutsche Rundschau', CXCVIII, 1924); and *Die seelischen und geistigen Quellen der Renaissancebewegung* ('Historische Zeitschrift', CXLIX, 1934). Finally, the student should refer to the introduction to *Petrarcas 'Buch ohne Namen' und die päpstliche Kurie* (Halle, 1925) and to *Cola di Rienzo* (Vienna, 1931), both by P. PIUR, who collaborated with Burdach.

In part reaffirming, but also developing – on the basis of a most minute philological examination of the terms 'Renaissance' and 'Reformation' – ideas already put forward by H. THODE (*Franz von Assisi und die Anfänge der Kunst der Renaissance in Italien*, Berlin, 1885) and R. HILDEBRAND (*Zur sogenannten Renaissance*, 'Zeitschrift für den deutschen Unterricht', VI, 1892, reprinted in 'Beiträge zum deutschen Unterricht', Leipzig, 1897), Burdach has closely associated the Renaissance, in its initial phase, with the great religious movement (Joachimite-Franciscan) of thirteenth-century Italy, with the concept of *renovatio*, and with those grandiose aspirations after a collective regeneration, religious and moral even before it was cultural, which had filled the Italian soul as a direct result of that movement.

This interpretation, according to which the Middle Ages and the Renaissance are seen to be closely connected, is therefore opposed, so far as the evaluation of origins and determining factors is concerned, to the classical thesis of Burckhardt, who had isolated the Renaissance, seeking in it no link with an earlier age and above all emphasizing its human, 'pagan' motifs. From this standpoint, therefore, while retaining his unmistakable originality of accent and clinging to his characteristically logical method of presentation, Burdach conforms to a widespread tendency to seek a link between the Renaissance and an earlier age. At the same time, however, he supports Burckhardt's thesis as to the originality, importance and essential progressiveness of the Renaissance itself, which he always looks upon as the dawn of the modern world. His interpretation may be regarded as a notable part of a whole embracing on the one hand the writings of E. GEBHARDT (*Les origines de la Renaissance en Italie*, Paris, 1879; *La Renaissance italienne et la philosophie de l'histoire*, 'Revue des Deux Mondes', LXXII, 1885; *L'Italie mystique, histoire de la Renaissance religieuse au moyen âge*, Paris, 1890), who also sought to emphasize the importance of the Franciscan movement viewed as a reawakening not merely religious but also cultural and artistic in character, and on the other hand the works of Volpe, who, writing almost contemporaneously with Burdach, described the Renaissance as the Italian people's spiritual emancipation, emphasizing above all the latter's economic, social and political features. (Besides the essay already cited, *La Rinascenza in Italia e le sue origini*, see also VOLPE's *Il medio evo*, Florence, 1926, 3rd edition, Milan, 1943; and for similar observations on the links between culture and politics cf. L. SALVATORELLI, *L'Italia comunale. Dal secolo XI alla metà del secolo XIV*, Milan, 1940; N. VALERI, *L'Italia nell'età dei principati dal 1343 al 1516*, Milan, 1950.)

Burdach's interpretation (reaffirmed by E. BENZ, *Ecclesia Spiritualis. Kirchenidee und Geschichtstheologie der Franziskanischen Reformation*, Stuttgart, 1934) has been and remains the subject of heated discussion. But there is no doubt that it constitutes a singularly important episode in the historiography of the Renaissance.

III

That the reality and the true greatness of the Renaissance are to be sought outside the 'academic and erudite systematizations', in other words outside any recognized 'philosophical systems' (to use the term in its strict connotation), that they reside, in fact, far more in the concrete expressions of art and of political and moral thought, is a conclusion which some of the most notable of contemporary scholars have reached by dint of philological analysis and the skilful application of their acquired knowledge. Led by E. GARIN and H. BARON, these enlightened scholars, while generally recognizing with Burckhardt the greatness of the Renaissance and its all-embracing originality as compared with the Middle Ages, are not content with generalities or with formulas, and try to analyse in detail the facts relevant to the notions of Humanism and Renaissance.

The following writings of E. GARIN should be consulted: *Giovanni Pico della Mirandola. Vita e dottrina* (Florence, 1937); *Dal Medioevo al Rinascimento* (Florence, 1950); and especially *L'Umanesimo italiano. Filosofia e vita civile nel Rinascimento* (Bari, 1952), and *Medioevo e Rinascimento*, Bari, 1954; also numerous essays, articles and introductions to collected works, including: *La 'dignitas hominis' e la letteratura patristica* ('La Rinascita', I, 1938); *Aristotelismo e platonismo del Rinascimento* (*ib.*, II, 1939); the introductions to *Il Rinascimento italiano* (Milan, 1941), *Filosofi italiani del Quattrocento* (Florence, 1942), *Coluccio Salutati: De nobilitate legum et medicinae. De verecundia* (Florence, 1947), and to *L'educazione umanistica in Italia* (2nd edition, Bari, 1953); the essay entitled *Umanesimo e Rinascimento* in the miscellaneous volume *Questioni e correnti di storia letteraria* (Milan, 1949); and the two volumes dealing with the general history of philosophy, *La Filosofia* (Milan, 1947).

In Garin's view, 'the future historian of the philosophical culture of the Italian Renaissance will be forced to read

works of politics, ethics, rhetoric, logic and science rather
than books dealing with that scholastic philosophy which
was already utterly discredited'. Universal values 'would be
sought in vain in the academic and erudite systematizations
of scholars. They are better revealed in the self-conscious
individuality present in every form of practical research. And
this in truth represents the dawn of modern thought.'

The writings of H. Baron are devoted to the study of
Florentine humanism in its bearing on civil life, and therefore essentially in its historical and political manifestations.
Baron published in 1955 a comprehensive work on the political ideals of the early Renaissance, entitled *The Crisis of the
Early Italian Renaissance. Civic Humanism and Republican
Liberty in an Age of Classicism and Tyranny* (2 vols., Princeton), to which should be added the volume *Humanistic and
Political Literature in Florence and Venice at the Beginning of
the Quattrocento* (Cambridge, Mass., 1955). Among his
many essays and articles the student should particularly consult the introduction to *Leonardo Bruni Aretino: Humanistisch-
philosophische Schriften* (Leipzig, 1928) and the articles entitled *Das Erwachen des historischen Denkens im Humanismus
des Quattrocento* ('Historische Zeitschrift', CXLVI, 1932);
*La rinascita dell'etica statale romana nell'umanesimo fiorentino
del Quattrocento* ('Civiltà Moderna', VII, 1935); *Cicero and
the Roman Civic Spirit in the Middle Ages and the Early Renaissance* ('Bulletin of the John Rylands Library', XXII, 1938);
*Franciscan Poverty and Civic Wealth as Factors in the Rise of
Humanistic Thought* ('Speculum', XIII, 1938); *The Historical
Background of the Florentine Renaissance* ('History', New
Series, XXII, 1938 and 'La Rinascita', I, 1938); *A Socio-
logical Interpretation of the Early Renaissance in Florence* ('The
South Atlantic Quarterly', XXXVIII, 1939); *A Struggle for
Liberty in the Renaissance: Florence, Venice, and Milan in the
Early Quattrocento* ('American Historical Review', LVIII,
1953); *Dekadenz im Italien des Quattrocento?*, ('Bibliothèque
d'Humanisme et Renaissance', XVII, 1955).

P. O. Kristeller, whose assiduous researches are most

useful because they yield such an abundance of data, concerns himself more especially with the analysis of strictly philosophical problems and speculative traditions. In this field he denies the originality of the 'philosophical' thought of 'Renaissance Humanism', seeing in Humanism only a 'limited sector of Renaissance thought'. See especially *The Philosophy of Marsilio Ficino* (New York, 1943); *Augustine and the Early Renaissance* ('Review of Religion', VIII, 1944); *The Place of Classical Humanism in Renaissance Thought* ('Journal of the History of Ideas', IV, 1943); *Ficino and Pomponazzi on the Place of Man in the Universe* ('Journal of the History of Ideas', V, 1944); *Humanism and Scholasticism in the Italian Renaissance* ('Byzantion', XVII, 1944–1945); *Francesco da Diacceto and Florentine Platonism in the Sixteenth Century* ('Miscellanea Giovanni Mercati', IV, Rome, 1946); *The Philosophy of Man in the Italian Renaissance* ('Italica', XXIV, 1947); the general introduction (written in collaboration with J. H. RANDALL JR.) to *The Renaissance Philosophy of Man* (Chicago, 1948); *Movimenti filosofici del Rinascimento* ('Giornale Critico della Filosofia Italiana', XXIX, 1950); *Umanesimo e filosofia nel Rinascimento italiano*, in the miscellaneous volume already cited, *Umanesimo e scienza politica. Atti del Congresso Internazionale di Studi Umanistici* (Milan, 1951); *The Classics and Renaissance Thought* (Cambridge, Mass., 1955). Almost all the articles cited above, together with others previously unpublished, have now been brought together in the volume *Studies in Renaissance Thought and Letters* (Rome, 1956).

IV

Ample reference has been made in the text to the tendency, which has become apparent in recent decades, to deny the originality and importance of the Renaissance, and instead to extol the greatness, profundity and power of mediaeval thought (especially that of the twelfth and thirteenth centuries), ascribing in particular to the so-called French Renaissance of the twelfth century the credit for having opened up new vistas to Western civilization.

This thesis is not entirely new: for even before 1900 L. COURAJOD had attributed the discovery of the 'new art' to the Flemish and North French artists of the fourteenth century (*Leçons professées à l'école du Louvre, 1887–1896*, II, *Origines de la Renaissance*, Paris, 1901). But it has undoubtedly been accorded an unprecedented measure of support in the last few decades, and not only in connection with art. An indication has already been given in the text of what the reader should think of these assertions, in part due to the 'revolt of the Medievalist' (as Ferguson has called it), which had its justification in the desire to demolish the legend of the 'barbarous' Middle Ages; but also deriving some of their vigour from nationalistic tendencies, mainly though not exclusively French, and from a militant religious, and especially Catholic, 'confessionalism'. Those who embrace this line of thought endeavour to destroy the picture created by liberal laymen of the nineteenth century (though they base their arguments on opinions and sentiments first expressed four hundred years previously!) and, fully justified when they seek to explode the myth – which in any case is by now thoroughly discredited – of a benighted and ignorant *Medium Aevum*, find themselves on less sure ground when they try instead on the one hand to uphold the argument that everything essential had already been said before the Renaissance, and on the other to deny the latter a vigorous individuality of its own.

It is certainly significant that, in these attacks on the Renaissance, theologians and men of faith belonging to different religions today find themselves in agreement (cf. H. WEISINGER, *The Attack on the Renaissance in Theology Today*, 'Studies in the Renaissance', II, 1955): for this provides an instance of how the change in the general spiritual climate since the age of Burckhardt influences the judgment of history.

In addition to the works already mentioned in the text, the following illustrations of this anti-Renaissance trend (apropos of which cf. I. SICILIANO, *Medio Evo e Rinascimento*, Rome, 1936) are deserving of notice:

(*a*) C. H. HASKINS, *The Renaissance of the Twelfth Century*, Cambridge, Mass., 1927); *Studies in the History of Mediaeval Science* (Cambridge, Mass., 2nd ed., 1927); *Studies in Mediaeval Culture* (Oxford, 1929). (On the so-called 'Renaissance' of the twelfth century v. also G. PARÉ, A. BRUNET, P. TREMBLAY, *La Renaissance du XIIe siècle. Les écoles et l'enseignement*, Paris-Ottawa, 1933; W. A. NITZE, *The So-Called Twelfth Century Renaissance*, 'Speculum', XXIII, 1948; H. LIEBESCHÜTZ, *Mediaeval Humanism in the Life and Writings of John of Salisbury*, London, 1950 (an important work); E. M. SANFORD, *The Twelfth Century—Renaissance or Proto-Renaissance?*, 'Speculum', XXVI, 1951; U. T. HOLMES, *The Idea of a Twelfth Century Renaissance, ib.*, XXVI, 1951). Although the above-mentioned works by Haskins have a special bearing on the so-called 'Renaissance' of the twelfth century they maintain an extremely cautious and by no means radical attitude towards the Italian Renaissance.

The question of the 'Northern Renaissance' of the twelfth and thirteenth centuries, and of the 'ascendances médiévales de l'humanisme italien' has been taken up again by P. RENUCCI, *L'aventure de l'humanisme européen au Moyen-Age (iv–xiv siècle)*, (Clermont-Ferrand, 1953). Cf. also T. GREGORY, *Anima mundi. La filosofia di Guglielmo di Conches e la scuola di Chartres* (Florence, 1955).

(*b*) In general: E. GILSON, *La philosophie au Moyen Âge des origines patristiques à la fin du XIVe siècle* (2nd edition, Paris, 1952) (a particularly important work); *L'esprit de la philosophie médiévale* (2nd edition, Paris, 1944; English translation, *The Spirit of Medieval Philosophy*, New York, 1936); *L'humanisme de Saint Thomas* ('Atti del V Congresso Internazionale di filosofia', Naples, 1924); *Humanisme médiéval et Renaissance*, in the volume 'Les idées et les lettres' (Paris, 1932); *Héloïse et Abélard* (Paris, 1938; English translation, Chicago, 1951). The above-named works are especially noteworthy both on account of the writer's scholarship and for the uncompromising nature of his thesis.

In Gilson's view the difference between the Middle Ages and the Renaissance is a negative one. The Renaissance is not the Middle Ages plus Man, but the Middle Ages minus God; and in losing God the Renaissance has also lost Man. Modern philosophy has not had to fight to ensure the triumph of reason over mediaeval superstitition. On the contrary, it was the Middle Ages that asserted the claims of reason on behalf of modern philosophy.

In the scientific field, P. Duhem's *Le système du monde. Histoire des doctrines cosmologiques de Platon à Copernic* (five volumes, Paris, 1913–1917), which eulogizes the scientific spirit of the Middle Ages (see also *Études sur Léonard de Vinci, ceux qu'il a lus et ceux qui l'ont lu*, three series, Paris, 1906–1913), has been followed by another remarkable and monumental work, L. Thorndike's *A History of Magic and Experimental Sciences* (six volumes, New York, 1923–41), in which it is maintained that the scientific thought of the Renaissance lacks originality and that the fourteenth and fifteenth centuries mark a step backward rather than a step forward by comparison with the two preceding centuries. (See also the same author's *Science and Thought in the Fifteenth Century*, New York, 1929, and *Renaissance or Prenaissance?*, 'Journal of the History of Ideas', IV, 1943.)

A negative attitude towards the originality of the science of the Renaissance is also adopted by G. Sarton, *Science in the Renaissance* (in *The Civilization of the Renaissance*, by J. W. Thompson, G. Rowley, F. Schevill and G. Sarton, Chicago, 1929); cf. *Introduction to the History of Science*, (three volumes, Washington-Baltimore, 1927–48, of which Volume III, in two parts, is concerned with *Science and Learning in the Fourteenth Century*). In his recent work, *The Appreciation of Ancient and Medieval Science during the Renaissance* (Philadelphia, 1955), Sarton maintains that, in the field of science,

the Renaissance continues the Middle Ages, without fundamental changes, and without giving rise to 'modern' experimental science – though, in the sixteenth century, new and
progressive elements are to be found in some fields, such as,
for example, anatomy. These new elements were emphasized
by Sarton in 1952, in the *Symposium on the Renaissance*,
already cited, where he gives a more positive evaluation of the
results also achieved in the field of science.

V

While the problem of the link between the Middle Ages
and the Renaissance has assumed a place of primary importance in recent historiography, very little attention has been
paid to the other problem, that which relates to the ultimate
rejection of Renaissance ideas and particularly to the revolutionary influence of the great geographical discoveries on
Europe's mode of thought. As has been indicated in the
text, this mode of thought changes profoundly after the
middle of the sixteenth century. The ensuing era of rela-
tivism opens men's minds to the philosophy of methodical
doubt and the idea of progress – the two main pillars of European thought between 1600 and 1700. Partly because of
this, partly as a result of the Reformation and the Counter-
Reformation, by the second half of the sixteenth century the
Continent has already entered a phase in which its intellectual perspective is seen to have altered profoundly. This is
a fact of which, generally speaking, people to-day take little
account when they speak of the Renaissance in France,
England, etc. (which in fact reaches its climax in the second
half of the sixteenth century), as if the moral and spiritual
climate of the Italian Renaissance had persisted until the
third or fourth decade of the Cinquecento. So far as Italy
herself is concerned, the thought of Giordano Bruno, for
example – not to mention Campanella – makes it impossible
for us to forget that we are now in a different age, one that is
exposed to the influence of historical forces – moral, relig-

ious and political – quite unlike those of the fifteenth and early sixteenth centuries.

This, then, is one of the problems which would most handsomely repay investigation and discussion. For the moment, however, it will be enough to refer to the following studies:

G. CHINARD, *L'exotisme américain dans la littérature française au XVIe siècle* (Paris, 1911); A. REIN, *Das Problem der europäischen Expansion in der Geschichtsschreibung* (Hamburg, 1929); F. CHABOD, *Giovanni Botero* (Rome, 1934); G. ATKINSON, *Les nouveaux horizons de la Renaissance française* (Paris, 1935); F. DE DAINVILLE, *La géographie des humanistes* (Paris, 1940); G. TOFFANIN, *Montaigne e l'idea classica* (cited above); R. GONNARD, *La légende du Bon Sauvage* (Paris, 1946); A. DUPRONT, *Espace et humanisme* 'Bibliothèque d'Humanisme et Renaissance', VIII, 1946); A. GERBI, *Viejas polémicas sobre el Nuevo Mundo* (3rd edition, Lima, 1946. The theme is re-examined and amplified in *La disputa del Nuovo Mondo. Storia di una polemica, 1750–1900* (Milan-Naples, 1955); this book contains certain helpful suggestions, although as a whole it is concerned with the controversies of the eighteenth and nineteenth centuries); A. PINCHERLE, *La dignità dell'uomo e l'indigeno americano* ('Atti del Congresso Internazionale di Studi Umanistici', Rome, 1952); R. ROMEO, *Le scoperte americane nella coscienza italiana del Cinquecento* (Milan-Naples, 1954); also, for certain initial observations – though the work as a whole is concerned with a later period (1609–1851) – R. H. PEARCE, *The Savages of America. A Study of the Indian and the Idea of Civilization* (Baltimore, 1953).

As to the precise manner in which those who attempted to portray the characteristics of different peoples were influenced by the literature of travel, see the remarks in B. W. BATE's *Literary Portraiture in the Historical Narrative of the French Renaissance* (New York, 1945).

For the Turks and 'Orientals' (Chinese, etc.) in European thought cf. C. D. ROUILLARD, *The Turk in French History,*

Thought and Literature (1520–1660) (Paris, undated but published in 1938); F. CHABOD, *Paolo Giovio* ('Periodico della Società Storica Comense', XXXVIII, 1954).

VI

Having thus briefly indicated the main lines along which the recent historiography of the Renaissance has developed, I will now mention a few of the more important writings to be consulted by those who wish to study individual aspects and problems of the Renaissance.

I

On the continuity of cultural traditions v. K. BORINSKI, *Die Antike in Poetik und Kunsttheorie vom Ausgang des klassischen Altertums bis auf Goethe und Wilhelm von Humboldt*, 2 vols. (Leipzig, 1914–1924); A. GOLDSCHMIDT, *Das Nachleben der antiken Formen im Mittelalter* ('Vorträge der Bibliothek Warburg', I, 1921–1922); F. VON BEZOLD, *Das Fortleben der antiken Götter im mittelalterlichen Humanismus* (Bonn-Leipzig, 1922); A. DOREN, *Fortuna im Mittelalter und in der Renaissance* ('Vorträge der Bibliothek Warburg', II, 1, 1922–1923); F. SAXL, *Antike Götter in der Spätrenaissance* (Leipzig-Berlin, 1927); *id.*, *Pagan Sacrifice in the Italian Renaissance* ('Journal of the Warburg Institute', II, 1939); H. R. PATCH, *The Goddess Fortuna in Mediaeval Literature* (Cambridge, Mass., 1927); A. WARBURG, *Die Erneuerung der heidnischen Antike. Kulturwissenschaftliche Beiträge zur Geschichte der europäischen Renaissance* ('Gesammelte Schriften', two volumes, Leipzig, 1932); J. SEZNEC, *La survivance des dieux antiques. Essai sur le rôle de la tradition mythologique dans l'humanisme et dans l'art de la Renaissance* (London, 1940; but cf. B. CROCE, *Gli Dei antichi nella tradizione mitologica del medio evo e del rinascimento*, 'Varietà di storia letteraria e civile', 2nd series, Bari, 1949, E. GARIN, *Le favole antiche*, in *Medioevo e Rinascimento*, cited above, and F. GAETA, *L'avventura di*

Ercole, 'Rinascimento', V, 1954); D. BUSH, *Classical Influences in Renaissance Literature*, (Cambridge, Mass., 1952); R. R. BOLGAR, *The Classical Heritage and its Beneficiaries*, (Cambridge, 1954). Cf. also P. RENUCCI, *Dante disciple et juge du monde gréco-latin* (Clermont-Ferrand, 1954).

On the Roman tradition in particular v. T. ZIELINSKI, *Cicero im Wandel der Jahrhunderte* (Leipzig, 4th edition, 1929); V. ZABUGHIN, *Vergilio nel Rinascimento italiano da Dante a Torquato Tasso* (two volumes, Bologna, 1921–1924); F. SCHNEIDER, *Rom und Romgedanke im Mittelalter. Die geistigen Grundlagen der Renaissance* (Munich, 1926); P. E. SCHRAMM's most important *Kaiser, Rom und Renovatio* (two volumes, Leipzig-Berlin, 1929); E. DUPRÉ THE-SEIDER's long introduction to the miscellany entitled *L'idea imperiale di Roma nella tradizione del Medioevo* (Milan, 1942); W. HAMMER, *The Concept of the New or Second Rome in the Middle Ages* ('Speculum', XIX, 1944); N. LENKEITH, *Dante and the Legend of Rome* ('Mediaeval and Renaissance Studies', Supplement II, London, 1952); also W. REHM, *Der Untergang Roms im abendländischen Denken* (Leipzig, 1930); and finally, of course, the standard works by A. GRAF (*Roma nella memoria e nelle immaginazioni del Medio Evo*, two volumes, Turin, 1882–83, now available in GRAF, *Opere Critiche*, Turin, 1923) and D. COMPARETTI (*Virgilio nel Medio Evo*, Leghorn, 1872; 2nd edition, in two volumes, Florence, 1896; new edition edited by G. Pasquali, two volumes, Florence, 1937–41).

For the 'Caesar' and 'Alexander' motifs v. F. GUNDOLF, *Caesar. Geschichte seines Ruhms* (Berlin, 1925); P. Treves, *Il mito di Alessandro e la Roma d'Augusto* (Milan-Naples, 1953); and also G. MARTELLOTTI, *Il Petrarca e Cesare*, ('Annali della Scuola Normale Superiore di Pisa', 2nd Series, XVI, 1947); A. MOMIGLIANO, *Per un riesame della storia dell'idea di Cesarismo* ('Rivista Storica Italiana', LXVIII, 1956).

The following general works on Antiquity, the Middle Ages and the Renaissance should also be consulted: E. NORDEN, *Die antike Kunstprosa vom VI. Jahrhundert v. Chr.*

bis in die Zeit der Renaissance (4th edition, Leipzig, 1923); F. J. E. RABY, *A History of Secular Latin Poetry in the Middle Ages* (two volumes, Oxford, 1934); *id.*, *A History of Christian-Latin Poetry from the Beginnings to the Close of the Middle Ages* (Oxford, 1927); E. R. CURTIUS, *Europäische Literatur und lateinisches Mittelalter* (2nd ed., Berne, 1954); as well as W. GOETZ's *Renaissance und Antike* ('Historische Zeitschrift', CXIII, 1914), which remains an important contribution to the subject, and M. MANITIUS's classic *Geschichte der lateinischen Literatur des Mittelalters* (three volumes, Munich, 1911–1931). Cf. L. SPITZER, *The Problem of Latin Renaissance Poetry* ('Studies in the Renaissance', II, 1955).

On the pre-classical civilizations v. K. H. DANNENFELDT, *The Renaissance and Pre-Classical Civilizations* ('Journal of the History of Ideas', XIII, 1952).

On the influence of Arabian civilization cf. especially M. ASÍN PALACIOS, *La escatología musulmana en la Divina Comedia* (Madrid, 1919; 2nd edition, Madrid-Granada, 1943); E. CERULLI, *Il 'Libro della Scala' e la questione delle fonti arabo-spagnole della Divina Commedia* (Vatican City, 1949). Cf. K. H. DANNENFELDT, *The Renaissance Humanists and the Knowledge of Arabic* ('Studies in the Renaissance', II, 1955).

2

On Humanism, the following are standard works: G. VOIGT, *Die Wiederbelebung des classischen Altertums oder das erste Jahrhundert des Humanismus* (Berlin, 1859; 3rd edition in two volumes, 1893); L. GEIGER, *Renaissance und Humanismus in Italien und Deutschland* (Berlin, 1882); R. SABBADINI, *Storia del Ciceronianismo e di altre questioni letterarie nell'età della rinascenza* (Turin, 1886); *id.*, *Le scoperte dei codici latini e greci ne' secoli XIV e XV* (two volumes, Florence, 1905–1914); *id.*, *Il metodo degli umanisti* (Florence, 1922); P. DE NOLHAC, *Pétrarque et l'humanisme* (two volumes, 2nd edition, Paris, 1907). A very important general work is the recent book by M. P. GILMORE, *The World of Humanism, 1453–1517* (New York, 1952).

Recent works to be consulted include: H. Rüdiger,
Wesen und Wandlung des Humanismus (Hamburg, 1937); J.
H. Whitfield, *Petrarch and the Renascence* (Oxford, 1943);
P. Van Tieghem, *La littérature de la Renaissance* ('Biblio-
thèque d'Humanisme et Renaissance', IV, 1944); U. Bosco,
Petrarca (Turin, 1946); W. Rüegg, *Cicero und der Humanis-
mus. Formale Untersuchungen über Petrarca und Erasmus*
(Zürich, 1946); G. Billanovich, *Petrarca letterato. I. Lo
scrittoio del Petrarca* (Rome, 1947); *id., Petrarch and the Tex-
tual Tradition of Livy* ('Journal of the Warburg and
Courtauld Institutes', XIV, 1951); *id., I primi umanisti
e le tradizioni dei classici latini* (Fribourg, 1953); R.
Weiss, *The Dawn of Humanism in Italy* (London, 1947);
id., Il primo secolo dell'Umanesimo (Rome, 1949); *id.,
Lo studio di Plutarco nel Trecento* ('La Parola del Passato',
XXXII, 1953); G. Martellotti, *Linee di sviluppo dell'-
umanesimo petrarchesco* ('Studi Petrarcheschi', II, 1949); A.
Renaudet, *Dante humaniste* (Paris, 1952). Cf. R. Spongano,
L'Umanesimo e le sue origini ('Giornale Storico della Letteratura Italiana', CXXX, 1953). A very important volume is
that of B. Ullman, *Studies in the Italian Renaissance* (Rome,
1955), cited above.

On the concept of 'humanitas' v. R. Pfeiffer, *Humanitas
Erasmiana* (Berlin-Leipzig, 1931).

For 'imitatio' v. H. Gmelin, *Das Prinzip der Imitatio in
den romanischen Literaturen der Renaissance* ('Romanische
Forschungen', XLVI, 1932).

On the Byzantine erudites and their influence v. L.
Mohler, *Kardinal Bessarion als Theologe, Humanist und
Staatsmann* (three volumes, Paderborn, 1923–1942); G.
Cammelli, *I dotti bizantini e le origini dell'Umanesimo*, I (M.
Crisolora), II (G. Argiropulo) (Florence, 1941), III (D.
Calcondila) (Florence, 1954); *id., Andronico Callisto* ('La
Rinascita', V, 1942; K. M. Setton, *The Byzantine Back-
ground to the Italian Renaissance* ('Proceedings of the Ameri-
can Philosophical Society', C, 1956).

The following works, dealing with particular individuals

and problems, are of fundamental importance, not least for the light which they shed on Humanism in general: E. WALSER, *Poggius Florentinus. Leben und Werke* (Leipzig-Berlin, 1914); *id.*, *Lebens- und Glaubensprobleme aus dem Zeitalter der Renaissance. Die Religion des Luigi Pulci, ihre Quellen und ihre Bedeutung* (Marburg a.L., 1926); the essays published in the volume *Gesammelte Studien zur Geistesgeschichte der Renaissance* (cited above), especially *Christentum und Antike in der Auffassung der italienischen Frührenaissance*; and the article entitled *Der Sinn des Lebens im Zeitalter der Renaissance* in 'Archiv für Kulturgeschichte', XIV (1926). The student should also refer constantly to the essays of W. GOETZ, now reprinted in *Italien im Mittelalter* (two volumes, Leipzig, 1942); P. JOACHIMSEN, *Aus der Entwicklung des italienischen Humanismus* ('Historische Zeitschrift', CXXI, 1920); A. VON MARTIN, *Mittelalterliche Welt- und Lebensanschauung im Spiegel der Schriften Coluccio Salutatis* (Munich, 1913); *id.*, *Coluccio Salutati und das humanistische Lebensideal* (Berlin-Leipzig, 1916); *id.*, *Petrarca und die Romantik der Renaissance* ('Historische Zeitschrift', CXXXVIII, 1938).

On the moral doctrines of the humanists v. C. E. TRINKAUS, *Adversity's Noblemen. The Italian Humanists on Happiness* (New York, 1940).

On Salutati cf. L. BORGHI, *La dottrina morale di Coluccio Salutati* and *La concezione umanistica di Coluccio Salutati* ('Annali della R. Scuola Normale Superiore di Pisa', New Series, III, 1934); W. RÜEGG, *Entstehung, Quellen und Ziel von Salutatis 'De fato et fortuna'* ('Rinascimento', V, 1954). On Poggio Bracciolini see also C. S. GUTKIND, *Poggio Bracciolinis geistige Entwicklung* ('Vierteljahrschrift für Literaturwissenschaft und Geistesgeschichte', X, 1932). On Valla, see F. GAETA, *Lorenzo Valla. Filologia e storia nell'umanesimo italiano* (Naples, 1955). On Alberti, v. P. H. MICHEL, *Un idéal humain au XVᵉ siècle. La pensée de L. B. Alberti (1404–1472)* (Paris, 1930). On Aeneas Sylvius, apart from the classic work by G. VOIGT, *Enea Silvio de' Piccolomini als Papst Pius*

der Zweite und sein Zeitalter, 3 vols. (Berlin, 1856–1863), cf.
G. PAPARELLI, *Enea Silvio Piccolomini (Pio II)* (Bari, 1950);
G. BÜRCK, *Selbstdarstellung und Personenbildnis bei Enea
Silvio Piccolomini (Pius II)* (Basle, 1956). On Pomponius
Laetus v. V. ZABUGHIN, *Giulio Pomponio Leto* (three volumes,
Rome, 1909–12).

On Humanism and the Renaissance in Piedmont v. G.
VINAY, *L'umanesimo subalpino nel secolo XV* (Turin, 1935);
in Venice, A. FERRIGUTO, *Almorò Barbaro, l'alta cultura nel
Settentrione d'Italia nel '400, i 'sacri canones' di Roma e le
'santissime Leze' di Venezia* ('Miscellanea di storia veneta',
3rd Series, XV, 1922); L. LAZZARINI, *Paolo de Bernardo e i
primordi dell'Umanesimo in Venezia* (Geneva, 1930) and the
works of P. Gothein cited in the section on political thought;
in the south of Italy, E. GOTHEIN, *Die Culturentwicklung
Süd-Italiens* (Breslau, 1886) (still an indispensable work);
various writings of B. CROCE, especially *I teatri di Napoli dal
Rinascimento alla fine del secolo XVIII* (4th edition, Bari,
1947); *La Spagna nella vita italiana durante la Rinascenza*
(4th edition, Bari, 1949); *Storie e leggende napoletane* (4th
edition, Bari, 1948); *Uomini e cose della vecchia Italia* (1st
Series, 2nd edition, Bari, 1943); *Aneddoti di varia letteratura*,
I (2nd edition, Bari, 1953); and, with special reference to
Sannazzaro, *Varietà di storia letteraria e civile* (2nd Series,
Bari, 1949). V. also A. ALTAMURA, *L'Umanesimo nel Mezzo-
giorno d'Italia* (Florence, 1941).

On the 'courtier', see E. Loos, *Baldassare Castigliones
'Libro del cortegiano'. Studien zur Tugendauffassung des Cinquecento* (Frankfurt a. M., 1955), as well as V. CIAN, *Un illustre
nunzio pontificio del Rinascimento: Baldassare Castiglione* (Vatican City, 1951). On Leonardo, v. C. LUPORINI, *La mente di
Leonardo* (Florence, 1953).

3

'Christian Humanism' is a phrase frequently on the lips of
contemporary scholars. On the one hand, it signifies a return
to the controversy about the dividing-line between the

Middle Ages and the Renaissance, and the advocates of 'Christian' Humanism are those who regard the two periods merely as different stages of a continuous historical process and who minimize the revolutionary character of the Italian Renaissance. There was a Christian humanism which declared itself in the early centuries of the Church. This humanism associated Antiquity with the Gospel and reached its peak during the Carolingian Renaissance and the Renaissance of the twelfth century. It was a humanism which St. Thomas, in face of the new Averroistic, anti-Christian and anti-humanistic trends, firmly established in the thirteenth century on the basis of a synthesis of reason and Revelation, of nature and super-nature. This is the humanism postulated by Gilson. It is the 'eternal' humanism of Bremond and Renaudet.

In this 'eternal' humanism there was, however, a second phase, clearer and more precise, which specifically concerned the Renaissance and the 'Christian' humanism of the fifteenth and sixteenth centuries. Here the problem has been studied chiefly in so far as it affects the countries north of the Alps, in particular the Netherlands and France; and the figure that commands most attention is Erasmus.

Important in this connection are the studies of P. MEST-WERDT, *Die Anfänge des Erasmus: Humanismus und 'Devotio Moderna'* (Leipzig, 1917); A. HYMA, *The Christian Renaissance. A History of the 'Devotio Moderna'* (Grand Rapids, Michigan, 1924), and the same author's recently-published *Renaissance to Reformation: A Critical Review of the Spiritual and Temporal Influences on Medieval Europe* (Grand Rapids, 1951). V. also F. CASPARI, *Erasmus on the Social Functions of Christian Humanism* ('Journal of the History of Ideas', VIII, 1947); W. K. FERGUSON, *Renaissance Tendencies in the Religious Thought of Erasmus* (*ibid.*, XV, 1954).

The student should consult H. BREMOND, *Histoire littéraire du sentiment religieux en France depuis la fin des guerres de religion*, I, *L'humanisme dévot* (Paris, 1916); *id.*, *Autour de l'humanisme. D'Érasme à Pascal* (Paris, 1937); above all, A.

RENAUDET, *Préréforme et humanisme à Paris pendant les premières guerres d'Italie (1494–1517)* (Paris, 1916; 2nd edition, 1953); *id.*, *Érasme, sa pensée religieuse et son action d'après sa correspondance (1518–1521)* (Paris, 1926); *id.*, *Études érasmiennes (1521–1529)* (Paris, 1939); *id.*, *Érasme et l'Italie* (Geneva, 1954).

Much less valuable is V. ZABUGHIN's *Storia del Rinascimento cristiano in Italia* (Milan, 1924).

Conversely, on the connection between certain humanistic trends and the 'libertinism' of the sixteenth and seventeenth centuries v. H. BUSSON, *Les sources et le développement du rationalisme dans la littérature française de la Renaissance (1533–1601)* (Paris, 1922); R. PINTARD, *Le libertinage érudit dans la première moitié du XVIIᵉ siècle* (two volumes, Paris, 1943); G. SPINI, *Ricerca dei libertini* (Rome, 1950). All the above-mentioned works are of greater value to the student than J. R. CHARBONNEL's *La pensée italienne au XVIᵉ siècle et le courant libertin* (Paris, 1919).

On the 'conceptual' links between the Renaissance and the Reformation and the similarities of outlook between humanists and heretics v. especially D. CANTIMORI, *Eretici italiani del Cinquecento* (Florence, 1939; German translation, *Italienische Häretiker der Spätrenaissance*, Basle, 1949); *id.*, *Anabattismo e neoplatonismo nel secolo XVI in Italia* ('Rendiconti R. Accademia dei Lincei', 6th Series, XII, 1936); v. also P. ROSSI, *Giacomo Aconcio* (Milan, 1952).

For general observations on the connection between the Renaissance and the Reformation v. D. CANTIMORI, *Ulrico von Hutten e i rapporti tra Rinascimento e Riforma* (Pisa, 1930); *id.*, *Umanesimo e Luteranesimo di fronte alla Scolastica: Caspar Peucer* ('Studi Germanici', II, 1937); *id.*, *Incontri italo-germanici nell'età della Riforma*, I, *Lutero e Savonarola* (*ib.*, III, 1938); *id.*, *Note su Erasmo e l'Italia* (*ib.*, II, 1937); R. W. BATTENHOUSE, *The Doctrine of Man in Calvin and in Renaissance Platonism* ('Journal of the History of Ideas', IX, 1948); C. TRINKAUS, *The Problem of Free Will in the Renaissance and the Reformation* (*ib.*, X, 1949); *id.*, *Renaissance*

Problems in Calvin's Theology ('Studies in the Renaissance', I, 1954); and J. BOHATEC, *Budé und Calvin. Studien zur Gedankenwelt des französischen Frühhumanismus* (Graz, 1950); G. RADETTI, *Umanesimo e Riforma nella prima metà del sec. xvi* ('Giornale Critico della filosofia italiana', XXXV, 1956).

Important for the interpretation of the Cinquecento is L. FEBVRE's *Le problème de l'incroyance au XVIᵉ siècle: la religion de Rabelais* (Paris, 1942; 2nd edition, 1947). V. also the same author's *Autour de l'Heptameron: amour sacré, amour profane* (Paris, 1944).

Finally, see A. CORSANO, *Il pensiero religioso italiano dall'Umanesimo al Giurisdizionalismo* (Bari, 1937).

4

For the philosophic thought of the period see W. DRESS, *Die Mystik des Marsilio Ficino* (Berlin-Leipzig, 1929); R. HÖNIGS-WALD, *Denker der italienischen Renaissance: Gestalten und Probleme* (Basle, 1938); E. CASSIRER, *Giovanni Pico della Mirandola* ('Journal of the History of Ideas', III, 1942); A. CORSANO, *Studi sul Rinascimento* (Bari, 1949).

For the neo-scholastic interpretation v. F. OLGIATI, *L'anima dell'Umanesimo e del Rinascimento* (Milan, 1924).

B. NARDI, whose work is rich in scholarship, rejects the thesis that the philosophic thought of the humanists is original and modern in character. Cf. his *Saggi di filosofia dantesca* (Milan, 1930); *Dante e la cultura medievale* (Bari, 2nd ed., 1949); *Nel mondo di Dante* (Rome, 1944); *Sigieri di Brabante nel pensiero del Rinascimento italiano* (Rome, 1945); *Il problema della verità. Soggetto ed oggetto del conoscere nella filosofia antica e medievale* (Rome, 1951). The two volumes *Medioevo e Rinascimento. Studi in onore di Bruno Nardi* (Florence, 1955), contain an important collection of studies by various authors.

For Platonism and the Platonic tradition in the Renaissance v. (apart from A. DELLA TORRE's *Storia dell'Accademia Platonica di Firenze*, Florence, 1902) N. A. ROBB, *Neoplatonism of the Italian Renaissance* (London, 1935); B.

KIESZKOWSKI, *Studi sul platonismo del Rinascimento in Italia* (Florence, 1936); W. MOENCH, *Die italienische Platonre-naissance und ihre Bedeutung für Frankreichs Literatur- und Geistesgeschichte, 1450–1550* (Berlin, 1936); R. KLIBANSKY, *The Continuity of the Platonic Tradition During the Middle Ages* (London, 1939; reprinted 1951); *id.*, *Plato's Parmenides in the Middle Ages and the Renaissance* ('Mediaeval and Renaissance Studies', I, 1941–1943); E. GARIN, *Per la storia della tradizione platonica medievale* ('Giornale Critico della Filosofia italiana', XXVIII, 1949). Cf. F. E. CRANZ, *Saint Augustine and Nicholas of Cusa in the Tradition of Western Christian Thought* ('Speculum', XXVIII, 1953).

For Averroism – which inspired one of the most cele-brated works of the nineteenth century, E. RENAN's *Aver-roès et l'Averroïsme* (Paris, 1852), in which the School of Padua is also discussed at length – v. B. KIESZKOWSKI, *Averroismo e Platonismo in Italia negli ultimi decenni del secolo XV* ('Giornale Critico della Filosofia italiana', 1933); E. TROILO, *Averroismo e aristotelismo padovano* (Padua, 1939) and *Averroismo o aristotelismo 'alessandrista', padovano* ('Rendic. Acc. Lincei', 1954); J. H. RANDALL JR., *The Development of Scientific Method in the School of Padua* ('Journal of the History of Ideas', I, 1940).

On stoicism, v. L. ZANTA, *La renaissance du stoïcisme au XVIᵉ siècle* (Paris, 1914).

On epicureanism, v. D. C. ALLEN, *The Rehabilitation of Epicurus and His Theory of Pleasure in the Early Renaissance* ('Modern Philology', XLI, 1944).

An interesting study is H. S. WILSON's *Some Meanings of 'Nature' in Renaissance Literary Theory* ('Journal of the His-tory of Ideas', II, 1941).

5

For the history of literary criticism, v. the observations of B. CROCE in *Estetica* (9th edition, Bari, 1950); see also J. E. SPINGARN, *A History of Literary Criticism in the Renaissance* (New York, 2nd ed., 1908) (still an indispensable work on the subject); G. SAINTSBURY, *A History of Criticism and Literary Taste in Europe* (three volumes, Edinburgh-London, 1900–1904); and C. S. BALDWIN, *Renaissance Literary Theory and Practice: Classicism in the Rhetoric and Poetic of Italy, France and England, 1400–1600* (New York, 1939). Cf. W. F. PATTERSON, *Three Centuries of French Poetic Theory. A Critical History of the Chief Arts of Poetry in France, 1328–1620* (two volumes, Ann Arbor, 1935); V. HALL JR., *Renaissance Literary Criticism: A Study of Its Social Content* (New York, 1945). An important recent work is A. BUCK, *Italienische Dichtungslehren vom Mittelalter bis zum Ausgang der Renaissance* (Tübingen, 1952). Cf. also G. MORPURGO TAGLIABUE, *Aristotelismo e Barocco*, in *Retorica e Barocco. Atti del III Congresso Internazionale di Studi umanistici* (Milan, 1954), and the writings of E. Garin, P. Rossi and C. Vasoli on Renaissance rhetorical theories in '*Archivio di filosofia*', III, 1953.

With regard to literature itself, I would refer the student who seeks more detailed indications of sources to the essays of A. MONTEVERDI (*Le origini*), M. BARBI (*Dante*), S. A. CHIMENZ (*Trecento*), and E. CARRARA (*L'età del Rinascimento*), also to *Un cinquantennio di studi sulla letteratura italiana (1886–1936). Saggi dedicati a Vittorio Rossi*, I (Florence, 1937); and G. PREZZOLINI, *Repertorio bibliografico della letteratura italiana dal 1902 al 1932* (two volumes, Rome, 1937–1939); and for the years 1933–42, two volumes, New York, 1946–48. Meanwhile, I will content myself here with mentioning a few essential works of a general character.

First, F. DE SANCTIS's classic and indispensable *Storia della letteratura italiana* (Bari, two volumes, 1925), which should be referred to for the elucidation of all problems connected with the Renaissance. Next, the volumes of the 'Storia Letteraria Vallardi' (N. SAPEGNO, *Il Trecento*, 3rd edition, Milan, 1938; V. ROSSI, *Il Quattrocento*, Milan, 1949; G. TOFFANIN, *Il Cinquecento*, Milan, 1954) and F. FLORA, *Storia della letteratura italiana*, I and II (Milan, 1940).

But see especially A. SCHIAFFINI, *Tradizione e poesia nella prosa d'arte italiana, dalla latinità medievale a G. Boccaccio*

(Genoa, 1934; 2nd edition, Rome, 1943); B. CROCE, *Poeti e scrittori del pieno e del tardo Rinascimento* (three volumes, Bari, 1945–52); M. FUBINI, *Studi sulla letteratura del Rinascimento* (Florence, 1948); L. RUSSO, *Ritratti e disegni storici*, 3rd series, *Studi sul Due e Trecento* (Bari, 1951). For Dante and Boccaccio, cf. also E. AUERBACH, *Mimesis: the Representation of Reality in Western Literature* (Engl. transl., Princeton, 1953). Concerned with maintaining 'the typically medieval character of the artistic experience of Boccaccio' is V. BRANCA, *Boccaccio medievale* (Florence, 1956).

6

On the history of art see especially G. VON SCHLOSSER, *Die Kunstliteratur. Ein Handbuch zur Quellenkunde der neueren Kunstgeschichte* (Vienna, 1924); L. VENTURI, *History of Art Criticism* (New York, 1936) (in addition, of course, the writings of Weisbach, Haseloff, etc., cited above).

E. PANOFSKY's *Idea. Ein zur Beitrag Begriffsgeschichte der älteren Kunsttheorie* (Leipzig-Berlin, 1924) is essential reading. See also the same writer's *Studies in Iconology. Humanistic Themes in the Art of the Renaissance* (New York, 1939).

For the general problem of the relationship and of the difference between Gothic art and the 'classical' art of the Renaissance, see W. WORRINGEN, *Formprobleme der Gotik* (Munich, 1910); and above all the fundamental study by M. DVOŘÁK, *Idealismus und Naturalismus in der gotischen Skulptur und Malerei*, in the volume *Kunstgeschichte als Geistesgeschichte* (Munich, 1924). See also D. FREY, *Gotik und Renaissance als Grundlagen der modernen Weltanschauung* (Augsburg, 1929).

For the relationship and the difference between Renaissance and Baroque art, see H. WÖLLFLIN's classic *Renaissance und Barock. Eine Untersuchung über Wesen und Entstehung des Barockstil in Italien* (Munich, 1888; 4th ed., 1926); *id.*, *Kunstgeschichtliche Grundbegriffe: das Problem der Stilentwickelung in der neueren Kunst* (Munich, 1915; 6th ed., 1923); still to be consulted is the same author's *Die classische Kunst. Eine Einführung in die italienische Renaissance* (Munich, 1898;

6th ed., 1914, preferable to the 7th: cf. the preface by Wölfflin to the Italian edition, *L'arte classica del Rinascimento*, Florence, 1941). Cf. also W. WEISBACH, *Der Barock als Kunst der Gegenreformation* (Berlin, 1921), and *Barock als Stilphänomen* ('Deutsche Vierteljahrschrift für Literaturwissenschaft und Geistesgeschichte', II, 1925). For music I will content myself with indicating the general article by E. E. LOWINSKY, *Music in the Culture of the Renaissance* ('Journal of the History of Ideas', XV, 1954), which provides references to the fundamental works of Besseler, Bukofzer, Reese and others.

7

For the sociological interpretations of the Renaissance, and on its economic and social aspects, see F. SCHNEIDER, *Zur sozialen Genesis der Renaissance* ('Festschrift Oppenheimer. Wirtschaft und Gesellschaft', Frankfurt, 1924); H. KOHT, *Le problème des origines de la Renaissance* ('Revue de synthèse historique', XXXVII, 1924); F. ENGEL-JÁNOSI, *Soziale Probleme der Renaissance* (Berlin, 1924); above all, A. VON MARTIN, *Soziologie der Renaissance. Zur Physiognomik und Rhythmik bürgerlicher Kultur* (Stuttgart, 1932; 2nd edition, Frankfurt-am-Main, 1949; English translation, London, 1944; 2nd edition, 1945); *id.*, *Bürgertum und Humanismus* ('Archiv für Kulturgeschichte', XXXII, 1944); A. FANFANI, *Le origini dello spirito capitalistico in Italia* (Milan, 1933); A. SAPORI, *Il problema economico*, in *Il Rinascimento. Significato e limiti* (cited above), 'Atti del III Congresso Internazionale sul Rinascimento', Florence, 1953 (including the discussion). See also G. BARBIERI, *Ideali economici degli Italiani all'inizio dell'età moderna* (Milan, 1940), and the bibliographical article by F. L. NUSSBAUM, *The Economic History of Renaissance Europe* ('The Journal of Modern History', XIII, 1941).

F. ANTAL's *Florentine Painting and Its Social Background: The Bourgeois Republic before Cosimo de' Medici's Advent to Power: Fourteenth and Early Fifteenth Centuries* (London,

1948) represents an attempt at a 'social' interpretation of Florentine painting in particular.

This inquiry into the 'social' connections of Humanism has been well carried out, as far as England is concerned, by F. CASPARI, *Humanism and the Social Order in Tudor England* (Chicago, 1954). In Italy, E. Conti has been working for several years on a detailed study of Florentine society in the Trecento and Quattrocento, which will certainly be of importance for the history of the 'social connections' of Humanism.

8

The political thought of the Renaissance has been the subject of a great deal of intensive research. Together with that of historiography, it is one of the fields in which the creative capacity and the originality of the period are most clearly displayed. No one has yet ventured to put forward the thesis that the political ideas of a Machiavelli or the historiography of a Guicciardini are already implicit in the writings of the twelfth and thirteenth centuries; and recent attempts to discover Machiavelli's 'sources' (A. H. GILBERT, *Machiavelli's 'Prince' and Its Forerunners. 'The Prince' as a Typical Book 'de Regimine Principum'*, Durham, 1938, and the commentary by Father L. J. WALKER, S.J., on *The Discourses of Niccolò Machiavelli*, Translation and Commentary, two volumes, London, 1950) merely serve to emphasize the gulf that divides the political thought of Machiavelli from that of the various writers of the Middle Ages.

Here, however, I will refrain from giving references to individual authors, in particular to Machiavelli, apropos of whom an exhaustive bibliography of works published up to 1936 has been included by A. NORSA in *Il principio della forza nel pensiero politico di Niccolò Machiavelli seguito da un contributo bibliografico* (Milan, 1936).[1] Among the many

---

[1] More up-to-date information is given in G. SASSO's *Recenti studi sul Machiavelli* ('Rassegna di filosofia', I, 1952) and in W. PREISER's *Das Machiavelli Bild der Gegenwart* ('Zeitschrift für die gesamte Staatswissenschaft', CVIII, 1952).

works on Machiavelli that have appeared since this biblio-
graphy was compiled the following are especially worthy of
mention: G. RITTER, *Machtstaat und Utopie. Vom Streit um
die Dämonie der Macht seit Machiavelli und Morus* (Munich-
Berlin, 1940; now available under the title *Die Dämonie der
Macht*, 6th edition, Munich, 1948); A. RENAUDET, *Machia-
vel* (Paris, 1942, 2nd ed., 1956); the third edition of L.
RUSSO's *Machiavelli* (Bari, 1949), which includes a note on
Italian criticism from Cuoco to Croce; L. HUOVINEN, *Das
Bild vom Menschen im politischen Denken Niccolò Machiavelli*
('Annales Academiae Scientiarum Finnicae', b. 74, 2, Hel-
sinki, 1951). Among works in English, the following should
be especially noted: H. BUTTERFIELD, *The Statecraft of
Machiavelli* (London, 1940; 2nd ed., 1955); the writings of
J. H. WHITFIELD, *Machiavelli* (Oxford, 1947), *Savonarola
and the Purpose of the Prince* ('The Modern Language Re-
view', XLIV, 1949), *Machiavelli and Castruccio* ('Italian
Studies', VIII, 1953), *On Machiavelli's Use of 'Ordini'* (*ib.*,
X, 1955), *The Politics of Machiavelli* ('The Modern Lan-
guage Review', L, 1955); and those of F. GILBERT, *The
Humanist Concept of the Prince and the 'Prince' of Machiavelli*
('The Journal of Modern History', XI, 1939), *On Machia-
velli's Idea of Virtù* ('Renaissance News', IV, 1951), *The
Concept of Nationalism in Machiavelli's Prince* ('Studies in the
Renaissance', I, 1954), and the essay on the *Discorsi* cited
above.

For the biography of Machiavelli, R. RIDOLFI, *Vita di
Niccolò Machiavelli* (Rome, 1954) is now fundamental. For
Guicciardini V. DE CAPRARIIS, *Francesco Guicciardini. Dalla
politica alla storia* (Bari, 1950).

Confining our attentions, then, to works of a comprehensive nature, we find that pride of place is still held by F.
MEINECKE's essential *Die Idee der Staatsräson in der neueren
Geschichte* (Munich-Berlin, 1924), which opens with a chapter on Machiavelli. V. also G. H. SABINE, *A History of Political Theory* (New York-London, 1937). For the Middle Ages,
apart from R. W. and A. J. CARLYLE's classic *History of*

R

Mediaeval Political Theory in the West (six volumes, Edin-burgh-London, 1903–36), see especially A. DEMPF, *Sacrum Imperium* (Munich-Berlin, 1929); G. DE LAGARDE, *La naissance de l'esprit laïque au déclin du Moyen Âge* (six volumes, Paris, I and II, 2nd edition, 1948; III–VI, 1942–46); A. P. D'ENTRÈVES, *The Medieval Contribution to Political Thought*, Oxford, 1939.

But see also (in addition to the studies of BARON, which have already been mentioned) F. VON BEZOLD, *Republik und Monarchie in der italienischen Literatur des 15. Jahrhunderts* (in *Aus Mittelalter und Renaissance*, Munich-Berlin, 1918); F. ERCOLE, *Da Bartolo all'Althusio* (Florence, 1932); C. CURCIO, *La politica italiana del '400* (Florence, 1932); *id.*, *Dal Rinascimento alla Controriforma* (Rome, 1934); *id.*, intro-ductions to *Utopisti e riformatori sociali del Cinquecento* (Bol-ogna, 1941) and *Utopisti italiani del Cinquecento* (Rome, 1944); N. VALERI, *L'insegnamento di Gian Galeazzo Visconti e i 'Consigli al Principe' di C. Malatesta* ('Bollettino Storico Bibliografico Subalpino', XXXVI, 1934); P. GOTHEIN, *Francesco Barbaro. Früh-Humanismus und Staatskunst in Vene-dig* (Berlin, 1932; cf. N. CAROTTI, *Un politico umanista del Quattrocento: Francesco Barbaro*, 'Rivista Storica Italiana', 5th Series, II, 1937); *id.*, *Zaccaria Trevisan* ('Archivio Veneto', XXI, 1937); D. CANTIMORI, *Rhetoric and Politics in Italian Humanism* ('Journal of the Warburg Institute', I, 1937); N. RUBINSTEIN, *The Beginnings of Political Thought in Florence* ('Journal of the Warburg and Courtauld Institutes', V, 1942) and *Florence and the Despots: Some Aspects of Florentine Diplomacy in the Fourteenth Century* ('Transactions of the Royal Historical Society', 5th Series, II, 1952); R. STADEL-MANN, *Persönlichkeit und Staat in der Renaissance* (in *Vom Erbe der Neuzeit*, I, Leipzig, 1942); A. RENAUDET, *Human-isme, histoire et politique au quattrocento*, in *Cultura e educa-zione. Studi in onore di Giovanni Calò* (Florence, 1955).

For the Cinquecento v. G. TOFFANIN, *Machiavelli e il 'Tacitismo' (La 'Politica storica' al tempo della Controriforma)* (Padua, 1921); J. W. ALLEN, *A History of Political Thought in the Sixteenth Century* (London, 1928; reprinted London, 1951); P. MESNARD, *L'essor de la philosophie politique au XVIe siècle* (Paris, 1936; 2nd edition, 1952); F. GILBERT, *Bernardo Rucellai and the Orti Oricellari: A Study on the Origin of Modern Political Thought* ('Journal of the Warburg and Courtauld Institutes', XII, 1949); R. DE MATTEI, *Fortuna e virtù dal Machiavelli al Lottini* ('Archivio di storia della filosofia italiana', VII, 1938).

An important general study, covering the period from Savonarola to the historians and political writers of the age of Cosimo I, is now provided by R. VON ALBERTINI, *Das florentinische Staatsbewusstsein im Übergang von der Republik zum Prinzipat* (Berne, 1955).

In order to obtain a complete picture of the mentality of the men of the Renaissance it is fitting that we should also ask ourselves what meaning the time-honoured and typically mediaeval concept of the *Respublica Christiana* continued to have for them and how much or how little importance they attached to the expression 'Europe'. In the writings of Machiavelli this expression is already used in its modern sense, viz. of a civilized lay community, politically conscious. On this problem v. R. WALLACH, *Das abendländische Gemeinschaftsbewusstsein im Mittelalter* (Leipzig-Berlin, 1928); W. FRITZEMEYER, *Christenheit und Europa* (Munich-Berlin, 1931); F. CHABOD, *L'idea di Europa* ('La Rassegna d'Italia', II, 1947). Cf. D. HAY, *Sur un problème de terminologie historique: 'Europe et Chrétienté'* ('Diogène', 17, Jan. 1957); also *From Roman Empire to Renaissance Europe* (London, 1953).

For the birth of the modern principle of the balance of power, which has its origins in the Italy of the second half of the fifteenth century, the student should consult, in addition to E. KAEBER's ever-useful *Die Idee des europäischen Gleichgewichts in der publizistischen Literatur vom 16. bis zur Mitte des 18. Jahrhunderts* (Berlin, 1907), W. KIENAST, *Die Anfänge des europäischen Staatensystems im späteren Mittelalter* ('Historische Zeitschrift', CLIII, 1936; but cf. F. CHABOD, 'Rivista Storica Italiana', 5th Series, I, 1936); C. MORANDI,

Il concetto della politica di equilibrio nell'Europa moderna ('Archivio Storico Italiano', XCVIII, 1940); E. W. NELSON, *The Origins of Modern Balance-of-Power Politics* ('Medievalia et Humanistica', I, 1943); N. VALERI, *La libertà e la pace orientamenti politici del Rinascimento italiano* (Turin, 1942) and *L'Italia nell'età dei Principati* (cited above); V. DE CAPRARIIS, *Il problema dell'equilibrio nel pensiero del Machiavelli* ('Atti dell'Accademia Pontaniana', New Series, II, Naples, 1950); G. MATTINGLY, *Renaissance Diplomacy* (London, 1955).

8

On the subject of historiography E. FUETER's *Geschichte der neueren Historiographie* (3rd edition, Munich-Berlin, 1936) and B. CROCE's observations in *Teoria e storia della storiografia* (6th edition, Bari, 1948) constitute essential reading. See also M. RITTER, *Die Entwicklung der Geschichtswissenschaft an den führenden Persönlichkeiten betrachtet* (Munich-Berlin, 1919); J. W. THOMPSON, *A History of Historical Writing* (two volumes, New York, 1942, Vol. I); K. BRANDI, *Geschichte der Geschichtswissenschaft* (Bonn, 1947; 2nd edition, Bonn, 1952); also the second chapter of H. VON SRBIK's *Geist und Geschichte vom deutschen Humanismus bis zur Gegenwart*, I (Munich-Salzburg, 1950). Still to be consulted are P. JOACHIMSEN's *Geschichtsauffassung und Geschichtschreibung in Deutschland unter dem Einfluss des Humanismus*, I (Leipzig, 1910).

See especially M. LUPO GENTILE, *Studi sulla storiografia fiorentina alla corte di Cosimo I de' Medici* (Pisa, 1905); E. SANTINI, *Leonardo Bruni Aretino e i suoi 'Historiarum florentini populi libri XII'* ('Annali della R. Scuola Normale Superiore di Pisa', XXII, 1910); *id.*, *La fortuna della Storia fiorentina di Leonardo Bruni nel Rinascimento* ('Studi Storici', XX, 1911); H. GMELIN, *Personendarstellung bei den Florentinischen Geschichtschreibern der Renaissance* (Leipzig, 1927); E. MEHL, *Die Weltanschauung des Giovanni Villani* (Leipzig, 1927); above all B. L. ULLMAN, *Leonardo Bruni and Human-*

istic Historiography ('Medievalia et Humanistica', IV, 1946, now in *Studies in the Italian Renaissance,* cited above); F. CHABOD, *Paolo Giovio* (cited above); N. RUBINSTEIN, *The 'Storie Fiorentine' and the 'Memorie di famiglia' by Francesco Guicciardini* ('Rinascimento', IV, 1953); A. R. REYNOLDS, *Latin Historiography: a Survey, 1400–1600* ('Studies in the Renaissance', II, 1955); G. ZIPPEL, *Lorenzo Valla e le origini della storiografia umanistica a Venezia* ('Rinascimento', VII, 1956).

For the attitude of the late Renaissance historians to such an episode as the Council of Trent v. H. JEDIN, *Das Konzil von Trient. Ein Überblick über die Erforschung seiner Geschichte* (Rome, 1948).

For Renaissance theories with regard to history and historical method v. SABBADINI, *Il metodo degli umanisti* (cited above); F. VON BEZOLD, *Zur Entstehungsgeschichte der historischen Methodik,* in *Aus Mittelalter und Renaissance* (cited above); J. L. BROWN, *The 'Methodus ad facilem historiarum cognitionem' of Jean Bodin. A Critical Study* (Washington, 1939); H. WEISINGER, *Ideas of History During the Renaissance* ('Journal of the History of Ideas', VI, 1945); F. LAMPRECHT, *Zur Theorie der humanistischen Geschichtsschreibung. Mensch und Geschichte bei Francesco Patrizi* (Zürich, 1950); E. GARIN, *La storia nel pensiero del Rinascimento,* in *Medioevo e Rinascimento,* cited above; M. P. GILMORE, *Freedom and Determinism in Renaissance Historians* ('Studies in the Renaissance', III, 1956).

The student will also find it helpful to consult M. SCHULZ, *Die Lehre von der historischen Methode bei den Geschichtschreibern des Mittelalters* (Berlin-Leipzig, 1909); E. MENKE-GLÜCKERT, *Die Geschichtschreibung der Reformation und Gegenreformation. Bodin und die Begründung der Geschichtsmethodologie durch Barthol. Keckermann* (Leipzig, 1912); G. SPINI, *I trattatisti dell'arte storica nella Controriforma italiana,* in the miscellaneous work entitled *Contributi alla storia del Concilio di Trento e della Controriforma* ('Quaderni di Belfagor', I, Florence, 1948).

On the concept of progress v. J. DELVAILLE, *Essai sur l'histoire de l'idée de progrès* (Paris, 1910); J. B. BURY, *The Idea of Progress* (London, 1924); E. ZILSEL, *The Genesis of the Concept of Scientific Progress* ('Journal of the History of Ideas', VI, 1945); E. L. TUVESON, *Millennium and Utopia. A Study in the Background of the Idea of Progress* (University of California Press, 1949); A. C. KELLER, *Zilsel, the Artisans and the Idea of Progress in the Renaissance* ('Journal of the History of Ideas', XI, 1950). Also H. BAKER, *The Wars of Truth. Studies in the Decay of Christian Humanism in the Earlier Seventeenth Century* (Chapter II) (London-New York, 1952).

Cf. H. GILLOT, *La querelle des anciens et des modernes en France de la Défense et illustration de la langue française aux Parallèles des anciens et des modernes* (Nancy, 1914).

VII

I

A number of comprehensive and well-arranged bibliographies are to-day available to keep the student abreast of the progress of Renaissance studies. Among them the following may be noted:

H. BARON, *Renaissance in Italien* ('Archiv für Kulturgeschichte', XVII and XXI, 1927 and 1931); P. O. KRISTELLER and J. H. RANDALL JR., *The Study of the Philosophies of the Renaissance* ('Journal of the History of Ideas', II, 1941); *Surveys of Recent Scholarship in the Period of Renaissance*. Compiled for the Committee of Renaissance Studies of the American Council of Learned Societies (First Series, Washington, 1945) (this work is divided into thirteen reprinted essays of various authors, and the subjects treated include Latin literature, philosophy, political thought, etc.); J. RUMMENS, 'Revue Internationale de Philosophie', V, 1951 (contains a bibliography covering the period 1930–

1950); E. R. CURTIUS, *Neuere Arbeiten über den italienischen Humanismus* ('Bibliothèque d'Humanisme et Renaissance', X, 1948).

Regular and general reviews are published (under the title of *Recent Literature of the Renaissance. A Bibliography*) in 'Studies in Philology'. Cf. also P. G. RICCI (*Studi sull'- Umanesimo e sul Rinascimento italiano*, in 'Rinascimento', Florence: the first article of the series, dealing with Italian and foreign studies published in 1950, appeared in Volume II, 1951, the second, on studies published in 1951, in Vol. III, 1952); E. GARIN (in 'Giornale Critico della Filosofia Italiana', XXIX, XXXI, XXXII, 1950, 1952, 1953); and – with special reference to art – A. CHASTEL (*Problèmes de l'art et de l'humanisme en Italie* or *Problèmes de l'art à la Renaissance*, in 'Bibliothèque d'Humanisme et Renaissance', Volume X, 1948, onwards).

The *Progress of Medieval and Renaissance Studies in the United States and Canada* is edited by S. H. Thompson and published at Boulder (Colorado). No. 19 includes a list of European works published between 1939 and 1945.

For Italian studies published between the end of the last century and 1950 v. CHABOD, *Cinquant' anni di vita intellettuale italiana* (cited above).

ANGELERI's *Il problema religioso del Rinascimento* (cited above) contains a wealth of useful information. The *Bibliographia philosophica, 1934–1945*, 2 vols. (ed. G. A. DE BRIE, Utrecht-Brussels-Antwerp, 1950–54) is also helpful, as is the *Bibliografia filosofica italiana dal 1900 al 1950*, 4 vols. (Rome, 1950–56).

Finally, for general indications of the progress of Renaissance studies, v. the bibliographies furnished by C. CARBONARA (in *Il secolo XV*, Milan, 1943); GARIN (especially in *Umanesimo e Rinascimento*, Milan, 1949, cited above); and SAITTA (in Volume III of *Il pensiero italiano nell'Umanesimo e nel Rinascimento*, cited above).

E. GARIN's admirable and well-chosen collection of significant passages from the writers of the Renaissance (in *Il*

Rinascimento italiano, Milan, 1941, cited above) constitutes an excellent introduction to the study of the period.

An instrument of information of an entirely new kind is provided by M. E. COSENZA, *Biographical and Bibliographical Dictionary of the Italian Humanists and of the World of Classical Scholarship in Italy, 1300–1800*, published in 29 rolls of microfilm by The Renaissance Society of America, 9 October, 1954 (copies can be purchased from the Society).

2

In recent decades a number of specialized reviews have appeared dealing explicitly with Humanism and the Renaissance. A beginning was made in France with *Humanisme et Renaissance* (Paris, 1934 onwards), renamed in 1941 *Bibliothèque d'Humanisme et Renaissance*. Under its new title this review was published first in Paris, then in Geneva, and by 1956 the number of volumes issued already amounted to eighteen. In Italy *La Rinascita* was published in Florence from 1938 to 1943 by the Centro Nazionale di Studi sul Rinascimento. It consisted of thirty-four parts plus a Supplement, published in 1940 and dedicated to Francesco Guicciardini on the four hundredth anniversary of his death. In 1950 it reappeared under the title of *Rinascimento*. In 1943 the review *Medievalia et Humanistica* was founded in America, where *The Renaissance News*, a periodical report published by the Committee of Renaissance Studies of the American Council of Learned Societies, made its first appearance in 1948. In 1954 The Renaissance Society of America was formed and, while continuing to publish *The Renaissance News*, which also contains useful bibliographical information, initiated the publication of an annual volume of essays entitled *Studies in the Renaissance* (I, 1954; II, 1955; III, 1956).

Published in London is the *Journal of the Warburg Institute*, founded in 1937. With the publication of Volume III (1939–40) it was renamed the *Journal of the Warburg and Courtauld Institutes*. Also published by the Warburg Institute is *Mediaeval and Renaissance Studies*. Indeed, all the Institute's publications should be consulted, from *Vorträge der Bibliothek Warburg* (nine volumes, Leipzig-Berlin, 1921–22 to 1930–31) to *Studien* (Leipzig-Berlin) (subsequently published in London under the title of *Studies*), which includes several of the more important books listed above (e.g. CASSIRER, *Individuum und Kosmos*; PANOFSKY, *Idea*.

INDEX

Absolutism, xv, 116
    Machiavelli as precursor of, 121n, 124n
Acciaiuoli, Roberto, 4–5
Accolti, Benedetto, 196
Albergaccio (villa), 10–11
Alberti, L. B., 165, 196
    cit., 183–4
Albertini, R. von, cit., xvi
Alexander VI, Pope, 94
Alginard, 167, 177, 178
Alvisi, cit., 106n
Amboise, Cardinal Georges D', 127
America, discovery of, 198
    Montaigne on (cit.), 199
Antiquity, *see* Roman world *and* Classical antiquity
Architecture, 155, 158
Ariosto, xi
Armies (national), 89n
Art,
    Christianity and, 153, 154, 155 : Mediaeval and Renaissance concepts of, 182–185
Art of War (Machiavelli's), 11, 16, 104, 108, 109
    cit., 73n, 84n–85n, 95n, 128, 147, 169
    origin and style of, 27–8
Arte della Guerra, see *Art of War*
Artillery, 197
Artisan class, 57
Asti, 42n

Balance of power, 13, 15, 60

Banking, 187
Barbarian concept, 199
Barbarossa, *see* Frederick I
Baumgarten,
    bibliographical theory of, 78n
Benoist, 164
Bergamo, 45
    marriage laws of, 48n
Blois, Pierre de, 168
Boccacio, cit., 152
Bologna, 43n
Borgia, Caesar, 69, 70, 73n, 76n
Boscoli's conspiracy, 135
Botero, cit., 198–9
Boulenger, J., 161
Bourgeoisie, 55–6, 58, 66, 98, 150,
Braccio, 49n
Brunelleschi, Filippo, 155, 158
Bruni, Leonardo, cit., 153, 169
Buonaccorsi, 3
Burckhardt, Jacob, xi, 157, 166
Bussolari, Friar Giacomo, 43n
Byzantine art, *see* Greek art

Calvinism, 187
Camino, Rizzardo da, 55n
Campanella, Thomas, cit., 199–200
Candida, Cardinal, cit., 171n
Capitalism, 58, 185, 188
Carpi, Republic of Friars of, 112
Casa, Francesco della, 126
Castruccio,
    dying speech of, 28n
Catholic Reformation, 150

249